RENEWALS   *Please quote:* date of return, your ticket number
and computer label number for each item.

MultiMate
STEP BY STEP

Bill Grout

Addison-Wesley Publishing Company, Inc.

Reading, Massachusetts • Menlo Park, California
Don Mills, Ontario • Wokingham, England • Amsterdam
Sydney • Singapore • Tokyo • Mexico City • Bogotá
Santiago • San Juan

MultiMate is a trademark of MultiMate International Corporation

Many of the designations used by manufacturers and sellers to distinguish their products are claimed as trademarks. Where these designations appear in the book and the author is aware of a trademark claim, the designations have been printed with initial capital letters—for example, MultiMate.

Library of Congress Cataloging in Publication Data

Grout, Bill.
  MultiMate step by step.

  Includes index.
  1. Word processing. 2. MultiMate (Computer program)
I. Title.
Z52.5.M84G76 1985   652'.5   85–6010
ISBN 0–201–11580–8

Cover design by Marshall Henrichs
Text design by Kenneth J. Wilson
Set in 10-point Palatino by Modern Graphics Inc., Weymouth, MA

ABCDEFGHIJ–HA–898765
First printing, September 1985

ACKNOWLEDGMENTS

I'd like to thank Kearney Rietmann, Amanda Hixson, Alan Goldstein, and Betsy Selfo for their kind support of this project.

MultiMate
STEP BY STEP

Contents

INTRODUCTION

What would make you want to toss your favorite typewriter off a cliff? Answer: word processing with MultiMate.

MultiMate can save you hours of work when it comes to typing and revising long documents. MultiMate makes using even the best typewriter seem like drudgery.

MultiMate is an excellent text processor and one that's easy to learn. If you've never word processed before, you'll be impressed with MultiMate's ability to rearrange and edit text, print multipage documents effortlessly, automatically number pages, and even check your spelling. "Get out the tranquilizers! It sounds complicated!" you're thinking. No need—you'll find learning to edit with MultiMate no trouble at all.

Check your pulse. Some people approach learning to use a word processor with a slight anxiety. Don't worry or hesitate. Learning to word process is like learning to drive a car: the task looks formidable at first, but it becomes second-nature with a little practice. And no one has ever hit a tree at fifty miles an hour while working at a word processor. You can't hurt yourself, the computer, or the program. This book never shrieks with laughter if you press the wrong key, either.

MultiMate Step by Step was written for people who want to learn MultiMate at their own speed. If you're a word-processing novice, you'll find all the explanations you need, as well as exercises that teach text editing, in this book. Word-processing experts or those who have experience with other word-processing programs can try out the exercises, quickly gleaning basic procedures, and skip any unneeded discussions. You can work slowly and thoughtfully through the book at your convenience or you can blitz it. (One speed reader completed the book in twelve minutes and learned absolutely nothing at all.)

You'll learn MultiMate while sitting at your computer, reading this book, and using the program. The book starts with the most basic editing procedures and builds upon them until almost all of MultiMate's features have been presented. Editing procedures are described in simple language, and the book allows for different styles of learning (as will be explained later). By the book's end, you'll have seen what MultiMate can do for you and you'll be ready to use it on your own. You may not be an expert, but you'll have had the training you need to begin using MultiMate in your work.

MultiMate Step by Step is a tutorial that teaches you to use the program. Although you might refer to this book for procedural explanations, it isn't meant to take the place of MultiMate's reference manual. As you read this book, you'll perform exercises that teach you to create and edit real documents. People with Digitophobia (a strangulating fear of pressing keys at computer keyboards) will have to get over it quickly.

REQUIREMENTS

To use this book, you must have the MultiMate disks that were supplied when you purchased the program and a blank disk to hold documents that you create and edit during exercises.

The appendices that are included in the back of this book give instructions for creating documents used in some of the exercises. Early in each chapter, a section devoted to preparations tells you which document(s) are needed for the exercises and which appendices provide instructions for creating them. You create the exercise documents as you need them. Don't try to create all the documents listed in the appendices before you start this book. (To do so, you'd already have to know how to word process with MultiMate.) Each chapter will provide you with the skills needed to create the next exercise document.

If your computer system has a hard disk drive, you may place the exercise documents that you create on the hard disk drive.

GETTING READY

Using this book requires some preparation. You must install MultiMate so that it works with your computer and printer. Because many different types of equipment, such as printers, are used with MultiMate, this book can't give installation directions. You'll have to refer to MultiMate's reference manual to install the program.

For Systems with Two Floppy Disk Drives

If your computer has two floppy disk drives, you should set up MultiMate to record documents on the disk in drive B (refer to your manual to learn which is A and which is B—B is usually the one on the right). Your MultiMate program disk will be used in drive A, as will the dictionary disk, which you'll use in the last exercises.

Part of installing MultiMate is designating which disk drive will hold specific disks. Different drives may be used to access documents, the program, the dictionary disk, and special documents called *libraries.* To set these disk designations, refer to the topic "Other Utilities" in the MultiMate reference manual. For this book, you should set up the "drive defaults" as follows:

System drive:	A
Document drive:	B
Library drive:	B
Dictionary drive:	A

The system drive is the disk drive that normally holds the program disk, in this case the A drive. The document drive normally holds disks used for recording documents. You'll be using the exercise disk as a document disk in drive B. The library drive holds special documents that you'll learn to create later. These documents will be stored on the exercise disk in drive B. Finally, MultiMate supplies you with a dictionary on disk (you'll learn about this later). MultiMate has to know the dictionary disk's location to look up words. The dictionary disk drive will be drive A.

If your system has only one disk drive, your only choice, of course, is to set all the drive designations to A.

For Hard-Disk Systems

Some people will have computers that have one floppy disk (drive A) and a hard disk. The hard disk is most often named drive C. Because hard disks can hold a great deal of information, you might transfer the MultiMate program, dictionary, and contents of the exercise disk all to drive C. All drive designations (program, document, library, and dictionary) would then be C. To set these disk designations, refer to the topic "Other Utilities" in the MultiMate reference manual. For this book, you should set up the "drive defaults" as follows:

System drive:	C
Document drive:	C
Library drive:	C
Dictionary drive:	C

You might also choose to set up MultiMate to use the C drive as the program, document, and library drive and the A drive as the dictionary drive. If you designate the dictionary drive as drive A, you must insert the dictionary disk in drive A when you need to use it.

Alternate hard disk specifications:

System drive:	C
Document drive:	C
Library drive:	C
Dictionary drive:	A

You might configure MultiMate to use other combinations of drives, but for carrying out the exercises in this book, the two settings above are probably the simplest.

The book's exercise instructions assume that you're using a system that has two floppy disks, with drive B as the document disk drive. With a hard-disk system, your document disk will likely be the C drive (as you choose). During exercises, you will sometimes be asked to type the drive specification for the document drive. You should ignore the instruction to type "B" as the document-drive specification if you are using a hard disk for the document drive; type "C" instead. If you've set up the document drive differently, you must use the corresponding drive specification during the exercises.

For Networked Systems

Your computer may be linked to a central system connecting many terminals. You might be able to use the disk drives found on your specific computer (perhaps two floppy disk drives or a floppy disk and hard disk as just described) or your computer might be configured to store documents on a large central storage device. You should consult with the computer system technician or someone who knows how to set up MultiMate for your terminal and how to access the information on the exercise disk.

HOW TO USE THIS BOOK

Each chapter presents information in the same way. After a short general discussion of the chapter's topic, preparatory notes that describe requirements for completing the chapter are presented. You'll be told which documents and disks are needed for the exercises, which appendices apply (if any), and generally what needs to be done before you start.

Each chapter provides an overview of word-processing topics and procedures to be learned. You'll be introduced to concepts and procedures that the exercises focus upon.

Following the overview, chapters present several exercises that are broken down into modules. Modules begin with an objective and a brief introduction to the concept or procedure used in an exercise.

Each exercise is presented with explicit instructions for which keys to press, the results you'll see, and brief explanations of each step. Exercises provide practice at the keyboard but do not explain everything you need to know about the text-processing procedures being taught. More detailed information and advice about using MultiMate is provided following each exercise.

Chapters may contain three or more exercise modules, depending upon the procedures and concepts to be learned. Finally, each chapter ends with a summary that illustrates the concepts or procedures presented.

If you're experienced with other word-processing programs, you might not need to read every line of the explanations. It might suffice for you to read the objective and introduction to a procedure, then try out an exercise briefly. Once familiar with MultiMate's editing methods, you might skim or skip the explanations. Sometimes you might just refer to a chapter summary to learn a particularly common editing procedure and skip the exercises and explanations altogether. Relying on your experience, you can pick and choose as you breeze through the book, experimenting with the exercises as you wish.

Some people prefer to try out a tool and then read the details of how it works. If you learn by doing, you too might read the objective and brief introductions that present a procedure, then do the exercise and get the hang of MultiMate on your own. If you have questions, you can read the explanations that follow the exercise when you need them. Otherwise, if you understand MultiMate from using it in the exercise, you might just browse the explanations for important details.

If you're a novice and need things clearly explained before undertaking an exercise, you might do better to use the following method: First, read the objective and the introduction to each exercise. Next, read the explanation following the exercise. With all the conceptual groundwork laid, try out the exercise to confirm for yourself how MultiMate works. Certainly, you should read the explanations first if you find that you don't quite understand what's happening in exercises. You might skip back and forth between explanations and exercises as you wish.

Know-it-alls, of course, can just play at the keyboard until they get in trouble, or they can start with the last chapter and work toward the front of the book.

However you like to learn, take the exercises and explanations at your own pace. You'll find that the chapters teach editing in small increments, each topic building upon earlier topics. It's not a good idea, therefore, to skip chapters (unless a chapter covers a topic that you never expect to use). You might complete the course in several hours or several weeks, as best suits you. The first chapter will teach you how to load MultiMate and how to stop it later, so you can stop taking the tutorial at the end of any chapter.

ABOUT PRESSING KEYS

As you perform the exercises, you'll be asked to press keys on the keyboard and to type information. This book assumes that you have a basic familiarity with your computer and equipment—it doesn't bother teaching what a disk drive is or how to connect a printer to the computer. Instructions will refer to function keys, cursor-movement keys, and various other keys, such as the TAB key, backspace, and ESCAPE key (marked ESC on the IBM keyboard). MultiMate's manual provides a diagram of the keyboard and keys used. You might want to keep this diagram handy for easy reference if you're unfamiliar with the keyboard.

If you see an instruction such as the following:

1. Type "book" and press ENTER

you should type the word "book" (without quotation marks) and press the ENTER key marked (←—). Likewise, if you are told to press F1, you should press the function key marked F1 (you don't type an "F" and then a "1").

Some keys are used in combination. For example, to type a capital S, you must hold down the SHIFT key and type "S". MultiMate uses a great many key combinations with keys such as ALT and CTRL instead of SHIFT. Most often you'll be given an instruction such as "Hold down ALT and press F1". You then press and continue to hold down the ALT key until you press the F1 key function once. Explanations sometimes take a short cut, saying that a feature is performed with ALT F1. This still means you should hold down ALT and press F1; it does not mean that you should press ALT, release it, then press F1.

Before you begin, get familiar with the key names. Find the TAB key, the ENTER key, the backspace key, the space bar, the ESCAPE key, marked ESC (this is the panic button and may save you if something unexpected happens), and the cursor-arrow keys on the numeric keypad.

Now find the key marked DESTROY. There isn't one, is there? Does that make you feel confident? You'll never accidentally press the DESTROY key and see the computer steam and pop its lid. There's also no key marked SERIOUS MISTAKE or PICK UP YOUR CHECK, YOU'RE FIRED. This is a no-risk keyboard. Now you're ready to start using MultiMate.

Chapter 1

THE SCREEN TOUR

You should have a working copy of the MultiMate program disk that you created from the master MultiMate boot/system disk. You don't need the utility or spelling disks for now. You should also have a formatted exercise disk.

You should have installed the disk operating system (DOS) on the working copy of the MultiMate program disk. If you haven't installed DOS, refer to the section called "Preparing Your Word Processing System" in the beginning of the MultiMate manual. If you have a monitor with an ON/OFF switch, you should turn it on now.

If you have installed DOS and MultiMate on a hard disk drive, you do not need to insert the working copy of the MultiMate program disk in the A drive when the instructions tell you to. You can load the program from the hard disk, and your exercises will be stored on the hard-disk drive as well. All drive specifications in the instructions should be "C:" (not "B:" or "A:") to designate the hard disk.

When you move to a new house, you first take a brief tour from room to room to see what it's like. Let's take a similar walk-through to see what MultiMate is like. Instead of viewing living room, bedroom, and kitchen, we'll look at different MultiMate screens. Just as a bedroom and a kitchen have different functions, MultiMate screens allow you to perform different word-processing functions. After you take this tour, you'll be comfortable knowing MultiMate's screen layout, and moving in will be that much easier.

**WHAT YOU WILL
LEARN AND SEE**

You'll create your first document as we take the tour. You'll see the following screens:

MULTIMATE'S MAIN MENU, which allows you to select a variety of word-processing functions;

DOCUMENT SPECIFICATION SCREEN, which you use to tell MultiMate which document you want to use;

DOCUMENT SUMMARY SCREEN, which provides information about the document's contents;

MODIFY DOCUMENT DEFAULTS SCREEN, which tells MultiMate how to act as you edit; and

EDITING SCREEN, which is your work area, in which you type and edit text.

**LOADING
MULTIMATE**

**Objective: Starting up
the Program**

As you must unlock the front door before you can tour a house, you must load the program before you can tour MultiMate. After you turn on the computer and load DOS, type "WP" (for "word processing") and press ENTER to open MultiMate's front door. After MultiMate loads, the first thing you see is—you might have guessed—a commercial.

During the loading procedure, your screen will look similar to figure 1.1.

Procedure

1. Place the MultiMate program disk in drive A and close the drive door. (Ignore this step if you have transferred the MultiMate

```
Current date is Tue 1-01-1980
Enter new date: 07/20/84
Current time is: 0:00:14.11
Enter new time: 12:00:00

The IBM Personal Computer DOS
Version 2.0 (C) Copyright IBM Corp 1981, 1982, 1983


A>WP
```

Figure 1.1
Loading MultiMate from DOS

program to your hard disk.) (See figure 1.2 for how to insert the disk.)

2. Place your exercise disk in drive B. (Ignore this step if you are using a hard disk.)

3. Turn on the computer.

4. If a "Date" prompt appears, type a date in the format MM/DD/YY (for example, 07/20/84 for July 20, 1984) and press ENTER. If no prompt appears, skip this step.

5. If a time prompt appears, type a time in the format HH:MM:SS (for example, 12:00:00 for noon in hours, minutes, and seconds) and press ENTER. If no prompt appears, skip this step.

6. When the DOS A> prompt appears, load MultiMate by typing "WP" and pressing ENTER. MultiMate's "commercial" appears.

7. Press any key to stop the "commercial screen" and continue the tour.

Computers don't bite, so don't worry about starting up MultiMate. **Explanation**
    You begin by inserting the MultiMate disk in the A drive. The A drive is left of the B drive or hard disk. You insert the disk as shown in figure 1.2. Notice the positioning of the label and the read/write oval. If you've transferred the MultiMate program to your hard disk, you don't need to insert the MultiMate program disk in the A drive. You can start the program without it.

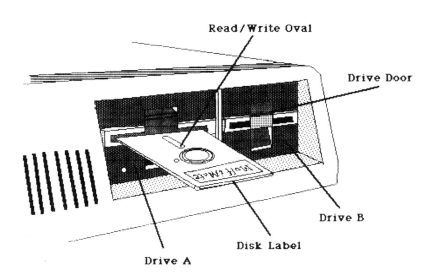

Read/Write Oval

Drive Door

Drive B

Disk Label

Drive A

Figure 1.2
Inserting the MultiMate Disk

On the IBM PC/XT, the ON/OFF switch is located at the back right corner. On other computers, the switch may be in different positions. Once turned on, the computer may appear to do nothing for several seconds. It is simply doing some internal testing, and there is nothing to worry about. The computer will finally wake up and load the disk operating system (DOS) automatically and perhaps display a prompt asking you to type the date. If nothing happens after a prolonged time, check to see the computer is plugged in or try turning it off and on again.

During the loading procedure, you may be asked to type a date and time. If you make a mistake before pressing ENTER, you can backspace and retype the date or time. If you made a mistake and pressed ENTER, the program may ask you to type the date or time again.

The MultiMate program is named WP.EXE on disk. You need only type "WP" to load it, however. After you type "WP" (for "word processing") at the DOS A> (or C>, if you're using a hard disk), the disk drive begins pumping the program into the computer's memory. After a few moments, you will see a screen that identifies the MultiMate program; this screen appears every time the program starts up (see figure 1.3).

Figure 1.3
MultiMate's Commercial

You've now successfully loaded the program. After you press any key, MultiMate's main menu appears.

MultiMate's main menu is like a hallway that leads to all the other rooms of a house. You usually return to the main menu to go from one word-processing function to another. The main menu is a numbered list of nine places where you can go to perform various text-editing, printing, and file-maintenance functions (see figure 1.4).

To make a selection, you type a number (1–9) and press ENTER. For example, when you start a new document, you select "Create a New Document" from the menu by typing "2" and pressing ENTER. If you want to edit a document you created previously, select "Edit an Old Document" by typing a "1" and pressing ENTER.

1. To select "Create a New Document, type "2" and press ENTER. Another screen appears that you'll learn about shortly. When you create a document, this screen enables you to assign the document a name of your choice.

MAIN MENU

Objective: Making Selections from the Main Menu

Procedure

```
┌─────────────────────────────────────────────────┐
│                                                   │
│     ┌───────────────────────────────────┐        │
│     │          M u l t i M a t e          │        │
│     │           Version 3.30              │        │
│     └───────────────────────────────────┘        │
│                                                   │
│         1) Edit an Old Document                   │
│         2) Create a New Document                  │
│                                                   │
│         3) Print Document Utility                 │
│         4) Printer Control Utilities             │
│         5) Merge Print Utility                   │
│                                                   │
│         6) Document Handling Utilities           │
│         7) Other Utilities                       │
│         8) Spell Check a Document                 │
│         9) Return to DOS                         │
│                                                   │
│           DESIRED FUNCTION: □                     │
│     Enter the number of the function; press RETURN│
│     Hold down SHIFT and press F1 for HELP menu    │
│                                          S:4 N:4  │
└─────────────────────────────────────────────────┘
```

Figure 1.4
MultiMate's Main Menu

2. Press ESCAPE (ESC) to cancel this selection. (Any time you make the wrong selection, you can press ESCAPE to return to the main menu.)

3. Type "3" and press ENTER to select "Print Document Utility". This main menu option is used when you want to print a document. The screen that appears enables you to specify the name of the document to be printed.

4. Press ESCAPE to cancel the selection.

5. Type "9" and press ENTER to select "Return to DOS". This option essentially turns off MultiMate when you're finished word processing. You see the "DOS" prompt (e.g., A>) appear. You can now run another program or turn off the computer. Let's load MultiMate again.

6. Type "WP", press ENTER, and press the space bar to view the main menu again.

Explanation   MultiMate's main menu enables you to do all of the following:

Edit an Old Document   You select "Edit an Old Document" to update or add to documents you've already stored on disk. If you typed a letter yesterday, for example, and now you want to change the wording, you would insert the disk containing the letter in the B drive. Next, you select "Edit an Old Document". MultiMate then knows it must find a document on disk. It displays a Document Specification screen (which you'll see next) that enables you to tell MultiMate which document you want.

Create a New Document   New documents are created with "Create a New Document". You cannot use this option to see or edit documents already on disk. After you select this option, MultiMate displays a Document Specification screen used to give the new document a name. The procedures for naming documents will be discussed later, but if you happen to specify the name of a document previously saved on disk, MultiMate will stop you. It won't allow you to create two documents with the same name on the same disk.

Print Document Utility   To print a document, you select "Print Document Utility". MultiMate then displays screens that allow you to specify which document to print and how to print it. MultiMate's procedure for printing documents is easy to learn and will be discussed later.

You don't have to wait for a document to finish printing before you specify another to be printed. MultiMate can line up your documents (in what's called a *print queue*) and hold them until the printer's free. You can specify as many documents as you want to be printed and MultiMate will print them out in sequence. You can even continue editing other documents as MultiMate prints the documents in the print queue.

If a printer is tearing up paper, printing your document askew, or generally misbehaving, you may want to stop it. Or you may decide not to print a document after all and therefore need to take it out of the printing line-up or queue. To stop the printer or change the order of documents in the print queue, select "Printer Control Utilities". (If you need to stop the printer quickly—if it's got you by the tie or scarf and is pulling you in—you can stop it without making this selection from the main menu. Later you'll read about stopping the printer this way.)

     "Printer Control Utilities" also lets you specify how you want routine documents printed. You can tell MultiMate the left margin, top margin, line spacing, and many other printing specifications you usually use, and MultiMate saves and uses them until you change them.

Printer Control Utilities

Merge-printing enables you to do mass mailings. With MultiMate, you can specially code a form letter and a list of names and addresses and print the letter repeatedly with a different name and address in each letter. (You can actually include more information than just names and addresses.) Merge-printing gets its name from the process of creating two documents, typically a form letter and a list of names and addresses, and merging the addresses into the letter during printing. A chapter in the latter part of this book is devoted to merge-printing.

Merge-Printing Utility

"Document Handling Utilities" helps you manipulate the documents saved on disk. You can rename, make copies of, or erase documents you don't need. You can also take a document off one disk and move it to another. If you just can't remember a document's name, "Document Handling Utilities" also lets you search for a document using special criteria, such as the author's name or a keyword that identifies the document (more about this later). You can also print out summaries of documents' contents.

     With MultiMate, you can have the program automatically make back-up copies of documents. (This will be explained a little later.) Once you've asked it to do so, any time you begin editing an old document, MultiMate will automatically make a copy and keep it safe on disk for you. Later, if you make a terrible mistake and wreck

Document Handling Utilities

the document that you're working on, you can tell MultiMate to use the old back-up copy and start over. To reuse the back-up copy of a document, you select an option called "Restore a Backed-Document" from the document handling utilities.

Other Utilities

"Other Utilities" lets you set up MultiMate to run the way you want it to. The utilities enable you to set routine specifications, called *defaults*, that MultiMate uses every time you load it. For example, you can tell MultiMate that you always store documents on the disk in drive B, that you want certain margins and tab stops, and that you want each page to have 55 lines. Once set, MultiMate uses these specifications each time you load it. You can still set up individual documents to any specifications you desire, of course. Naturally, you use these utilities when you first set up MultiMate and rarely after that.

Spell Check a Document

MultiMate can check the spelling of every word in a document. To check finished documents saved on disk, you place the MultiMate spelling disk in a disk drive (not necessary if you've transferred the MultiMate dictionary to a hard disk) and select "Spell Check a Document". You specify a document name and MultiMate looks at every word in the document, checking it against an 80,000-word dictionary. Words that are misspelled are marked in the text, and the spelling-checker program even helps you correct them.

You can also spell-check parts of a document as you edit. The spelling-checker is a great help in proofreading. You'll learn to use the spelling-checker in a later chapter.

Return to DOS

To stop using MultiMate, you select "Return to DOS". The MultiMate program shuts down and the DOS prompt appears, enabling you to run another program if you wish.

That's a quick run-down of the main-menu options. You'll get more familiar with each of these menu options as you work more with MultiMate. By the way, if you select an option by mistake, you can quickly return to the main menu by pressing ESCAPE (as you did for practice in the second step of the procedure).

DOCUMENT SPECIFICATION SCREEN

Objective: Creating a Document and Specifying a Document Name

After you type "1", "2", "3", or "8" from the main menu and press ENTER, you must tell MultiMate the name of the document that you wish to create, edit, print, or spell-check. The Document Specification screen enables you to specify a document name and the drive that holds the document disk. It also shows you a list of other documents already on disk.

When you create a new document, you use the Document Specification screen to name it. When editing, printing, or spell-checking a document, you use this screen to designate which document you wish to work with.

Each document must be identified by a unique name. A Document Specification screen similar to figure 1.5 appears when you select "Edit an Old Document", "Create a New Document", "Print Document Utility", or "Spell Check a Document" from the main menu.

Try creating a new document with the name MEMO. You'll only type your name in it during this screen tour, but in the next chapter you'll use it to type a memo.

1. Select "Create a New Document" by typing "2" and pressing **Procedure** ENTER. The Document Specification screen appears.

2. At the "Document" prompt, type "MEMO". (Don't type quotation marks. It makes no difference if the letters are upper- or lower-case. Use the backspace key to back up and type over mistakes.)

3. Press SHIFT and TAB to move the cursor to the "Drive" prompt. This prompt tells MultiMate which disk drive to use for storing and accessing documents.

4. Type the letter of the drive on which the document should be stored. Type "B", if you have the blank exercise disk in drive B, "A" if it's in drive A, or "C" if you're using a hard disk. The drive specification may already be correct; but we wanted to show you how to change it.

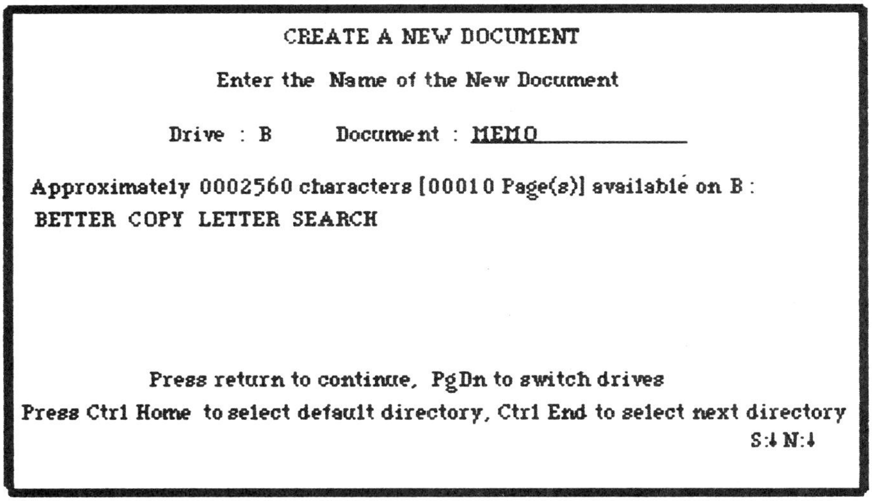

```
                    CREATE A NEW DOCUMENT
                Enter the Name of the New Document

        Drive : B       Document : MEMO_____

Approximately 0002560 characters [00010 Page(s)] available on B :
BETTER COPY LETTER SEARCH




            Press return to continue, PgDn to switch drives
     Press Ctrl Home to select default directory, Ctrl End to select next directory
                                                    S:↓ N:↓
```

Figure 1.5
Document Specification
Screen

5. To see a list of document names for disks in other disk drives, press the PGDN key several times. Each time you press PGDN, MultiMate displays a list for a different drive, appearing at about mid-screen. Keep pressing PGDN until the "Drive" prompt displays the correct drive designation for the exercise disk again.

6. Once you've specified a document name (and drive specification), press ENTER to move on.

Explanation

All God's children have to have names and so do MultiMate documents.

You can type a document name up to twenty characters long, but MultiMate only uses the first eight characters to store the document on the disk. Later, when you want to recall a document for editing, select "Edit an Old Document" from the main menu and type the exact eight-letter name at the Document Specification screen. You can use upper- or lower-case letters when you type the name; to MultiMate, the names MEMO and memo are identical.

When you specify names for new documents, you should try to use names that are meaningful. Meaningful names can help you remember which document is which. Although you can use characters other than just letters (@, $, !, for example), you shouldn't use blank spaces in a name. MultiMate is unable to read names with spaces in them. If you type a name with invalid characters or spaces, MultiMate will stop and ask you to retype the name.

If you make a mistake when typing a document name, you can simply backspace and retype. You can also use the arrow keys to move the cursor under a character and then delete that character by pressing the DELETE key (DEL). You can insert a character in a name by positioning the cursor where the character should be and pressing the INSERT key (INS), which inserts a blank space. You can then type letters in those spaces.

The "Drive" prompt specifies where the finished document will be stored. If it says "B", for example, MultiMate will save the document on the disk in drive B. By changing the letter following the "Drive" prompt, you direct MultiMate to use a specific disk drive. To change the "Drive" prompt, press SHIFT and TAB and type a letter.

Under the "Drive" and "Document" prompts you see a sentence starting "Approximately . . .". MultiMate is telling you how much space is left on the disk. Although the actual number of characters available may not mean much to you, knowing the number of pages a disk can hold enables you to judge if the disk has enough free space for a document. Of course, you can't store a ten-page document on a disk with room for only two pages.

Under the disk-space-available notice, you may see a list of documents already stored on the disk. This list is called a *directory*. When you create a new document, the new name will be added to the list. If you want to edit an old document, you can check the directory to see if the desired document is on the disk and to find out how to spell its name.

You can see directories for other disks by pressing the PGDN key. Each time you press it, MultiMate will show you a directory for a disk in a different drive. You can keep pressing PGDN until MultiMate comes full circle and shows you the directory for the disk you started with. Notice, however, that the "Drive" prompt changes each time you press PGDN, you should be sure that the drive prompt is correct after checking other directories using PGDN. You can also change from one directory to another on the same disk by pressing CTRL END. To automatically see the documents in the default directory, press CTRL HOME.

It makes no difference which directory is displayed on the screen if you know the document you want is located on a disk in one of the drives. Just be sure the "Drive" prompt shows the desired drive when you type the document name and press ENTER.

MultiMate sometimes tries to save you a little typing. After you create or edit a document, MultiMate will automatically display the document's name in other Document Specification screens. If you want to work with a different document, just type a document name over the displayed one. You must be sure to erase any extra letters that appear on the "Document" prompt line; otherwise, MultiMate may be unable to find the desired document.

Remember, the Document Specification screen simply tells Multi-Mate which drive and document to use. When creating a document, you use this screen to name the document. To edit a document, you use this screen to say which document you want to edit. For printing, the Document Specification screen designates the document to be printed, and the same goes for spell-checking a document.

After you type the name MEMO in the procedure, MultiMate creates a blank document on disk and displays the next screen in the tour: the Document Summary screen.

DOCUMENT SUMMARY SCREEN

Objective: Completing the Document Summary Screen

When visiting someone for the first time, you might check the mailbox to see if you've got the right address. The Document Summary screen is MultiMate's mailbox; it tells you if you've got the right document. You can record information in the Document Summary screen that tells you about the document.

As a file card might, the Document Summary screen displays the document name, author, addressee, operator (who typed the document), the length of the document, when it was created, and various other items of information you can choose whether to record or not (see figure 1.6).

When you first create a document, of course, the Document Summary screen is blank, and you must fill in the information. After that, whenever you specify that document for editing, the Document Summary screen appears, informing you about the document.

Procedure

1. To complete the "Author" line, type your name and press ENTER. If you make a typing mistake, just backspace and type over. You can also move the cursor from line to line with the cursor arrow keys.

2. To complete the "Addressee" line, type "John Brown" and press ENTER.

3. To complete the "Operator" line, type your name and press ENTER.

4. To enter a keyword, type "Employment" and press ENTER three

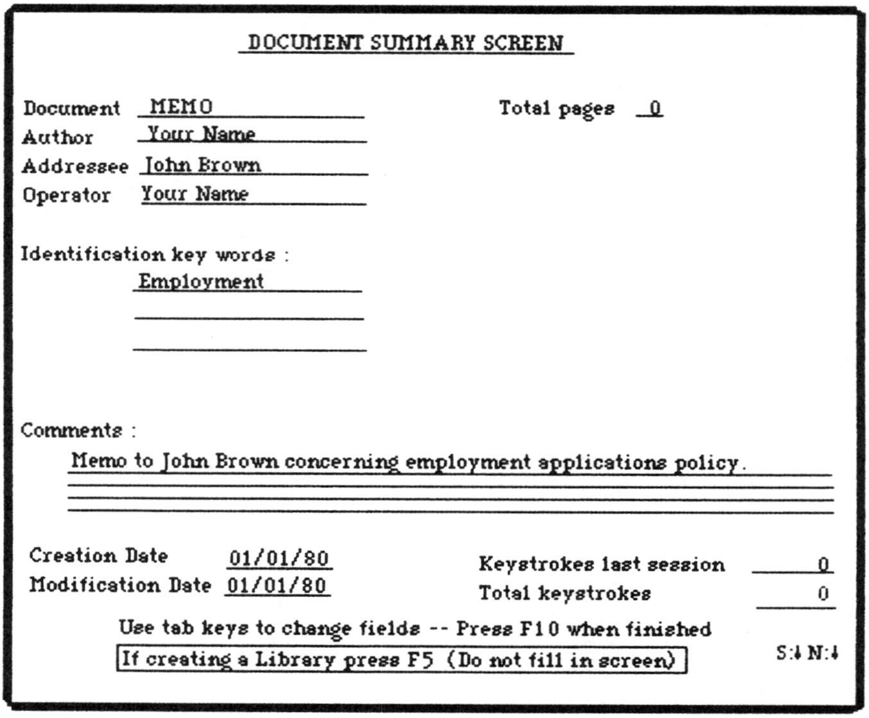

```
                    DOCUMENT SUMMARY SCREEN

    Document   MEMO                    Total pages  _0_
    Author     Your Name
    Addressee  John Brown
    Operator   Your Name

    Identification key words :
               Employment




    Comments :
          Memo to John Brown concerning employment applications policy.



    Creation Date    01/01/80       Keystrokes last session      0
    Modification Date 01/01/80      Total keystrokes             0

         Use tab keys to change fields -- Press F10 when finished
        │ If creating a Library press F5  (Do not fill in screen) │   S:↓ N:↓
```

Figure 1.6
Document Summary
Screen

times to move the cursor to the comment line. (You could list three keywords, but just add one for now.)

5. To complete a descriptive comment, type "Memo to John Brown concerning employment applications policy."

6. When the information for the Document Summary screen is complete, press F10 to move ahead.

Not sure what a document is about? Check its Document Summary screen.

Explanation

The Document Summary screen provides information about the document you are about to create or edit. After you complete this screen, MultiMate shows it to you each time you edit the document. The information in the Document Summary screen is part of the document, but it doesn't print with the document. (If desired, you can print the Document Summary screen with the document, as will be explained later.)

The Document Summary screen shows the document name and provides lines where you can record the author, addressee, and operator's name. (The operator's name refers to the word-processing operator—who may be different from the author of the document.) MultiMate also shows you the document length in pages. Naturally, the total page number is zero at first, because you haven't typed the document yet.

You can also record three keywords to help you identify the document. If the document was an invoice to John Brown about a housing contract, you might record the words "invoice" and "housing" as keywords.

The "Comment" line enables you to record a brief statement of the document's contents or perhaps a reminder to yourself about things remaining to be done to the document.

At the bottom of the Document Summary screen, MultiMate shows you the date on which the document was created, when it was last edited, the length of the document in characters (total keystrokes), and how many keys you pressed the last time you edited the document (keystrokes last session). If you made 250 key presses while editing, MultiMate eagerly informs you of the total keystrokes—useful, right? (If it's a really big number, you can look at it and feel tired.)

You can move the cursor from line to line by pressing ENTER or the cursor-arrow keys. You can also just press ENTER repeatedly to cycle the cursor through all the lines until it starts over at the top line again. You do not have to complete the information on this screen. You can press F10 at any time to move ahead.

You can also change information recorded in the Document Summary screen when you next edit the document.

After examining the Document Summary screen, you may find that you have accessed the wrong document. You can press ESCAPE to return to the main menu.

After pressing F10 at the Document Summary screen, you will see the Modify Document Defaults screen, which governs some of MultiMate's editing capabilities.

MODIFY DOCUMENT DEFAULTS SCREEN

Objective: Completing the Modify Document Defaults Screen

MultiMate is smarter than the average typewriter. With a typewriter, you must keep track of how many lines of text fit a page and decide when to end one page and start another. MultiMate can do those things for you once you tell it how by completing the Modify Document Defaults screen.

You see the Modify Document Defaults screen only once, when you first create a document (see figure 1.7). When it appears, the Modify Document Defaults screen is already filled out for you. If the specifications are correct (which they usually will be), you can press F10 without changing anything.

The Modify Document Defaults screen essentially asks you four questions:

1. Should MultiMate allow *widows* and *orphans* (single lines separated from the rest of the paragraph at the top or bottom of a page)?

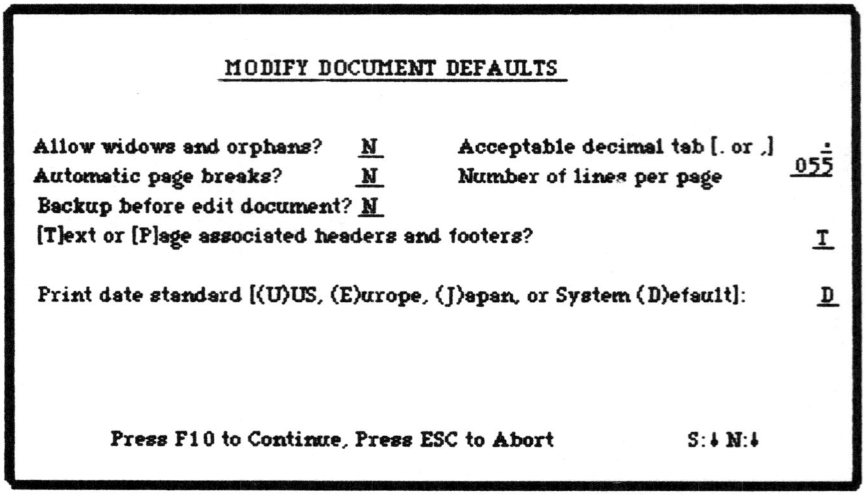

```
          MODIFY DOCUMENT DEFAULTS


   Allow widows and orphans?   N       Acceptable decimal tab [. or ,]    ·
   Automatic page breaks?      N       Number of lines per page         055
   Backup before edit document? N
   [T]ext or [P]age associated headers and footers?                      T

   Print date standard [(U)US, (E)urope, (J)apan, or System (D)efault]:   D



          Press F10 to Continue, Press ESC to Abort        S:↓ N:↓
```

Figure 1.7
Modify Document Defaults Screen

2. Should MultiMate automatically create a new page when the one you're editing is full?

3. Should columns of numbers line up on a comma or decimal point?

4. How many lines of text should appear per page?

MultiMate also asks whether you want a back-up copy of the document made automatically each time you edit it, where special sections of text called *headers* and *footers* (explained later) will appear, and how dates are to be printed (that is, in European, Japanese, or standard American format).

Use the cursor key or ENTER to move the cursor to the specification you want to change; then type a new entry. When the Modify Document Defaults screen is correct, press F10 to move ahead.

1. At the "Widows and orphans" prompt, type "N" for "no." (If **Procedure** all the prompts are set as seen in figure 1.7, simply press F10 to complete the procedure.)

2. At the "Automatic page breaks" prompt, type "N" for "no."

3. At the "Acceptable decimal tab" prompt, type a period. (Use the arrow keys to move the cursor from option to option.)

4. At the "Number of lines per page" prompt, type "055" and press F10. The rest of the options will be skipped for now to avoid burdening you with too much detail that might prove distracting.

The Modify Document Defaults screen is made to be ignored. Because **Explanation** it is completed automatically, you will usually just press F10 when you see it. You can set the defaults to those you routinely use by selecting the main menu's "Other Utilities". (See your reference manual for how to set up defaults.) Then, whenever you create a document, you need only change the Modify Document Defaults screen for special cases.

To explain this screen's options, let's start with the last prompt, "Number of lines per page". To complete it you simply type the number of text lines you want per page. If you specify 55 lines per page (a standard number for an 8½-by-11-inch sheet of paper), MultiMate will tell you when you've typed the 55th line during editing. With MultiMate a page can hold up to 150 lines.

Once MultiMate knows the number of lines per page, it can automatically stop when a page is full and create a new one. If you don't want MultiMate to create new pages, but wish to do so yourself when you judge that a page is full, you set the "Automatic page breaks" prompt to "N" for "no." You can then type up to 150 lines per page and MultiMate will wait for you to specify when a page is full.

As you type, MultiMate keeps track of the number of lines per page for you. Sometimes, a page may end or begin inappropriately. For example, the first line of a paragraph may be stranded at the bottom of a page, separated from the rest of the paragraph on the following page. This line is called a "widow." It is also possible for a paragraph's last line to dangle at the top of a new page; such a line is called an *orphan*.

After you've typed a document of several pages, you may want MultiMate to readjust how the text fits on each page. MultiMate can automatically prevent widowed and orphaned lines if you set the "Allow widows and orphans" prompt to "N" for "no." If you set it to "Y" for "yes," MultiMate simply fits as many lines per page as it can without worrying about how paragraphs break. (You'll learn more about widows and orphans in chapter 8.)

MultiMate has a special tab function that can automatically line up numbers in columns. If numbers are dollar amounts, for example, MultiMate can line them up on the decimal point (denoting cents) as you type them. Alternatively, you might want MultiMate to line up numbers on dividing commas. You'll learn about MultiMate's number-aligning tabs, called Dectabs, later. For now, the "Acceptable decimal tab" prompt lets you specify whether numbers will align on a decimal point or comma.

The "Backup before edit document" option is used to tell MultiMate to make automatic back-up copies of documents before editing them. If you type a "Y" at this option, MultiMate will copy the document, giving it a slightly different name. If something goes wrong during editing, you can then use the back-up copy of the document.

The next option, regarding "headers" and "footers," determines where MultiMate prints special sections of text called *headers* and *footers*. A header, for example, is a section of text, perhaps one to five lines, that appears at the top of every page in a document. You'll learn about headers and footers in detail later. For now, all you need to know is that the "Text or page" option of the Modify Document Defaults screen enables you to specify whether these sections of text start at a particular point in the text or on a particular page of a document.

The final "Print date" option of this menu enables you to select a format for printing dates. You can insert a special code in your documents that tells MultiMate to automatically print the current date during printing. You can select from four choices of date formats, including USA, European, Japanese, and the computer's DOS format. See your reference manual for a description of these formats.

Once the default prompts are set, you press F10 to see the editing screen.

EDITING SCREEN

Last stop on the tour! The editing screen you see in figure 1.8 is the work area in which documents are typed. Most of your word-processing effort will be spent viewing and changing text on this screen.

Objective: Viewing the Editing Screen

The top line of the screen is the status line. It displays the document name and cursor-position indicators that tell you the cursor's position in a document.

Below the status line is the format line, which sets up line spacing, tab stops, and the right margin (or line width).

The status and format lines are references only. They aren't part of your document, and they do not print. You type the first line of a document under the format line.

Procedure

1. Review the elements of the editing screen.

2. Type your name. If you make a mistake, backspace and retype over the characters. Don't type anything else for now. Pretend you finished this document.

3. To save the entire document, press F10. MultiMate stores MEMO on disk and displays the main menu once more.

4. If you wish, you can stop using the MultiMate program now by typing "9" to select "Return to DOS" and pressing ENTER.

5. You can optionally remove your disks and turn off the computer.

Explanation

The editing screen is your electronic chalkboard, on which it's easy to type, erase, and rearrange text. On the screen you can see about 22 lines of text at a time; about a third of a standard sheet of typing paper. (Your pages, of course, can be much longer.) You view different parts of a document by moving the cursor to them. You'll learn about moving the cursor through documents later, because the current document consists of only your name.

At the editing screen's top you see a status line and a format line. These two lines are not part of the text, but act as references as you create a document. They do not print with the rest of the document.

The status line identifies the document name and the cursor's present position. The cursor-position indicators appear to the right of the document name. The "Page" indicator tells you which page you're currently editing. Because this is the first page, the indicator says "1". The "Line" indicator tells you the cursor position in relation to the top of the page. If it says 7, the cursor is on line seven of your text. The "Col" indicator stands for "column" and shows the cursor's horizontal position on the screen. If you want to indent a paragraph five spaces, you move the cursor right until the "Col" indicator shows "5". Thus, you don't have to count spaces when positioning text on screen; MultiMate's cursor-position indicators display the cursor's exact position.

The format line serves as a reference for line spacing, tab stops, and the right margin. The "1" you see now in the format line indicates that MultiMate is set for single spacing. To create a double-spaced document, you change this number to "2". (You'll learn other ways to change the format line later.) The right-pointing brackets (≫) on the format line show where tab stops have been set. In figure 1.8, tab stops have been set at columns 5, 10, and 15 (column 1 is on the left edge of the screen).

The format line also shows where the right margin is, or, more accurately, what the line length is for the document. As you type, MultiMate won't let you type a line longer than the specified line length. At the end of the format line, you see left-pointing brackets (≪) that show how wide the text can be. In figure 1.8, the line length is set at 65, although your format line may be set differently. You'll

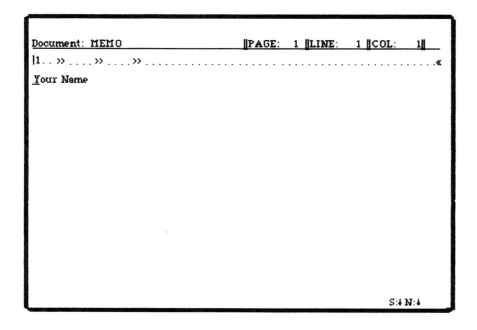

Figure 1.8
Editing Screen

learn more about setting these elements of the editing screen later.

You've now successfully created a document called MEMO. Your name appears as the first line of the document. When you're finished with a document, you tell MultiMate to save it on disk by pressing the F10 key. After you press F10, the main menu appears on the screen.

When you wish to stop using MultiMate, make sure you always save your work on disk. You should never just turn off the computer with the editing screen still displayed. Simply turning off the computer will cause you to lose whatever editing you did on the current screen. Information already on disk won't be hurt, however.

The best method of stopping MultiMate is to save the document and then select "Return to DOS" from the main menu. Once MultiMate shuts down and the DOS prompt appears, you can remove the MultiMate disks and run other programs or shut off the computer.

To create or edit a document using MultiMate, you move through a sequence of screens as illustrated in figure 1.9. First, you make an initial selection from the main menu. Next, you are asked to specify a document name using a Document Specification screen. After you specify the document, a Document Summary screen appears, providing information about the document's contents.

SUMMARY

When creating a document, you must set or accept the settings of a Modify Document Defaults screen. If you are editing a previously created document, this screen will not appear. Notice that the sequence of screens is almost identical for creating and editing a document, except for this Modify Document Defaults screen. Last, the Editing screen, the word-processing work area, comes to view. You type your document and finally save it on disk by pressing F10.

You have now been through the general cycle of creating a document with MultiMate. Now, let's go back and edit that MEMO document and learn some editing basics.

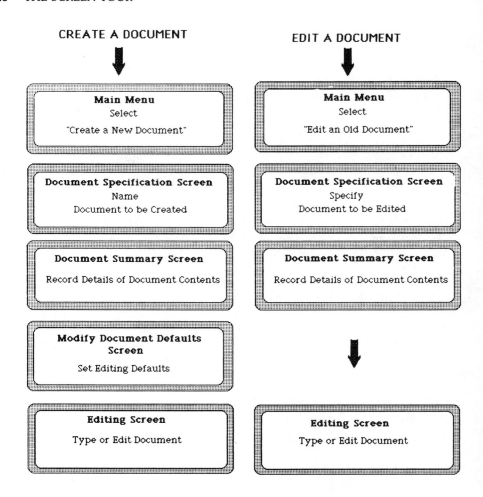

CREATE A DOCUMENT

EDIT A DOCUMENT

Main Menu
Select
"Create a New Document"

Main Menu
Select
"Edit an Old Document"

Document Specification Screen
Name
Document to be Created

Document Specification Screen
Specify
Document to be Edited

Document Summary Screen
Record Details of Document Contents

Document Summary Screen
Record Details of Document Contents

Modify Document Defaults Screen
Set Editing Defaults

Editing Screen
Type or Edit Document

Editing Screen
Type or Edit Document

Figure 1.9
MultiMate Screen
Sequence

Chapter 2

BASIC EDITING

Preparation

Your computer should be turned on and the MultiMate main menu should be on the screen. (See chapter 1 for instructions if you've forgotten how to load MultiMate.) Your exercise disk with the document called MEMO should be in drive B (this is not necessary if you are using MultiMate on a hard disk).

In this chapter we put you to work: you'll type a short memo. Once you've saved a document by pressing F10, MultiMate relays it to disk for safekeeping. To edit it later, you must use "Edit an Old Document", the first selection of the main menu. You cannot access a previously created document using "Create a New Document". If you accidentally try to see a document using "Create a New Document", MultiMate stops you and tells you the document already exists.

Once you've used "Edit an Old Document" to bring the document up on the editing screen, you can add, delete, or change text as you wish. When the document is finished, you save it on disk again under the same name. The original document on disk is replaced with the newly updated one.

MultiMate has a variety of editing procedures. If you happen to forget one, you can call to the screen "Help" information that describes the procedure. MultiMate's Help facility is a great alternative to looking things up in the manual, and you'll try it out in this chapter.

You'll also learn basic editing techniques. You'll learn to arrange text on screen and to insert and delete single characters. Because the screen is your electronic paper, you'll find that it's easy to change text with MultiMate.

The memo you're going to type will look like figure 2.1 when finished. You'll use MultiMate's simplest editing procedures to create it. Later, you'll learn more sophisticated and faster editing techniques, but for now you should start with the basics.

Objective: Accessing a Document Stored on Disk

Once a document is safely saved on disk, you can remove the disk from the disk drive and keep it in a safe place for later editing. You can also create and edit new documents on the same disk. A disk might hold dozens of documents.

To edit a previously saved document, you must tell MultiMate which document you want. You insert the disk containing the document in a drive (not necessary if you're storing documents on a hard disk) and select "Edit an Old Document" from the main menu. After you tell MultiMate the document's name, MultiMate finds the document on the disk for you.

The next exercise shows you how to access the MEMO document that you created in chapter 1.

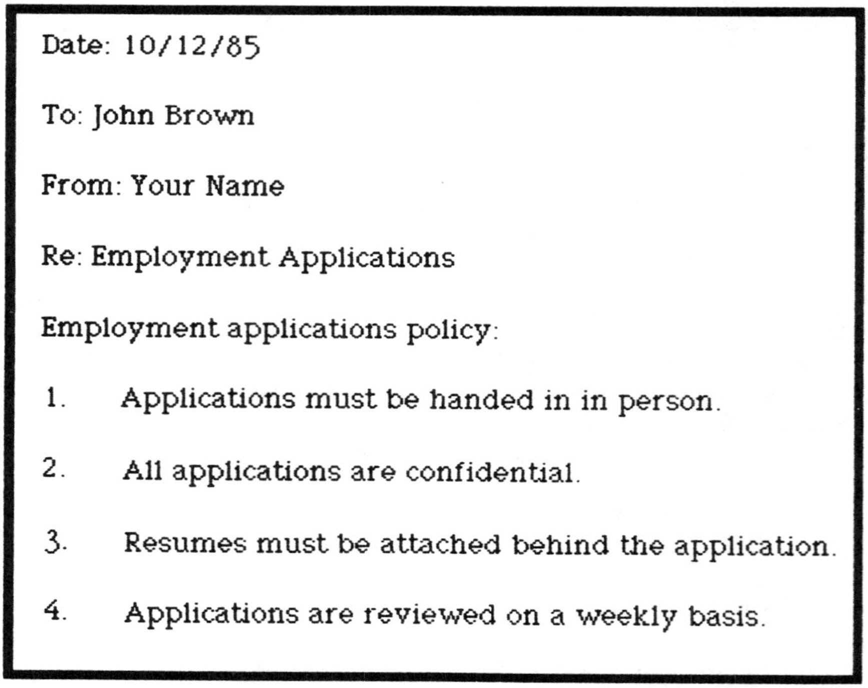

Date: 10/12/85

To: John Brown

From: Your Name

Re: Employment Applications

Employment applications policy:

1. Applications must be handed in in person.

2. All applications are confidential.

3. Resumes must be attached behind the application.

4. Applications are reviewed on a weekly basis.

Figure 2.1
Finished MEMO
Document

1. To select "Edit an Old Document" from the main menu, type   **Procedure**
   "1" and press ENTER. The Document Specification screen appears (it will look similar to figure 2.2).

2. To specify the document name, type "MEMO" at the "Document" prompt, as shown in figure 2.2. If you make a typing
   mistake, simply backspace and type over the incorrect letter.
   Make sure no extra letters are on the "Document" prompt line.

3. Check that the drive specification for the disk holding the MEMO
   document is correct. For example, if your exercise disk is in drive
   B, the "Drive" prompt should read "B". If you're using a hard
   disk, it should read "C".
       To change the drive specification, press SHIFT and TAB. Type
   the letter of the disk drive in which the MEMO document is
   located.

4. Press ENTER to tell MultiMate to find the document.

5. When the Document Summary screen appears, press F10 to move
   ahead to the editing screen.

MultiMate needs to know two things to find a document. You must   **Explanation**
specify the document name and indicate which drive holds the disk
containing the document.
    After selecting the "Edit an Old Document" option, you will see

---

```
        EDIT AN OLD DOCUMENT

      What is the Name of the Old Document?

     Drive : B     Document : MEMO_____

Approximately 0002560 characters [00010 Page(s)] available on B :
BETTER COPY LETTER SEARCH




      Press return to continue, PgDn to switch drives
 Press Ctrl Home to select default directory, Ctrl End to select next directory
                                              S:↓ N:↓
```

Figure 2.2
Document Specification
Screen for MEMO

the Document Specification screen. It asks you the question "What is the name of the old document?" You must type a name on the line following the "Document" prompt.

MultiMate inserts the name of the last document edited in the document prompt to save you some typing time. If the displayed document's name isn't the one you want, you type a different document name over it. Only the name of the document you want to edit should appear on the line; no extra letters should appear there.

It doesn't matter if you type the document name in upper- or lower-case letters (or a mix of both). You must spell the name correctly, however, or MultiMate won't be able to find the document on disk. To check the spelling, refer to the directory in mid-screen that lists the names of documents on disk. If you don't see the document you want among the names listed, you can press PGDN to see a directory for a disk in a different disk drive. You can continue pressing PGDN until you see the directory for the desired disk. You can also press CTRL END to see a different directory on the same drive.

Basically, you type a document's name and space over any extra letters that appear on the line. To delete letters from a name, you can also move the cursor under a letter and press the DEL (delete) key. Similarly, to insert letters, move the cursor where the letter is to appear and press INS (insert). A blank space will be inserted on the prompt line. You can then type the desired letter into it.

After typing a document name, check to see that the correct drive is specified in the "Drive" prompt. If it is correct, you can press ENTER to tell MultiMate to find the document. If the wrong drive is specified, you press SHIFT and TAB and type the letter of the drive holding the document disk, or just press PGDN a few times until the correct drive designation appears. If you type the correct document name but the wrong drive, MultiMate will not locate the correct document and may tell you the document doesn't exist. In this case, you simply specify the correct drive and press ENTER.

After you complete the Document Specification screen, the Document Summary screen appears. Notice that the same information you originally typed in chapter 1 is displayed. You can change this information if you wish. You then press F10 to see page one of the document.

If, after reading the Document Summary screen, you find that you've accessed the wrong document, you can press ESCAPE to return to the main menu.

Before you type the memo, you should know how to get help when you need it.

Stumped? If you can't remember which key to press or how to perform a specific editing procedure, MultiMate's Help facility can often
provide the answer. MultiMate has many keyboard and procedural
explanations stored on disk, and you can refer to them easily. It's as
if MultiMate carried around its own autobiography just waiting for
you to ask a question.

You access the Help Facility by pressing SHIFT F1. MultiMate
lets you choose from six general areas of information to review, or
you can press any key on the keyboard to view an explanation of
that key's function.

When you first access Help, a screen appears like that shown in
figure 2.3.

1. To access MultiMate's Help facility, press SHIFT and F1. A menu
   of six choices appears, as shown in figure 2.3.

2. To see information about "Editing Functions", type "2".

3. Examine the list of functions associated with keys. The list is not
   complete; to see more press the space bar.

**MULTIMATE'S HELP
FACILITY**

**Objective: Getting
Help Information
When You Need It**

Procedure

```
DOCUMENT:MEMO                 ‖PAGE:      1‖LINE:      1‖COL:   1‖
| 1 . . ≫ . . . . ≫ . . . . ≫ . . . . . . . . . . . . . . ≫ . . . . . . . . . . . . . . . . . . . . .≪

HELP MENUS

        Press the function key for the help desired.
        Example: Press the F8 key for help on the Copy function.
                 Press Alt F for help on the Footer function.
        To get help on more general topics, press one of the following keys:


        HELP DESIRED                        PRESS
        ----------------------------------  ------

        CURSOR POSITIONING                    1
        EDITING FUNCTIONS                     2
        FORMAT LINE CONTROLS                  3
        PRINTING FUNCTIONS                    4
        MISCELLANEOUS FUNCTIONS               5
        LIST OF ALL HELP TOPICS AND KEYS      6




 Press Escape to exit                                    S:↓N:↓
```

Figure 2.3
Help Menu

4. To see an explanation of a specific key's function, you press that key after the list of functions appears. For example, press the minus key (-) next to the key marked "9" on the numeric keypad (*not* the one on the top row of numbers). An explanation of the minus key's function appears.

5. To stop viewing the explanation, press ENTER. The list of keys returns. You can now choose another editing function to read about or return to the Help menu by pressing ENTER.

6. Press ENTER to return to the Help menu. You can also get information directly by pressing the key about which you have a question when the Help menu appears.

7. After the Help menu reappears, press the plus key (+) (on the numeric keypad—not the one on the top row on the keyboard) to find out about its function.

8. When you have finished reading about the plus key, press ESC. The information about the plus key disappears, and the editing screen reappears as it originally was.

Explanation

With MultiMate, Help is always at hand. You can access the Help facility at MultiMate's main menu or during editing, as you did here. The information displayed on screen doesn't become part of your text. Once you're finished viewing it, your document returns to the way it originally was before you asked for Help.

The Help menu provides a list of Help topics and keys, as well as information about the keys used for cursor positioning, editing functions, setting format lines, specifying special kinds of printing, and miscellaneous editing functions.

Once you see the Help menu, you can either select one of the general topic areas or press the key (or key combination) about which you have a question. If you select a general topic area, information about that topic appears. For example, if you select "Editing Functions", a list of editing functions and their associated keys appears. If the editing function you have a question about is listed, you press the key or key combination associated with that function; an explanation then appears on screen.

When the Help menu appears, you can also just press the key in question, and MultiMate will display an explanation for that key. You read the explanation and when done, press ENTER to see the Help menu again or press ESC to stop using the Help facility and continue editing.

As you learn to use MultiMate, don't worry about memorizing what all the different keys do. Now that you know about the Help facility, you can quickly look up their functions any time you wish.

Let's type the memo shown in figure 2.4. Typing on screen is easier than typing on paper. If you make a simple typing error, just back-space and type the correct character over it. If you leave out characters in a word, you can insert them by positioning the cursor where the letters should appear and pressing the plus key (on the numeric keypad) to insert spaces. Then you can type the missing characters into the blank spaces. You can also erase characters by moving the cursor under them and pressing the minus key (on the numeric keypad) to delete one character at a time.

You move the cursor around the screen with the arrow keys. You can't move the cursor, however, until you've typed something on the screen. Unlike when you use a typewriter, you shouldn't try to move the cursor by holding down the space bar. The space bar puts blank spaces in your text and will actually space over (and erase) text if you try to move the cursor this way.

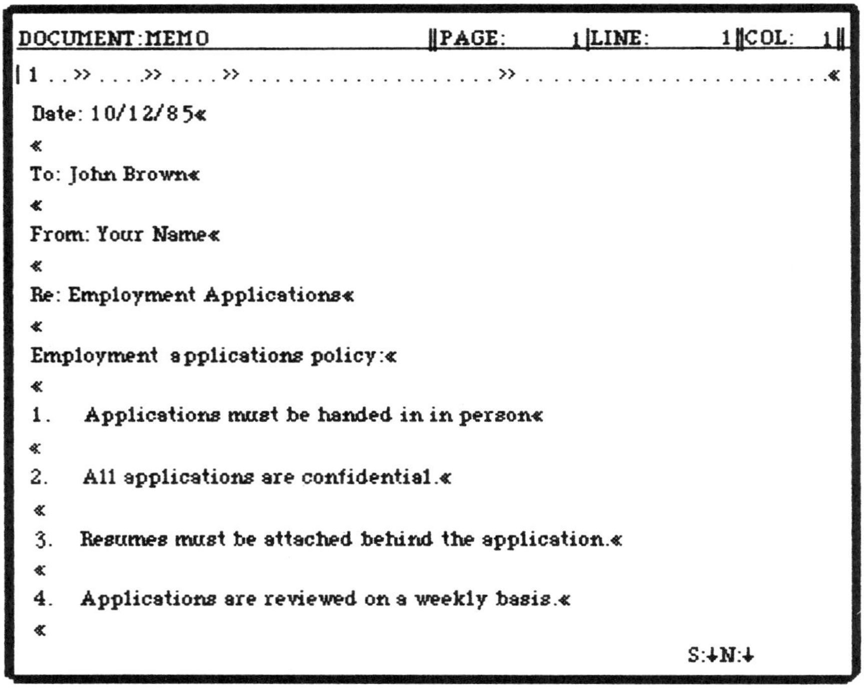

EDITING A DOCUMENT

Objective: Typing a Short Document

```
 DOCUMENT:MEMO                    ‖PAGE:      1│LINE:      1‖COL:   1‖
│ 1 . . ≫ . . . .≫ . . . .≫ . . . . . . . . . . . . . . .≫ . . . . . . . . . . . . . . . . . . . . .«
   Date: 10/12/85«
   «
   To: John Brown«
   «
   From: Your Name«
   «
   Re: Employment Applications«
   «
   Employment applications policy:«
   «
   1.    Applications must be handed in in person«
   «
   2.    All applications are confidential.«
   «
   3.    Resumes must be attached behind the application.«
   «
   4.    Applications are reviewed on a weekly basis.«
   «
                                              S:↓N:↓
```

Figure 2.4
Editing Screen and Memo

When you come to the end of a line, and you want the cursor to go down one line, you press ENTER, the carriage return key, just as you would with a normal typewriter. (MultiMate has an editing feature that lets you avoid doing this for every line, as you'll learn later.)

If you want to skip a line, you also press ENTER. Whenever you press ENTER, MultiMate will put a special marker (≪) on the screen. This marker simply tells you where the line ends. It doesn't print with the rest of the text.

Procedure

1. With the cursor on line 1, column 1, press the minus key (on the numeric keypad) repeatedly until your name is deleted. Every time you press the minus key, the character above the cursor disappears.

2. Type "Date: 10/11/85" and press ENTER. If you make a typing mistake, backspace and type the correct letter. Notice the carriage-return marker (≪) that appears at the end of the line when you press ENTER.

3. With the arrow keys, move the cursor to line 1, column 1, under the "D" in "Date". (Remember, the cursor-position indicators at the top of the screen show the cursor's line and column position.)

4. Press the minus key twice (be sure to use the minus key on the numeric keypad). The "D" and "a" of "Date" are deleted. Notice how the rest of the line moves to fill up the deleted space.

5. Without moving the cursor, press the plus key (on the numeric keypad) twice. Two blank spaces appear and the characters of the rest of the line slide to the right. Now type "Da". The plus key inserts blank spaces, which can then be filled with any character you choose.

6. With the arrow keys, move the cursor down to line 2, column 1 and press ENTER to skip down a line. Only a carriage-return marker appears on line two.

7. Type "To: John Brown" and press ENTER twice, once to end the line and again to skip down a line.

8. Type "From:" and then type your name; press ENTER. Let's erase a carriage return marker to see what happens.

9. Move the cursor under the carriage-return marker in line 4, column 1. Let's delete this marker.

10. Press the minus key. The carriage-return marker disappears, and the lines beginning "To:" and "From:" are no longer separated

by a blank line. Carriage-return markers are just like letter characters and can be deleted. Let's insert a carriage return marker between the "To" and "From" lines to separate them again.

11. With the cursor on line 4, column 1 (under the "F" of "From:"), press the plus key to insert a space and then press ENTER. The two lines are separated again. Notice how MultiMate automatically adjusts the positioning of letters and lines of text for you.

12. Move the cursor to line 6, column 1, and press ENTER.

13. Type "Re: Employment Applications" and press ENTER twice.
    Let's make a mistake on purpose so that you know how to handle one on your own later.

14. Press the backspace key and then press the DEL key. That starts a deletion procedure that can delete large chunks of text. Up in the right corner of the screen, the message "DELETE WHAT?" will appear. Because you don't know the procedure, you don't know what to do next. To get out of this jam, you press ESCAPE. That cancels most procedures you might get into accidentally.

15. Press ESC. The "DELETE WHAT?" message disappears.

16. Continue typing the rest of the memo as you see it in figure 2.4. Press ENTER wherever you see a carriage-return marker. Remember to use the plus and minus keys to insert and delete characters. Also experiment with the arrow keys to see how they move the cursor through text. You hold down the cursor keys to make the cursor move continuously through text.

17. After typing the last line of the memo (beginning "4. Applications are reviewed . . ."), press ENTER and read over the memo text. If you spot a typing error, move the cursor up to the error and correct it by inserting, deleting, or typing over the mistake.

18. With the memo completed, save it on disk by pressing F10. MultiMate stores the memo, replacing the old document with the new one you just edited, and the main menu reappears on screen. Congratulations, you've just completed MultiMate's routine editing cycle.

Editing on a word-processing screen is a little different from typing on paper. First, MultiMate always displays text in a single-spaced format. You can print it out using double spacing, triple spacing, or several other types of spacing, but the text you see on the screen will always be single-spaced during editing. **Explanation**

Aside from line spacing, you position text on screen the way it is to be printed on paper. If you type text centered or indented on screen, it prints centered or indented on paper. With a few exceptions, the text as you see it formatted on screen closely resembles the printed version.

Usually, when you begin typing a document, you set the format line to the line spacing, tab stops, and line length you desire. Don't worry about setting up the format line for now; you'll learn to do that shortly. If the format line on your screen looks different from the one illustrated here, it makes little difference for learning the basic editing procedures.

The cursor marks the place where editing takes place. If you press a letter key, the letter appears at the cursor position on screen and the cursor moves over one space.

With a typewriter, you usually start at the top of a page and work down, typing line by line. The same is true with MultiMate. Once you've finished typing, however, you can move the cursor back through the text displayed on the screen and change it easily. If you want to perform an editing procedure, such as deleting a word, the first thing you do is move the cursor to the word to be deleted. Thus, a good deal of editing involves moving the cursor from place to place on screen.

In the exercise above, you moved the cursor up, down, left, and right one space at a time with the cursor arrow keys and the backspace key. MultiMate has many much faster methods of moving the cursor, as you'll learn later.

As you edit with MultiMate, some information appears on screen that doesn't print as part of the document. Chapter 1 mentioned the status line, with its cursor-position indicators, and the format line, which shows settings of line spacing, tab stops, and line length. These two lines, which appear at the top of the editing screen, serve only as references. Beneath them you type the actual text to be printed.

MultiMate also uses special screen markers that are visible within the text. These markers tell you when a certain key has been pressed. For example, each time ENTER is pressed, a carriage-return marker (≪) appears on the screen. If you examine figure 2.4, you can see where the ENTER key was pressed to end each line of the memo. The carriage-return marker also appears (by itself) where blank lines are to appear in the text.

Although the markers appear on screen for your reference, they don't print on paper. MultiMate uses a variety of screen markers, such as the carriage-return marker, that appear when formatting keys are pressed. The screen markers are just like any other character on the screen. You can erase and insert them to change the shape of your text. For instance, you can insert three blank lines in a document by inserting three carriage-return markers. You might delete a blank line between two paragraphs simply by deleting the carriage return marker that separates them. You'll learn more about using and changing these markers later.

The simplest way to delete a single character (or screen marker) is to move the cursor under the character and press the numeric keypad's minus key (it is located next to the 9 of the ten-key pad). The character disappears and the text to the right moves up to fill in automatically.

Similarly, to insert a blank space in the text, you position the cursor and press the plus key (again on the numeric keypad; you cannot use the plus and minus keys on the keyboard's top row). A space appears on the screen, and you can fill it with a character if you wish. If, for example, you typed "tee" instead of "tree", you could insert the missing "r" by positioning the cursor under the first "e" of "tee", pressing the plus key, and typing an "r". Thus, when you've left letters out of words, you can use the plus key to insert them.

MultiMate has much faster ways of inserting and deleting large chunks of text, but for now you should start off using the plus and minus keys for single-letter insertions and deletions.

If you've mistyped a character or two, you can also backspace and type the correct characters over them. Depending on how your version of MultiMate is set up, the cursor may or may not erase the characters it backs over when backspacing. If it erases characters, you'll want to stick to using the cursor arrow keys to move the cursor harmlessly across correctly typed text.

When you first begin editing, there are some things to watch out for. You might accidentally press a key and find MultiMate doing something unexpected. Don't worry. If a screen marker appears that you've never seen before, try moving the cursor under the marker and deleting it. Your text may go back to its original format. Or, if MultiMate displays an unfamiliar message, apparently starting an editing procedure you haven't learned, pressing ESCAPE usually cancels the procedure and returns the text to the way it was.

If you press ESCAPE one too many times, however (and everyone does this sooner or later), you'll see the message:

"Do you wish to escape without saving this page? (Y/N)"

MultiMate is asking you if you want to quit editing without saving your work. Type "N" for "no" to continue editing.

Don't worry about mistakes, you can't hurt the program or the computer.

Another common mistake that beginners make is to hold a key down too long. If you hold a key down longer than a second, it begins to repeat. Holding down the *A* key, for example, sends a string of *A*s spreading across the screen. Holding down the cursor keys moves the cursor continuously on the screen. Don't hold down a key unless you mean to start it repeating. If you hold a key down too long, and MultiMate can't execute the desired instruction repeatedly, the computer may squeak in complaint. A prolonged key press may also move you ahead in a procedure many steps farther than you intend.

SUMMARY

To edit a document already on disk, you perform the general steps outlined in figure 2.5. The keys shown in figure 2.6 are used to perform basic editing functions. When you're finished with a document, you press F10 to save it on disk. The newly edited document replaces the old version on disk.

Figure 2.5
Editing an Old Document

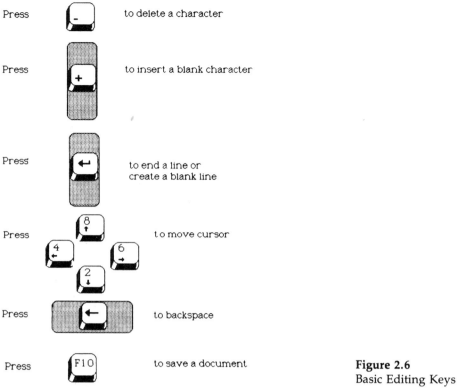

Press   to delete a character

Press   to insert a blank character

Press   to end a line or
         create a blank line

Press   to move cursor

Press   to backspace

Press   to save a document

Figure 2.6
Basic Editing Keys

Chapter 3

PRINTING

> Your computer should be turned on and the MultiMate main menu should be on the screen. (See chapter 1 for instructions if you've forgotten how to load MultiMate.) Your exercise disk with the document called MEMO should be in drive B (this is not necessary if you are using MultiMate on a hard disk.)
>
> Your printer should be turned on and loaded with 8½-by-11-inch typing paper or a comparable size continuous-form computer paper. Refer to your printer manual for instructions about loading and turning on the printer.
>
> You must also have set MultiMate's printer defaults for your type of printer. For instructions for setting the printer defaults see appendix A.

Now for a new skill: using a computer printer.

Unlike typewriters that print a character on paper with every key press, MultiMate prints documents in one long bout as fast as your printer allows. Printing can be a bit scary; as the printer furiously taps out a document you might not feel you're in control.

Don't worry. You'll tell MultiMate exactly how you want the document printed—the margins, line spacing, page numbering, paper size, and many other printing factors—and MultiMate will obediently do just as you say. Setting up a document for printing is as easy as making selections from a restaurant menu. You just choose the printing options you want from a list. You can also quickly stop the printer any time with just a key press or two. If your paper is misaligned, for example, you can stop and make adjustments.

In the beginning, don't be surprised if you have to print a document several times. It takes practice to learn to load paper into a

40

printer and align it so that printing consistently begins at the same place. Fortunately, with MultiMate you can print a document repeatedly with little effort.

Next, you'll print the document called MEMO.

To print a document, you select "Print Document Utility", the third option of the main menu. You tell MultiMate the name of the document to print, and MultiMate shows you a print menu similar to figure 3.1.

Objective: Printing a Document

How a document prints on paper depends on two things: how you arranged the document during editing, including the line spacing and line length chosen, and what settings you specify from the print menu.

If, during editing, you specified double-spacing, a line length of 60 characters, and 50 text lines per page, MultiMate prints the document using those specifications. But what top margin should MultiMate use? How wide a left margin? These types of decisions are made using the print menu.

You change the selections of the print menu by moving the cursor up and down through the options, using the arrow keys, and typing new settings. After specifying the printing parameters, you press F10 and MultiMate prints the document. If you decide not to print, press ESCAPE; the main menu returns to screen.

```
┌──────────────────────────────────────────────────────────────────────┐
│         Print Parameters for Document    B:MEMO                        │
│                                                                        │
│  Start print at page number    001   Lines per inch : 6 / 8       6    │
│  Stop print after page number  001   Justification: N / Y / M(icro) N  │
│  Left margin                    010   Proportional Spacing: N / Y   N   │
│  Top margin                     005   Char translate/width table  ____  │
│  Pause between pages : N / Y     N    Header/footer first page number 001│
│  Draft print : N / Y             N    Number of original copies    001  │
│  Default pitch (4=10 cpi)        4    Document page length         0 66  │
│  Printer Action Table Your Printer    Sheet Feeder Action Table Your Feeder│
│  Sheet Feeder Bin Numbers (0/1/2/3): First page: 0 Middle: 0 Last page:  0│
│  P(arallel) / S(erial) / L(ist) / A(uxiliary) / F(ile)             ?    │
│                            Device Number                          001   │
│                                                                        │
│  Print document summary screen: N/Y N Print printer parameters :  N/Y N │
│  Background / Foreground:      B/F B Remove queue entry when done:Y/N Y  │
│  Current Time is:    00:00:00     Delay Print until Time is: 00:00:00   │
│  Current Date is:    00/00/0000   Delay Print until Date is: 00/00/0000 │
│  Press F1 for Printers, F2 for Sheet Feeders - only the first 16 are displayed│
│        Press F10 to Continue, Press ESC to Abort        S:↓ N:↓        │
└──────────────────────────────────────────────────────────────────────┘
```

Figure 3.1
Print Menu

Procedure

1. With the printer turned on and paper loaded, select "Print Document Utility" from the main menu by typing "3" and pressing ENTER.

2. At the Document Specification screen, type "MEMO" as the document name. Check that the drive specification correctly identifies the location of the disk holding the MEMO document. To change the drive specification, press SHIFT and TAB and type the drive's identifying letter.

3. With the drive and document name specified, press ENTER.

4. Set the print-menu parameters as you see them in figure 3.1, with the exception of the following prompts:

    Printer Action Table
    Sheet Feeder Action Table

    Use the cursor keys to move the cursor from prompt to prompt. Type over the characters of the print specifications to change them.

    At "Printer Action Table" the name of the MultiMate print driver (that is, action table) for your printer should appear. You do not need to type anything at the "Sheet Feeder Action Table" prompt if you do not have a sheet feeder device. Otherwise, you must type the name of the sheet feeder driver at this prompt. (See appendix A for an explanation of drivers.)

    The four time and date prompts at the bottom of the menu— "Current Time is:", "Current Date is:", "Delay Print until Time is", and "Delay Print until Date is"—should display the current time and date (set when you started up the computer.) Don't change these prompts, use them as displayed.

5. With the print-menu specification set, press F10 to begin printing.

6. When printing is complete, repeat the procedure and try printing the memo with a different top and left margin.

Explanation

The print menu provides a formidable array of options, and squinting at them doesn't make them go away. Let's take a look at what they mean.

The print menu displays the document name and drive location at its top. Below are 27 printing specifications that you can change. These printing specifications are filled with automatic selections, called defaults. You need change a default setting on the menu only if the current specification is inappropriate.

Here's what the print menu specifications mean.

To start printing a document on a specific page, you type the starting page number at this prompt. MultiMate always displays "001" as a default, assuming you want printing to begin with page one. With a ten-page document, for example, you can start printing on page five by typing "005" at this prompt. MultiMate then prints the document from page five onward.

Start print at page number

This option specifies where printing should stop. A document's last page number is automatically displayed here. If you don't want to print an entire document, but want printing to stop after a specific page, you use this option to specify which page should be the last page printed.

Stop print after page number

    With a ten-page document, you might stop printing after page 6 by setting this option to 6. To print all ten pages of a document, you set "Start print at page number" to 1 and "Stop print after page number" to 10. To print just two pages of a ten-page document—pages 5 and 6, for example—you tell MultiMate to start printing on page 5 and stop printing after page 6. The "Start print" and "Stop print" options enable you to print part of a multiple-page document.

This option tells the printer how far from the paper's left edge to start printing. You specify the left margin in characters (not inches). Typing "10" here tells the printer to print the memo with a left margin ten characters in from the paper's edge.

Left margin

    The right margin is determined by the line length you set during editing. If you are printing at 10 pitch, the standard typing sheet is 85 characters wide. If you set a left margin of 10 characters and a line length of 60 characters, for example, your right margin would be 15 characters wide [85 − (10 + 60) = 15], as shown in figure 3.2.

    When you set the left margin, you are essentially positioning the page in a block on the paper. Adjusting the left margin changes the right margin as well.

    You may be used to calculating margins in inches. To continue that practice, you'll have to convert characters to inches (according to the printing pitch you use) and do some fast adding and subtracting of paper size, line length, and left margin. It actually may be easier to get used to estimating margin size in numbers of characters than to bother with character-to-inches conversions.

The top margin tells the printer how many lines to skip down before printing the first line of text. With the MEMO document, you told the printer to space down 5 lines from the top of the page. If you were printing a ten-page document, the printer would space down

Top margin

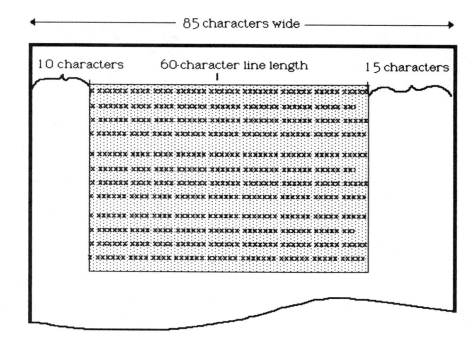

←————————————— 85 characters wide ————————————→

10 characters   60-character line length   15 characters

Figure 3.2
Left and Right Margins
and Line Length

five lines at the top of every page.

Setting the top margin automatically specifies the page's bottom margin. During editing, you typed a certain number of lines on a page. This number, plus the number of lines set as the top margin, determines the space left over at the page's bottom. An 11-inch typing sheet holds 66 lines of text. With a ten-line top margin and a page containing 48 text lines, the bottom margin would be 8 lines, as shown in figure 3.3.

Pause between pages

If you are printing on separate sheets of paper, you want the printer to stop printing after a page is finished so that you can load the next sheet. To make the printer pause between pages, you type a "Y" for "yes" at this option.

With continuous-form computer paper, however, one sheet is attached to the next and the paper feeds into the printer automatically. You don't need to stop the printer between pages in this case; MultiMate can print page after page without stopping (all with the proper top and bottom margins.) When using continuous form paper, you set this option to "N" for "no".

When you tell MultiMate to stop printing between pages, the computer will beep when each page is finished and stop the printing

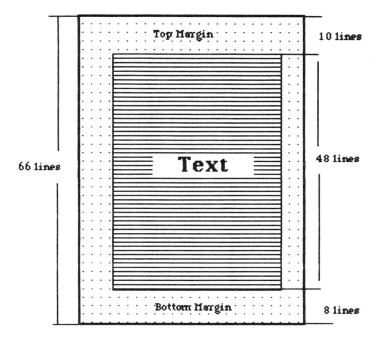

Figure 3.3
Top and Bottom Margins
of Typing Sheet

process. You then load the next sheet and press ESCAPE to continue printing.

Draft print

You will rarely use this option. It determines how dark the printer prints characters on the page. You set this option to "Y" for "yes" to print text in the normal manner.

To make text appear darker on the page, most printers print the same characters twice (or even three times) in the same place. It's the same principle as if you typed the letter A with a typewriter, then backspaced and typed it again. The letter A appears darker the second time you type it. With "Draft print", MultiMate lets you specify that the entire document be printed extra dark this way. If your printer can double-strike, or produce boldface printing, you can print darker text by typing an "N" at this prompt. Naturally, because each letter is being printed several times, printing takes longer. Because most printers print adequately dark text without double-striking, you will probably have few occasions to use this option.

Default pitch

Like some typewriters, most printers can print at 10 or 12 pitch, and some can even print at pitches from 5 to 17 pitch. Most often, however, your printing will likely be at 10 or 12 pitch.

To specify the printing pitch for a document, you type at this option a number corresponding to the desired pitch. For 10 pitch you type a "4", and for 12 pitch you type a "5". The other pitches that are possible won't be listed here, because it might be confusing. You can consult the MultiMate reference manual if you need to use an unusual printing pitch.

Printer Action Table

Most printers refuse to work correctly unless talked to in their own languages. That means that MultiMate must send a set of codes that a printer understands to make it print correctly. To speak the right language, MultiMate has to know what kind of printer you are using. The "Printer Action Table" option identifies your brand of printer and allows MultiMate to find information stored on disk regarding each type of printer's codes.

At the "Printer Action Table" option, you must type the name of the disk information, or print-driver file, associated with your printer. If you press F1 while viewing the print menu, a list of sixteen print driver files appears (MultiMate has dozens more that don't appear, however). If you recognize your printer among them, simply type the corresponding name. See appendix A for a list of these print driver names and for further instructions for configuring MultiMate to use your printer.

Lines per inch

The "Lines per inch" option specifies how close lines appear vertically on the page. Printing is commonly done at 6 lines per inch, which allows 66 lines of text per page (if you filled the entire page). Some printers may be capable of printing in smaller vertical increments, and MultiMate allows you to specify printing at 8 lines per inch if you wish. You could then put 88 lines of text on a standard typing sheet.

Justification

When you print justified text, text is printed with an even right margin up and down the page. Justification creates text that looks similar to the even margins used with most newspaper print.

To print a document with justified text, you type a "Y" for "yes" at this option. During printing, MultiMate inserts extra blank spaces between words, spreading them out, so that all lines are equally long. You can also have MultiMate place small spaces between letters and words to create justified lines (if your printer is capable of this). To create this type of justified text, you type an "M" at this option. If you don't want an even right margin, you type an "N" for "no."

Proportional Spacing

Each of the letters on most printers and typewriters takes up an equal amount of space on paper. The same amount of space is used whether a letter is a wide capital *W* or a slim *l*. Printers that are capable of proportional spacing can print letters next to each other according to the space individual letters take. This provides printed text with the finished look of typeset text, instead of the equally spaced appearance of text produced with a standard typewriter. If your printer is capable of proportional spacing, you can set this option to "Y" for "yes," and MultiMate will print proportionally spaced documents.

If your printer is capable of printing special characters (such as math symbols or foreign language characters), you can tell MultiMate to print them. You do that by creating a character-translation table that allows you to substitute special characters for other characters found on the keyboard.

Char translate/width table

You can also use these kinds of tables to tell MultiMate how much space to use between characters during proportionally spaced printing. A character translation/width table is actually part of the printer action table that you specify, and you don't need to specify another character translation/width table unless you want to use one that you've specifically designed.

Explaining how to set up and use these tables is technically beyond the scope of the discussion here. Refer to your MultiMate reference manuals if you care to investigate these tables further. There are also several other ways in which you can print special characters without creating one of these tables. Chapter 13 will discuss another method of printing special characters.

The "Header/footer first page number" option is related to a few word-processing concepts you may not have encountered before.

Header/footer first page number

MultiMate can automatically count and number pages for you during printing. With a multiple-page document, MultiMate can print page numbers on every page without your typing individual page numbers yourself.

MultiMate also can automatically print repeating text, such as report titles, at the top and bottom of every page in a document. Text that is printed at the top of every page is called a "header" and repeating text that is printed at the page's bottom is a "footer."

You set up automatic page numbering for a document by creating either a special header or footer. (Don't worry about understanding headers and footers for now; you'll learn more about them later.) If you print a thirty-page document, chapter one of a book, for example, the program can correctly number the pages from 1 to 30. Suppose you now want to print another document, the book's second chapter. The first page of this document should print as page 31 (because it follows the first thirty pages of chapter 1). The "Header/footer first page number" option tells MultiMate the starting page number to use.

A document's first page might be numbered 1, 10, 50, or whatever number you choose. The number you type at the "Header/footer first page number" prompt specifies the page number that will be assigned to the first page of the document, and thus controls every page number after that.

Because the MEMO document didn't use automatic page numbering, this prompt was left at 1 and had no effect on the document.

Number of original copies

At this option, you type a number corresponding to the number of times you want the document printed. If you type "1" here, MultiMate prints the entire document once. If you type "2", MultiMate prints the document twice consecutively. Although it's perhaps slower and less efficient than a copying machine, you can use this option to produce multiple copies of a document.

Document page length

This option tells MultiMate the length of the paper you're using. You type a number corresponding to the number of text lines that fit on a page. When you are printing at 6 lines an inch, a standard typing sheet is 66 lines long. To print on an 11-inch sheet, you set the page length at 66. If you are using legal-size, 14-inch sheets, you set this option to 84 lines (assuming your printing is set at 6 lines per inch). If you are using shorter or longer paper, you multiply the inch length of the sheets by 6 to determine the number of lines to fill in for this option.

You are specifying the physical length of the paper with this option, not the number of text lines you want printed on a page.

Sheet Feeder Action Table

A sheet feeder is a paper-loading device that loads separate sheets of paper into a printer. With a sheet feeder, you don't have to load typing sheets by hand. Just as you had to identify your brand of printer, you must also tell MultiMate the type of sheet feeder being used, if you have one. Press F2 with the print menu on screen to see a list of sheet feeders that MultiMate knows how to run. If you see your brand of sheet feeder among the list, type the corresponding name at this prompt.

Sheet Feeder Bin Numbers

Sheet feeders usually have one to three bins that hold different types of paper. In one bin, you might have letterhead stationery; another might hold blank stationery; and a third might hold colored paper of some sort. When you print a document, you tell MultiMate which bins and paper you wish to use.

For example, you might tell MultiMate to print a document's first page on letterhead stationery by setting "First page" to 1 (assuming letterhead paper is stored in bin 1). The second page of a letter might be printed on blank stationery by setting "Middle" to 2 (for bin 2, in which blank stationery is stored). To use a special type of paper for the last page of a document, you specify a number that tells MultiMate to use bin 1, 2, or 3 with the "Last page" option.

If you don't have a sheet feeder, these options are set to zero.

MultiMate needs to know if you are using a parallel or serial printer. The difference between parallel and serial printers has to do with the manner in which your documents are sent to the printer. You probably needn't bother learning the technical details of parallel and serial communications; all you need to know is which type your printer uses.   *P(arallel)/S(erial)/ L(ist)/A(uxiliary)/F(ile)*

Your printer manual will tell you if the printer is parallel or serial. You can't tell by simply looking at the printer. If you're using a parallel printer, this option should be set to "P"; otherwise set it to "S" for serial. You can set this option when you first set up your print menu defaults and avoid having to set it later.

In most cases, simply setting this option to "P" or "S" will suffice. In special cases, such as when a PC is connected to a network of other computers sharing a printer, you may need to use the "List" or "Auxiliary" options. Refer to MultiMate's reference manuals for further explanation of this technical topic. You can also create a special file that can be used with DOS commands if you select "F" (for "File") at this option. Your document will be stored on disk in a special format.

You may have more than one printer connected to the computer. You tell MultiMate which printer to use by specifying a number at this option. If you only have one printer attached to the computer, you naturally don't have to worry about this option.   *Device Number*

Printers are attached to the computer by cables connected to devices called *ports*. As far as you're concerned at this point, these ports are simply plugs in the back of the computer to which you hook printer cables. You tell MultiMate to use the first, second, or third printer port by specifying "001", "002", or "003" as the printer to use.

Each document that you create has a Document Summary screen in which you can record the author, addressee, operator, and various other pieces of information about the document, including keywords and comments. You completed the MEMO Document Summary   *Print document summary screen*

screen in chapter 1. You can print the information found in the Document Summary screen as a record of the document. If you type a "Y" for "yes" at the "Print Document Summary screen" option, the Document Summary screen prints as the first page of the document. Type "N" for "no" if you do not want to print this information.

Print printer parameters

This option enables you to print the print menu, as you've just set it up, as a reference. It's like taking a snapshot of the print menu so that you'll know how to print the same document later. To print the print menu, type a "Y" for "yes" here.

You'll probably rarely print the print menu specifications, however. Once you set up the print menu and print a document, MultiMate remembers and displays the same print menu specifications the next time you want to print that document. This saves you time and makes the "Print printer parameters" option of limited usefulness.

Background/Foreground

With MultiMate, you can print one document as you edit another. Because printing long documents can take many minutes, even hours, MultiMate enables you to keep working on other documents during printing. Printing one document as you edit another is called "background" printing; to initiate it, you type a "B" for "background" at the "Background/Foreground" prompt.

If you type "F" for "foreground" at this prompt, you must wait until the printer is finished printing before you can continue word processing. Naturally, you'll most often be using background printing. You must select "foreground", however, when you use Multi-Mate's merge-print functions for such things as printing form letters for mass mailings.

Remove queue entry when done

With MultiMate, you can line up several documents to be sent to the printer, and MultiMate keeps track of them and prints them one after the other. Documents that are waiting to be printed are said to be in a *print queue*.

The print queue is a list of documents waiting to be printed. After one document is finished printing, the next document in line moves up in the queue and is sent to the printer. Later in this chapter, you'll learn how to change the order of the documents waiting to be printed, stop printing a document before it's finished, and put a hold on a document if you temporarily want to stop it from being printed.

Normally, once a document is finished printing, you want to remove its name from the print queue. To do that, you set this option to "Y" for "yes." You will almost always delete the document from the print queue this way when it has finished printing.

If you set this option to "N" for "no," the document will stay in the print queue, but on "hold", meaning it won't print again until you specifically tell it to do so. Thus, you might use this option to print a document several times, at different intervals of time. Because it's easy to specify a document for printing, however, it's unlikely that you'll ever keep a document on hold in this way.

The "Current time is" and "Current date is" prompts act as references for the time and date and cannot be changed. The time and date are set when you first load the DOS program.

Current Time is/Current Date is

Unless you change the time displayed in this option, MultiMate begins printing the document immediately once you press F10. You can, however, delay printing a document until a specific time. For example, if you choose to delay printing until after a meeting adjourns, you would type here the time when you expect the meeting to end. MultiMate will hold the document in the print queue until the set time and then print it. You cannot edit or change a document that is on hold in the print queue, however.

Delay Print until Time is

If you can delay printing minutes or hours, why not days? After you fill in this option with a future date, MultiMate will hold the document in the print queue until its printing day arrives. You can even turn off the computer or exit MultiMate, and the program will hold documents in the queue for printing for days, months, years . . . perhaps a half century?

Delay Print until Date is

Once you've specified a document for printing, you can specify another right away without waiting. If you want to print five documents in a row, you can quickly perform this print procedure five times, and each document is put in the print queue until its turn to be printed arrives.

You cannot edit a document at the same time it is printing. If you try, MultiMate displays a message informing you that the document is printing and is unavailable for editing changes.

In a pinch, several ways exist for stopping the printer quickly. Printers often have switches that enable you to stop printing immediately without turning off the machine. You'll have to refer to your printer's manual for information about such switches. MultiMate also provides a way to stop the printer quickly and to manipulate the order of documents waiting to be printed in the print queue.

PRINTER QUEUE CONTROL

Objective: Stopping the Printer Quickly

If you press CTRL and SCROLL LOCK, the printer queue control menu (see figure 3.4) appears on screen.

```
        Printer Queue Control

   1. Remove a Document from the Queue
   2. Place a Document on Hold
   3. Release a Document from Hold
   4. Move a Document to the top of the Queue
   5. Restart the Document Currently Printing

MEMO




   File Status:   Printing  [Hold]   Errors will Blink

        Place the cursor next to the document name.
   Press the numeric key (1 to 5) for the function to be performed.
                Press F10 to return.
```

Figure 3.4
Printer Queue Control
Menu

Procedure

1. To see the printer queue control menu, hold down the CTRL key and press the SCROLL LOCK key.

2. Examine the menu selections and press ESCAPE when done. The main menu appears. Now try stopping the printer. First, you must start a document printing.

3. From the main menu, select "Print Document Utility" by typing "3" and pressing ENTER.

4. Type the document name MEMO and press ENTER at the Document Specification screen. Check that the drive specification is correct. You can just press ENTER if the MEMO document name already appears at the prompt.

5. Make sure that the printer is turned on and paper loaded. Read steps 6 and 7 before you perform them.

6. Press F10 at the print menu to start the printer.

7. Now, stop the printer, as follows: hold down CTRL and press SCROLL LOCK. Type "1". The printer stops. Of course, you must perform this step before the printer finishes printing the short MEMO document.

8.   Press ESCAPE to return to the main menu.

In case of printing panic, call printer queue control.   **Explanation**
    You can call the printer queue control menu to the screen any
time during editing or while performing other main menu options.
To stop a document from printing, you type a "1" to select "Remove
a Document from the Queue". This stops the printer and removes
the document that was printing from the print queue so that you
can edit it.
    You can also select "Place a Document on Hold" by typing "2".
This stops printing but does not remove the document from the print
queue. To resume printing again, you select "Release a Document
from Hold".
    When you release a document from hold, printing begins from
the first page (or from the page you selected to begin printing). It
doesn't pick up where printing left off. To pause the printer and
restart it at the same place in a document, you must use the On-line
or Select buttons on the printer itself. MultiMate will temporarily halt
printing. To restart printing, you press the On-line switch again and
then press ESCAPE.
    The names of the documents in the print queue appear under-
neath the menu options. The documents print in order from left to
right. The document name that is highlighted is the one currently
printing. To stop printing a particular document, you move the cursor
to the desired document's name and select the first or second option.
To take a document off hold, you position the cursor on the document
name and select the third option.
    The option "Move a Document to the top of the Queue" allows
you to select a document to be printed next. To change the print-
queue order, you move the cursor to a document name and type
"4". The selected document name will jump ahead in the queue for
printing after the currently printing document finishes.
    The last option, "Restart the Document Currently Printing", will
stop the document currently printing and immediately begin printing
it from the beginning.

To print a document, you make the menu selections as shown in   **SUMMARY**
figure 3.5.
    You can stop printing a document using either printer switches
or by selecting an option on the printer queue control menu (see
figure 3.6).

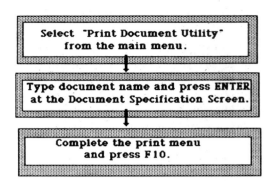

Figure 3.5
Printing Procedure

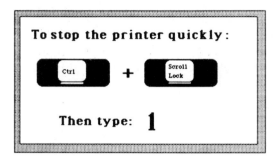

Figure 3.6
Calling Up the Printer
Queue Control Menu

Chapter 4

TYPING A LETTER

Preparation

Your computer should be turned on and the MultiMate main menu on screen. (See chapter 1 for instructions if you've forgotten how to load MultiMate.) Your exercise disk should be in drive B (this is not necessary if you are using MultiMate on a hard disk).

Now that you have created a short memo, some questions have probably come to mind: How do you set the line spacing, tab stops, right margin? How do you change the left margin within a page? How do you create a new page? How do you go from one page to another?

To answer these questions, this chapter will teach you to type the letter you see in figure 4.1. As you type it, you'll learn basic steps for formatting a document so that it prints on paper the way you want it.

You're probably wondering if MultiMate performs these procedures in a way similar to that used by a typewriter. The answer is yes and no. MultiMate's procedures are often similar, but MultiMate also does things a typewriter can't. After setting tab stops, for example, you press the TAB key to move the cursor in short leaps from tab stop to tab stop across the screen, a process similar to tabbing with a typewriter. But MultiMate can also automatically center words and phrases between margins as you type them, and MultiMate also has a feature called *word wrap* that lets you type line after line of text without pressing the ENTER key at the end of each line. Typewriters can rarely perform these last two editing functions.

June 30, 1984
24 Taylor Pl.
San Rafael, CA 94903

Linda Benson, Literary Agent
1111 Jackson Street
San Francisco, CA 92222

Dear Linda:

I've just finished revising my manuscript "Death in Dungarees." With your suggestions in mind, I cut two chapters from the beginning of the book and condensed and combined several others. I also went through the entire manuscript, taking out sections of background material that didn't move the plot along.

I have also done the following:

1. Clarified who killed whom and put some additional material at the end so that Jamal's situation is more clearly resolved.

2. Translated the excerpts lifted from Camus' books to make them more accessible to the reader.

3. Wrote a brief foreword that sets the book in a historical context.

I feel the book is strengthened considerably thanks to your reading.

Thank you!

Sincerely,

Bill Green

Figure 4.1
MultiMate Letter

In this chapter, you'll learn to set the format line, use tab stops, set a temporary left margin, use MultiMate's word-wrap feature, create new pages when you need them, and move the cursor from page to page.

When you first create a document, you'll likely begin by setting the format line. The format line sets the line spacing, tab stops, and line width.

As you remember from chapter 1, the format line appears at the top of the editing screen and looks something like this:

|1.....≫.....≫ ....≫........≪

The number on the left side governs line spacing, and you can switch between single, double, and triple spacing (other settings may be possible depending on your printer). The right-pointing brackets (≫) represent tab stops; you can set tab stops anywhere along the format line (you can also erase them). The left-pointing bracket (≪) marks where the line width (or right margin) is set.

To set the format line, you first press function key F9. The cursor jumps up into the format line and you can now make changes.

To change the line spacing, you backspace the cursor under the line-spacing number and type a new number corresponding to the desired line spacing (that is, 1 for single spacing, 2 for double spacing, or 3 for triple spacing).

To set tab stops, you position the cursor with the arrow keys and press the TAB key. A tab marker (≫) appears and a tab is then set at the cursor position. To erase a tab you move the cursor under the tab marker and press the space bar.

To set the line width, you use the arrow keys to position the cursor where text lines are to end and press ENTER. The line-width marker (≪) appears at the cursor position. To make the line width wider than it currently is, you simply push the marker to the right by holding down the right arrow key until the format line is as wide as you desire.

With your changes made, you press F9 to finish the procedure. Try setting the format line as you see it in figure 4.2.

1. Select "Create a New Document" from the main menu by typing "2" and pressing ENTER.

2. Type "LETTER" as the document name and press ENTER. (Check that the drive specification is B if your exercise disk is in drive B. You can change it by pressing SHIFT TAB and typing "B".)

3. At the Document Summary screen, press F10.

4. At the Document Defaults screen, change the "Automatic Page Break" option to "N" for "no" and press F10.

5. With MultiMate's editing screen in view, press F9 to begin changing the format line.

SETTING UP THE PAGE

Objective: Setting Line Spacing, Tab Stops, and Line Width on the Format Line

Procedure

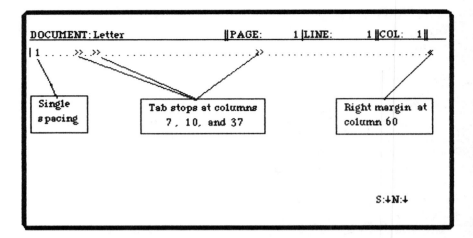

Figure 4.2
Format Line for LETTER
Document

6. Backspace once to move the cursor under the line-spacing number and type 1 for single spacing. (Skip this step if spacing is already set to 1.)

7. Press the space bar five times and press TAB to set a tab stop at column 7.

8. Press the space bar twice to position the cursor on column 10 and press TAB to set a second tab stop.

9. Press TAB to set a tab stop, then backspace and press the space bar to erase it. This is how you eliminate extra tab stops—space over them.

10. With the right arrow key, move the cursor to column 37. Erase any tabs between column 10 and 37 by spacing over them.

11. Press TAB to set a tab at column 37.

12. With the right arrow key, move the cursor to column 45 and press ENTER. (Space over any tabs that might appear after column 37.) This sets the line width. For this letter, make the line width 60 characters.

13. With the right arrow key, move the cursor right to column 60. Notice how the left-pointing bracket is pushed along. (If you go too far, just move the cursor back to the correct column position and press ENTER.)

14. With the format line looking like figure 4.2, press F9 to finish the procedure.

Although you began this letter by setting the format line, you can change it any time during or after editing a document. The text on the screen will automatically adjust to the line settings of the new format.

Remember, to change the format line, press F9, change the settings, and press F9 again to finish. You can change the format line with the cursor anywhere in your text. (You can actually insert several format lines in a page—you'll learn that procedure later.)

With the cursor in the format line, you backspace and type "1", "2", or "3" for single, double, or triple spacing. If your printer is capable of small increments of vertical movement, you might also set spacing to one-and-a-half or two-and-a-half line spacing by typing a plus (+) or equal sign (=) respectively. You can also print using half spacing if you type "H" and quarter spacing if you type "Q". This might be useful, for example, if you were creating some kind of special design or chart and wanted lines closely spaced together. Typing a "0" stops line spacing entirely.

With the right arrow key, you move the cursor right and the cursor position indicators display the current column position. To set a tab, you move the cursor right to the desired column and press TAB. To erase tabs you can move the cursor under the tab marker and press the space bar.

To set line width, you again position the cursor and press ENTER. You can set a line width as narrow as you like. You can also set a line width wider than the screen. You simply keep moving the cursor to the right until you reach the page width you desire. A page can be up to 156 characters wide, about 15½ inches at 10-pitch printing. During editing, lines stretch out of sight off the side of the screen, but when you move the cursor into the right screen margin, off-screen text comes into view. It's a strange computer phenomenon, and you should try setting up extra-wide documents on your own to get used to it.

If you change the format line after you have typed a page of text, the text will reshape itself to the new settings. Thus, when you finish typing a letter, for example, you can still change the line spacing, the amount of space allotted to paragraph indentation, and the line width.

Explanation

You're about to see a little word-processing magic. To move the cursor to the right one tab stop, you press the TAB key. The cursor jumps over one tab stop and a tab marker appears on screen. You can then type text or press TAB again to move the cursor over another tab stop. Unlike a typewriter, however, MultiMate also allows you to erase (or insert) tab markers on screen; the text will adjust to align

TYPING THE LETTER

Objective: Using the TAB Key and Automatic Word Wrap

with the new tabs. You'll try this to make the process clear to you.

When you type several lines of a paragraph, you don't have to press the ENTER key at the end of each line. MultiMate automatically adjusts words between lines for you. When you type paragraphs, you press ENTER only to end the paragraph's last line.

In the next exercise, you'll type the text you see in figure 4.3.

Procedure

1. Press the TAB key once. Notice that the tab marker appears at column 6. If you typed a character it would appear on column 7, where the first tab marker is set in the format line.

2. Press TAB again. The cursor jumps over one more tab stop and another tab marker appears.

3. Press TAB again and type "June 30, 1984" and press ENTER to end the line.

4. To see what happens when you erase a tab stop (which you might do purposefully or accidentally), position the cursor under the tab marker in line 1, column 6 and press the minus key. Notice that the date slides over one tab stop.

```
DOCUMENT: Letter           ‖PAGE:    1 ‖LINE:      1 ‖COL:   1‖
│ 1 . . . . ≫. ≫ . . . . . . . . .       ≫. . . . . . . . . . . . . . . . . . . .⋞
            ≫   ≫                  ≫ June 30, 1984⋞
            ≫   ≫                  ≫ 24 Taylor Pl.⋞
            ≫   ≫                  ≫ San Rafael, CA 94903⋞
⋞
Linda Benson, Literary Agent⋞
1111 Jackson Street⋞
San Francisco, CA 92222⋞
⋞
Dear Linda:⋞
⋞
I've just finished revising my manuscript "Death in
Dungarees ." With your suggestions in mind, I cut two
chapters from the beginning of the book and condensed and
combined several others. I also went through the entire
manuscript, taking out sections of background material that
didn't move the plot along.⋞
                                                    S:↓N:↓
```

Figure 4.3
Letter with First
Paragraph

5. To put the date back in position, insert a tab marker by positioning the cursor under the tab marker at column 6. Next, press the plus sign to insert a space and then press TAB to insert a tab marker. The date jumps back to its original position.

6. Move the cursor to line 2, column 1, press TAB three times and type "24 Taylor Pl." and press ENTER.

7. Press TAB three times and type "San Rafael, CA 94903" and press ENTER twice, once to end the line and again to skip a line.

8. Type the address and salutation you see in figure 4.3. Remember to press ENTER twice after the "Dear Linda:" of the salutation to end the line and skip a line.

9. Type the first line of the paragraph. As you are typing the phrase "Death in Dungarees", watch MultiMate automatically move the cursor and the word "Dungarees" down to the next line. That's word wrap.

10. Type the rest of the paragraph; don't press ENTER at the end of each line—use word wrap. Press ENTER only to end the last line of the paragraph.

You'll have to get used to using screen markers as you edit text. **Explanation** MultiMate has quite a variety of them.

When you press TAB a marker appears on screen. The marker holds your text in place—if you erase a tab marker, the text after it slides left to the next marker or to the left screen margin. As you type text, you use TAB the same way as you would with a typewriter. However, you might also occasionally reposition text by inserting and deleting tab markers.

If you accidentally erase a tab marker, for example, your text goes out of position on screen. You can fix the problem simply by inserting a tab marker where the old one appeared.

MultiMate uses several other kinds of screen markers similar to tab, two of which you'll use shortly. These screen markers all act as place holders on screen, and you can erase and insert them to change the formatting of text. During editing, if you make a mistake and an unwanted screen marker appears, simply move the cursor under a marker and erase it.

You will always want to use word wrap when you type paragraphs. Not only is it convenient not having to press ENTER to end each line, but it also helps your editing in other ways.

With word wrap, MultiMate tries to fit as many whole words on a line as possible. (A word is considered to be any group of characters separated by a blank space.) If you delete or insert text in a paragraph, word wrap will automatically adjust the positioning of every word to fit with the set line width. If you delete the first two words of a paragraph, for example, word wrap readjusts every line of the paragraph to take up the deleted space.

Unlike when using a typewriter, you must not press ENTER at the end of each line when typing paragraphs. With a carriage-return marker at the end of each line, word wrap can't function properly. If you insert or delete text later, text can't automatically readjust to properly fit words on lines. You'll have to either erase all the carriage-return markers or manually move words between long and short lines to make them fit the line length. This is a needless and tedious process at best; let word wrap work for you.

SIMPLE FORMATTING

Objective: Setting Temporary Left Margins and Centering Text

Next, you'll complete the letter so that it looks like figure 4.4. Notice the numbered text in figure 4.4. It is indented from the left margin. MultiMate provides an INDENT key, F4, that automatically sets the left margin to a new position (at a tab stop). As when you press TAB, pressing F4 will cause the cursor to jump to the next tab stop. That position also becomes the left margin. You can type many lines of text and word wrap will use the new left margin. Once you press ENTER the old left margin is reinstated.

You can also automatically center words and phrases, such as the "Thank you!" seen at the letter's bottom. You press F3, the CENTER key, and any text you type (up to one line) will center itself on screen. You press ENTER to stop the centering process.

Procedure

1. After pressing ENTER to end the first paragraph, press ENTER again to skip down one line and type:

   "I have also done the following:"

   and then press ENTER twice.

2. Press TAB and type "1." Include period as part of entry.

3. Press F4, the INDENT key; the cursor jumps to the next tab stop and puts a new screen marker on screen (→). This is the indent marker, and it marks the new left margin.

4. Type the three lines beginning "Clarified" as seen in figure 4.4. Just keep typing—word wrap will adjust the lines for you. Notice how word wrap adjusts the text to the next left margin. Also notice that when you run out of space MultiMate brings up blank lines at the screen's bottom, and lines of text at the screen's top disappear.

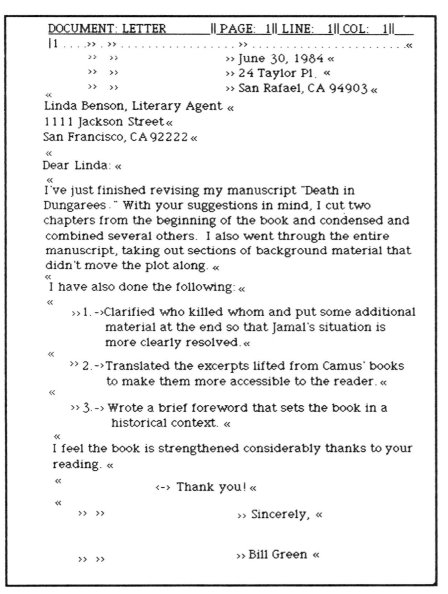

Figure 4.4
Completed Letter

5. After finishing the three lines, press ENTER twice. Notice that the old left margin comes back into effect.

6. Press TAB and type "2." Then press F4, the INDENT key.

7. Type the lines beginning "Translated". Press ENTER twice when finished.

8. Press TAB and type "3.", press F4, and type the text beginning "Wrote"; press ENTER twice to end the text.

9. Move the cursor to line 27, column 9, under the Indent marker (→).

10. Try changing this marker to a TAB marker to see what happens. Press TAB. Notice how the temporary left margin is eliminated.

11. To reinstate the temporary left margin, backspace and press F4 to change the marker to an INDENT marker. The text reshapes itself to the new left margin.

12. Move the cursor to line 30, column 1 and type the line beginning "I feel", ending it by pressing the ENTER key twice. The cursor is now on line 33.

13. To center the "Thank you!", press F3, the CENTER key. A new marker (↔) appears on screen.

14. Type "Thank you!" and press ENTER twice. Notice how the phrase centers itself as you type.

15. Type the closing to finish the letter. Press TAB three times, type "Sincerely," and press ENTER three times. Then tab over and type "Bill Green".

16. Press ENTER. Your letter is finished; read it over for typographical errors. Correct any errors you find. To see the parts of the letter that are out of sight above or below the screen, just move the cursor up or down into the screen's border. Text will scroll into view.

Explanation

INDENT is like a drill sergeant who orders troops to stand in a straight line.

INDENT temporarily sets a new left margin at a tab stop. When you need to indent a quotation in a research paper, for example, you press the INDENT key once at the start of the quote and a new left margin is in effect.

On the screen you see a screen marker—a right-pointing arrow—marking the new margin. You can insert or erase this marker to change text format, just as you could with the TAB marker. Except that it sets a new left margin, INDENT is similar to the TAB function, which moves the cursor right from tab stop to tab stop. You can set a left margin any number of tab stops to the right.

To center text before you type it, press F3, the CENTER key. As you type, characters adjust on screen and center themselves. You can center as much text as fits within one line. You press ENTER to stop the centering function. To center two lines of text, for example, you press F3 at the beginning of each line and press ENTER to end them.

If you decide that you no longer want the text centered, you can move the cursor under the centering marker and erase it. The centered text jumps immediately to the left margin. You can also center text that you have already typed. Move the cursor to the beginning of the line you want centered, insert a space and press F3. Text to the right of the center marker centers on screen. (The centered text must also end with an ENTER screen marker.)

By now, you can see the importance of the screen markers. They tell you which formatting keys have been pressed to create different text formats. Although the screen markers appear on screen, they don't print with the text. It's important to realize that you can insert and erase these screen markers just as you can any other character. Erasing and inserting these formatting markers is useful for rearranging your text after you've typed it.

If a page is longer than 24 lines, you can't see all of it at one time. If you're editing at the bottom of a page, you can think of text as being out of sight above the screen. To see text above the screen, you direct the cursor past the top visible text line; magically, line after line descends into view, like a scroll unwinding. This is called *scrolling*, and you can scroll up and down through a page with the up and down arrow keys.

CREATING NEW PAGES AND MOVING FROM PAGE TO PAGE

You can tell MultiMate to start a new page after you finish one. You create a new page by pressing F2, called the PAGE BREAK key. When the cursor is at the bottom of a finished page, pressing F2 saves the page on disk and a new blank editing screen appears (as illustrated in figure 4.5).

Objective: Creating a New Page and Moving between Pages

Some of your documents may be many pages long. To move to a specific page, you press the F1 key. MultiMate asks you to which page you want to go. You type a page number and press ENTER. MultiMate searches the document until it finds the correct page and displays it on screen for you.

Procedure

1. With the cursor at the bottom of your letter, on line 39, create a new page by pressing F2. The disk drive turns on as page 1 is saved, and a blank editing screen appears; it is marked page 2. Normally, you would now continue typing the second page of your document.

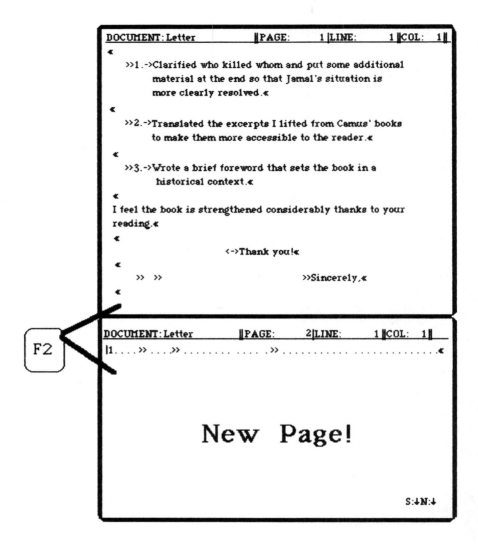

DOCUMENT:Letter   ‖PAGE: 1‖LINE: 1‖COL: 1‖
≪
    »1.->Clarified who killed whom and put some additional
        material at the end so that Jamal's situation is
        more clearly resolved.≪
≪
    »2.->Translated the excerpts I lifted from Camus' books
        to make them more accessible to the reader.≪
≪
    »3.->Wrote a brief foreword that sets the book in a
        historical context.≪
≪
I feel the book is strengthened considerably thanks to your
reading.≪
≪
            <->Thank you!≪
≪
  » »   »Sincerely,≪
≪

F2

DOCUMENT:Letter   ‖PAGE: 2‖LINE: 1‖COL: 1‖
|1....»....»..........»...................................≪

New Page!

S:↓N:↓

Figure 4.5
Creating a New Page

2. To go to page 1, press F1, the GO TO key. At the prompt, "Go To Page?", type 1 and press ENTER. Page 1 appears on the screen again.

3. Press F1, type a "2" and press ENTER. MultiMate shows you page 2. Now try telling MultiMate to go to page 3, which doesn't exist yet.

4. Press F1, type "3" and press ENTER. The message, "Invalid Page Number" appears, meaning that no page 3 exists. Although you haven't typed anything on page 2, try creating a third page.

5. Press F2 to create a new page. MultiMate saves the blank page 2 on disk and creates page 3. Let's go back to page 1.

6. Press F1, type 1, and press ENTER. Page 1 appears. The letter is now three pages long, although pages two and three are blank.

7. You're finished with the letter document for now, so press F10 to save it on disk. The main menu reappears.

One good page deserves another.   **Explanation**

 After typing a page with MultiMate, you press F2 to create a new blank page, if desired. MultiMate stores the page you were just working with on disk and brings up a blank editing screen as a new page. In word processing, ending a page this way is generally called making a "page break"—that is, breaking the current page to start another.

 You can type a page up to 152 lines long. After that MultiMate stops and asks you to create a new page to hold additional text. MultiMate will hold a maximum of 152 lines in memory (as one page) at a time.

 By pressing F2, you can manually create new pages any time, and pages can have any number of lines (up to 152). You type the last line that you want on the page and press F2 to create a new page. MultiMate keeps track of page numbers for you.

 Although you didn't use it here, MultiMate also has an automatic page-break feature that creates a new page for you whenever a page is full. At the Modify Document Default screen, for instance, you can tell MultiMate to create pages with 48 text lines each and to create new pages automatically. When you type more than 48 lines, MultiMate creates a new page without your pressing F2.

 Whether you use automatic or manual page breaks is up to you. The manual method was used here to help explain the concept. To use automatic page breaks, you set the "Automatic Page Breaks" option of the Modify Document Defaults screen to "Y" for "yes".

 As you create a multiple-page document, the program saves page after page on disk. You work with one text page at a time and the rest of the document is safe, waiting on disk for you. If something disastrous, such as a power outage, happens and your computer goes off, only the most recently edited page (which hasn't been saved on disk yet) will be lost. The rest of the document, which is already on disk, is safe.

 Instead of using F2 to create new pages, you can also use it to divide pages. Moving the cursor into the middle of a page, you can split the page into two parts by pressing F2. The text above the cursor will be on one page, and the text that was below the cursor will be on the next page. In later chapters, you'll learn to divide and combine pages. For now, remember that the cursor must be on the bottom line of a page when you press F2 to create a new blank page. Otherwise, you will divide the page on the screen.

With long documents, you need a way to jump from one page to another quickly. To get from page 5 to page 50, for example, you use the F1, or GO TO, key. You can jump forward or backward through a document with ease. You simply tell MultiMate the page number of the text you want to see. (You'll also learn other ways of moving from page to page later.)

Unfortunately, MultiMate doesn't tell you how many pages a document has during editing. If you tell MultiMate to show you page 15, and the document only has fourteen pages, MultiMate tells you it can't make the jump. If you're editing an old document, it's a good idea to check how many pages it has at the Document Summary screen before you begin editing.

Whenever you move from one page to another, the page most recently displayed on screen is saved on disk for you. When you press F10 to end editing, you are actually saving only the text of the page on which you are working.

Remember that during editing you mustn't remove the disk receiving the document from the disk drive. Without the document disk in the drive, MultiMate would have nowhere to record the text in memory if you created a new page or changed pages. You must keep the disk in the disk drive until you finally save it with F10.

You can, however, remove the MultiMate program disk from the drive if you need to. For example, you can take the program disk from drive A and replace it with the dictionary disk. You could then continue editing and check the spelling of words with MultiMate's dictionary. Some editing procedures, however, such as using the HELP function or creating a new document, will require you to replace the program disk in the system drive again. Fortunately, MultiMate displays a message asking you to replace the disk when it becomes necessary.

SUMMARY

To set the format line, you use the keys shown in figure 4.6.

Word wrap is an editing procedure that automatically adjusts the number of words that fit on a line. Unlike when using a typewriter, you shouldn't end each line with a carriage return. With a word processor, you can just keep typing line after line and the program will move words between lines for you.

You've seen how the TAB, INDENT, and CENTER functions put markers on the screen that affect text formatting. Like any character, such markers can be erased or inserted to rearrange text. You also learned to move from page to page with the GO TO key, and to create new pages with the PAGE BREAK key. These functions use the keys shown in figure 4.7.

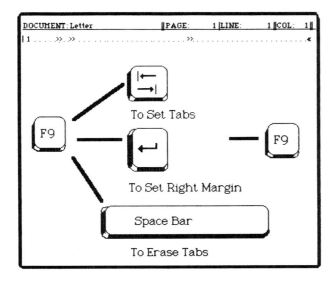

Figure 4.6
Keys Used to Set Format Line

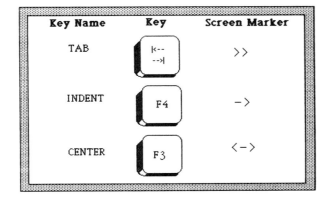

Figure 4.7
Editing Keys

Chapter 5

EDITING
THE BETTER WAY

Preparation

> Your computer should be turned on and the MultiMate main menu on screen. (See chapter 1 for instructions if you've forgotten how to load MultiMate.) Your exercise disk should be in drive B, and it should contain the document called LETTER, from the last chapter, and one called BETTER. Create the BETTER document according to the instructions in appendix B.

Now that you've had some practice, it's time to learn some faster methods of editing.

Most editing involves dragging the cursor around the screen. Up to now you've relied on the arrow keys and the GO TO key, F1, to position the cursor in a document. You can greatly speed up editing, however, with MultiMate's other cursor-movement functions.

You can send the cursor leaping through text word by word or from one side of the screen to the other. You can also move it to the top or bottom of a screen or page and ahead or back a page at a time in the document.

We've purposely held you back by teaching you to delete and insert single characters with the plus and minus keys. Now we're turning you free. MultiMate can easily insert and delete large chunks of text much faster than you can do it character by character. You can insert lines, paragraphs, and even whole pages as fast as you

70

can type them. You can delete them even faster. The insert function, using the numeric key marked INS, and the delete function, using the key marked DEL, are two of MultiMate's swiftest features—ones you'll rely on for efficient editing.

Let's try out some fast cursor-movement techniques with the LETTER document from chapter 4.

Several types of cursor movement are shown in figure 5.1. To move the cursor left or right one word, hold down the CTRL key and press the left or right arrow key. With each press of an arrow key, the cursor moves from word to word through text.

With the cursor positioned somewhere in the middle of a line,

FAST CURSOR MOVEMENT

Objective: Moving the Cursor Word by Word, to the End of a Line, and to the Screen's Top and Bottom

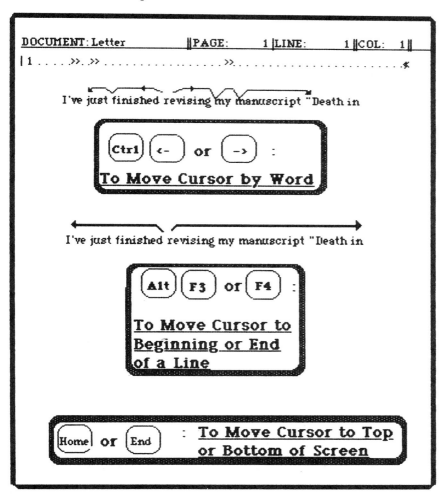

Figure 5.1
Cursor-movement Keys

you can jump it to the left margin by holding down ALT and pressing F3. To move the cursor to the right screen margin, hold down ALT and press F4.

On the numeric keypad are four keys marked HOME, END, PGUP (for "page up"), and PGDN (for "page down"). These four keys move the cursor in big jumps up and down through the text on the screen.

HOME jumps the cursor to the first character seen at the screen's top. END moves the cursor to the last character seen at the screen's bottom.

To see how these cursor functions work, let's try them out on the LETTER document.

Procedure

1. Select "Edit an Old Document" from the main menu by typing "1" and pressing ENTER.

2. At the Document Specification screen, type the document name—LETTER—and press ENTER.

3. At the Document Summary screen, press F10.

4. With the arrow keys, move the cursor down into the first line of the first paragraph under the "r" of "revising" (line 11, column 20). Let's move the cursor word by word through the text.

5. Hold down the CTRL key and press the right arrow key several times. Notice that the cursor jumps to the right one word with each key press.

6. Still holding down CTRL, press the left arrow key several times. The cursor jumps to the left word by word.

7. Move the cursor back under the "r" of "revising". Let's jump the cursor from one end of a line to another.

8. Hold down the ALT key and press F4. The cursor jumps to the right end of the line.

9. Still holding down the ALT key, press F3. The cursor jumps to the left end of the line. You can jump the cursor to either side of a document this way. Try it a few times—ALT F4 and ALT F3.

10. Press HOME. Notice that the cursor jumps to the top left corner of the screen.

11. Press END. Notice that the cursor jumps to the last character showing at the screen's bottom.

12. Practice these cursor movements before continuing.

Fast cursor movement is fundamental to comfortable editing. You must be able to move the cursor where you want it in a hurry.

You can now move the cursor word by word, to either side of the screen, or to the top or bottom of the current screen. When you need to position the cursor to the left or right several words, hold down CTRL and press the left or right arrow key. MultiMate considers a word to be any group of characters surrounded by spaces. When you tell the program to move the cursor ahead a word, MultiMate searches for the next space, then moves the cursor to the initial letter character of the group. You can also hold CTRL and the left or right arrow key down; the cursor will jump continuously from word to word through your text.

To jump the cursor from one side of the screen to the other, you hold down the ALT key and press F3 (to go left) or F4 (to go right). Although oddly positioned on the keyboard (most other cursor-movement functions use keys on the keyboard's right side), the ALT F3 and ALT F4 key combinations are often used during editing. Because MultiMate uses many function-key combinations, you should firmly register these two important cursor-movement functions in your mind now.

The home position of the cursor is the upper left corner of your screen. Whenever you press HOME, the cursor zooms home and waits. Likewise, the END key takes the cursor to the last character visible on screen. Neither HOME nor END move the cursor beyond the text currently visible. Remember that the text currently visible, about 24 lines at most, isn't necessarily the whole page. In the next section you'll learn how to move the cursor beyond the 24 lines of a screen.

Editing on a monitor can sometimes make you feel as if you're wearing a diver's face mask. As you edit, you can often only see part of a page. The top or bottom portion may be off screen and out of view. How do you bring the rest of the page into sight when you need to edit it? Figure 5.2 illustrates MultiMate's methods of moving the cursor beyond the currently displayed screen of text.

Holding down CTRL and pressing HOME launches the cursor to the top of a page.

Holding down CTRL and pressing END sends it diving to a page's bottom.

Pressing PGDN moves the cursor down nineteen lines (about one screen's worth of text). Holding down CTRL and pressing PGDN jumps the cursor ahead one page.

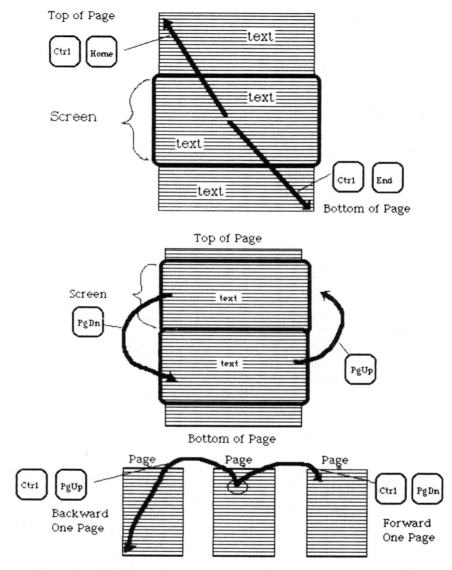

Figure 5.2
Cursor Movement
beyond the Screen

Pressing PGUP jumps the cursor up nineteen lines in the document. Holding down CTRL and pressing PGUP jumps the cursor back one page in a document.

Procedure

1. Move the cursor to line 27. Let's jump the cursor to the page's top.

2. Holding down CTRL, press HOME. The top of the page comes into view. Now direct the cursor to the page's bottom.

3. Holding down CTRL, press END. Now move the cursor up 19 lines by pressing PGUP.

4. Press PGUP. Notice how the document bumped down into view, but the cursor stayed in the same relative line on screen.

5. Press PGDN. MultiMate brings up the next 19 lines (or as much as exists) of the page. You can also use PGUP and PGDN in combination with CTRL to make a short hop to the next or previous page.

6. Holding down CTRL, press PGDN. Page 2 of the LETTER document (blank) appears on screen. You can also back up one page with CTRL PGUP. The cursor jumps to the *bottom* of the previous page, however, which may appear confusing.

7. Holding down CTRL, press PGUP. MultiMate moves the cursor to the last line of page 1.

8. Holding down CTRL, press PGUP again. MultiMate tells you that it can't back up another page: this is page 1.

9. Holding down CTRL, press PGDN three times. With each press of PGDN, MultiMate moves ahead one page. On the third press it tells you that you're already on the last page. Notice that you wouldn't necessarily want to page through a long document using CTRL PGDN. The GO TO key, F1, is best used to jump to specific pages.

10. Experiment with these cursor movements. When done, press F10 to save the document.

You can now make the cursor leap tall text in a single bound.   **Explanation**

To remember when to use CTRL with one of the cursor-movement keys—HOME, END, PGUP, or PGDN—think of CTRL as amplifying the effect that the cursor-movement key has when used by itself.

HOME, for example, moves the cursor to the top left of current screen. CTRL HOME jumps the cursor to the top of a page. Similarly, END moves the cursor to the last character of a screen, and CTRL END moves it to the last character of the page (see figure 5.3).

PGDN and PGUP scroll blocks of text into view. Think of PGUP and PGDN as similar to buttons on an elevator that raise your view of a page up or down a floor (19 lines). Used with CTRL, PGUP and PGDN move the cursor a page of text at a time. (If the cursor happens to be at the page's top when you press PGUP or the up arrow key, MultiMate will also back up to the previous page. If the cursor is at

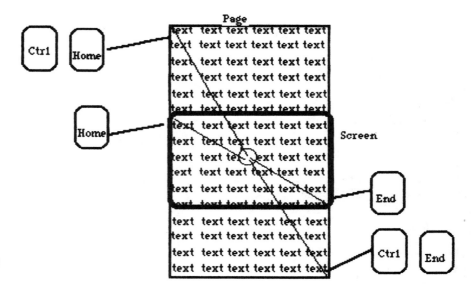

Figure 5.3
Use of CTRL and Cursor Keys

the bottom of the page when you press PGDN or the down arrow key, MultiMate moves the cursor forward a page.) Figure 5.2 illustrates how PGUP and PGDN affect cursor movement.

FAST INSERTIONS

Objective: Inserting Blocks of Text

Perhaps you've typed a page only to discover—whoa, you've left out a sentence or two. That's no disaster with MultiMate. You can easily insert words, sentences, and paragraphs in a document whenever you want.

You move the cursor to the position in the document at which the insertion should start. Press INS, the INSERT key. MultiMate opens a large blank space on the screen in which you can type as many text lines as you want. After typing the insertion, you press INS a final time and the text moves up and readjusts itself around the new insertion.

Should you change your mind halfway through an insertion and decide you didn't actually want to insert anything, you can press ESCAPE. The inserted text disappears and your document returns to its original condition.

Try inserting some text in the first page of the BETTER document to make it look like figure 5.4.

Procedure

1. From MultiMate's main menu, select "Edit an Old Document" by typing "1" and pressing ENTER.

2. Type the document name—"BETTER"—and press ENTER.

3. Press F10 at the Document Summary screen.

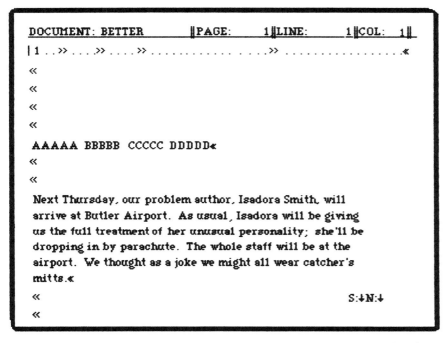

DOCUMENT: BETTER   ‖PAGE: 1‖LINE: 1‖COL: 1‖

| 1 . . » . . . . » . . . . » . . . . » . . . . «

«

«

«

«

AAAAA BBBBB   CCCCC DDDDD«

«

«

Next Thursday, our problem author, Isadora Smith, will
arrive at Butler Airport. As usual, Isadora will be giving
us the full treatment of her unusual personality; she'll be
dropping in by parachute. The whole staff will be at the
airport. We thought as a joke we might all wear catcher's
mitts.«

«   S:↓N:↓

«

Figure 5.4
Page 1 of BETTER
Document

4. With the editing screen in view, move the cursor under the first
   "C" in line 5, column 7. Let's insert some *B*s on this line.

5. Press INS. The screen opens up a blank space for the insertion.
   Notice the *C*s and *D*s are at the bottom of the screen as a reference.
   At the top right corner of the screen appears the message "Insert
   What?" MultiMate is asking you to type the insertion.

6. Type "BBBBB" and press the space bar. Notice that as you type
   the *B*s are brighter or highlighted. The highlighting tells you what
   text is being inserted.

7. Press INS a final time. The text closes up around the newly
   inserted characters. Let's try that again.

8. Press INS. The screen opens up.

9. Type "ZZZZZZ". Now, say you've decided not to insert the
   *Z*s. You cancel the insertion by pressing ESC.

10. Press ESC. The *Z*s disappear and the text returns to its original
    state. Now let's insert a sentence as you might during normal
    editing.

11. Move the cursor under the "T" of "The whole" in line 9, column
    28. You're going to insert a sentence here.

12. Press INS.

13. Type "As usual, Isadora will be giving us the full treatment of her unusual personality; she'll be dropping in by parachute."

    Space twice after the period ending the sentence. If you make a typing mistake, you can still use the plus and minus keys to insert and delete single characters and edit the text.

14. Press INS to complete the insertion. Your screen should look like figure 5.4.

Explanation

Insert is one of the main tools you'll use as you hammer text into shape. The key sequence to remember is:

Press INS—type the insertion—press INS.

You begin by positioning the cursor where the insertion is to appear. Remember the character under the cursor (before you press INS the first time) will follow the inserted text when the procedure is complete. Another tip: remember to type a blank space after the last word in an insertion. Then, when the text closes up around the insertion, the insertion's last word won't run together with the first word of the following text.

After you press INS, you type away. You can still move the cursor back and forth in the insertion itself, but only using the arrow keys. You can't use other methods of moving the cursor. You can type over characters, erase characters with the minus key and insert single characters with the plus key to edit the insertion.

No other editing procedures work during the insertion, however. You can't move the cursor into the surrounding text until you finish the insertion by pressing INS a final time.

After you press INS to complete the insertion, the highlighted text dims to normal intensity and all MultiMate's editing and cursor-movement functions can be used again. You can cancel an insertion at any time by pressing ESC.

FAST DELETIONS

Objective: Deleting Blocks of Text

MultiMate provides you with a set of killer keys when you need them. Whether you're deleting a word, a phrase, a sentence, or many pages of a document, MultiMate's procedure for deleting blocks of text is fast and easy to learn.

You begin a deletion by positioning the cursor under the first character to be deleted. You press the DEL (for DELETE) key.

Next, you tell MultiMate how much text to delete. This involves "marking" the amount of text to be deleted by positioning the cursor on the last character of the doomed text block. As you move the cursor during a deletion procedure, any characters marked for deletion become highlighted on the screen. With a simple glance at the screen, you can easily see how much text will be erased. A variety of ways exist to mark different amounts of text, and you'll try several in the exercise.

With the text marked, you press DEL a final time. Your text is then irreversibly erased. You can cancel a deletion procedure at any time (before pressing DEL the final time) by pressing ESC. The procedure stops and your text returns to its original condition.

The next exercise lets you practice some deletions on page 2 of the BETTER document (seen in figure 5.5).

1. With page one of the BETTER document on screen, press F1, **Procedure**
   type 2, and press ENTER.

2. Move the cursor under the ''a'' of line 2, column 4. We'll begin
   deleting here.

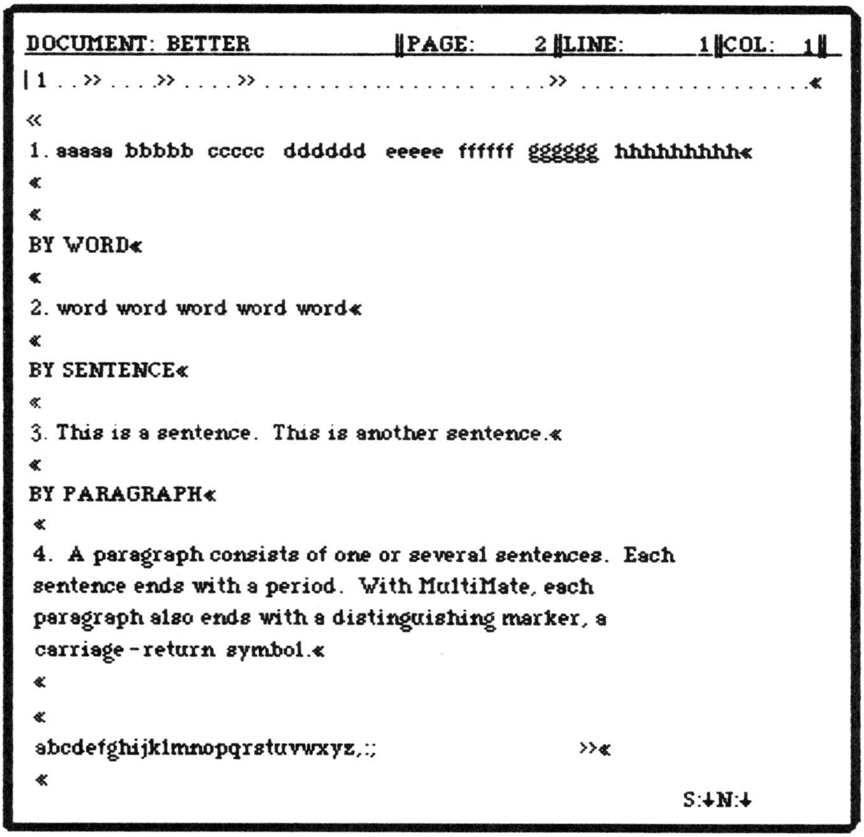

```
DOCUMENT: BETTER          ‖PAGE:     2‖LINE:      1‖COL:   1‖
| 1 . . >> . . . >> . . . . >> . . . . . . . . . . . . . . . >> . . . . . . . . . . . . . . ◄
«
1. aaaaa bbbbb ccccc dddddd eeeee ffffff ggggg hhhhhhhhh◄
«
«
BY WORD◄
«
2. word word word word word◄
«
BY SENTENCE◄
«
3. This is a sentence. This is another sentence.◄
«
BY PARAGRAPH◄
«
4. A paragraph consists of one or several sentences. Each
sentence ends with a period. With MultiMate, each
paragraph also ends with a distinguishing marker, a
carriage - return symbol.◄
«
«
abcdefghijklmnopqrstuvwxyz,:;                    >>◄
«
                                    S:↓N:↓
```

Figure 5.5
Page 2 of BETTER
Document

3. Press DEL. The message "Delete What?" appears on screen. MultiMate is asking you to mark the text to be deleted.

4. With the right arrow key, move the cursor to the first "d" on the line. Notice the characters getting brighter as they are marked for deletion?

5. Press DEL. The characters marked for deletion disappear. Try deleting from the first "d" to the last "g". If anything goes wrong, press ESC and try again.

6. Move the cursor under the "w" of "word" on line 7, column 4.

7. Press DEL. Instead of marking text using the arrow keys to move the cursor, try marking a word at a time.

8. Press the space bar three times to mark three words. MultiMate marks the next word ahead with each press of the space bar.

9. Press DEL to finish the deletion. Try marking a whole sentence for deletion in one blow.

10. Move the cursor under the "T" of "This" on line 11, column 4.

11. Press DEL.

12. To mark an entire sentence, type a period. MultiMate searches ahead for the next period it can find, which of course is at the end of this sentence. (Remember ESC if you make a mistake.)

13. Type another period. Now you've marked two sentences for deletion.

14. Press DEL to complete the procedure.

15. Move the cursor under the "A" on line 15, column 5. You can also mark entire paragraphs.

16. Press DEL.

17. To mark all the paragraph up to its ending ENTER symbol (≪), press ENTER. Notice that the cursor jumps to the carriage-return marker at the paragraph's end. Just as periods mark the end of a sentence, carriage-return markers mark the end of paragraphs in word processing. Let's pretend we've made a mistake and cancel this deletion procedure.

18. Press ESCAPE. The marked text dims on screen, returning to normal. Now let's actually delete it.

19. Press DEL, then press ENTER, and then DEL. Away it goes. You mark text by pressing a key, and MultiMate looks ahead for that

character in the text, marking all text in between for deletion. You can tell MultiMate to delete up to any letter, punctuation mark, or screen marker.

20. Move the cursor under the ''a'' of the alphabet typed at the bottom of the page.

21. Press DEL. Now let's try MultiMate's search ahead capability.

22. Type an ''f''. MultiMate marks text up to the ''f''.

23. Type an ''o''. MultiMate marks text up to the ''o''. By now you get the idea that MultiMate will automatically mark up to the next character you press.

24. Type a comma. When you type a comma, MultiMate might automatically mark a whole clause for deletion. You can also delete up to a specific screen marker, such as a tab marker.

25. Press TAB. The character you type when marking text gives MultiMate the signal for how much text to mark.

26. Press DEL. The deletion is complete.

27. Experiment with inserting and deleting text. When you are done, press F10 to stop editing this document.

The general deletion procedure follows this sequence: **Explanation**

Press DEL—mark the text to be deleted—press DEL.

You begin by positioning the cursor on the first character to be deleted and press DEL to initiate the procedure. The next step, called *marking the text* or *highlighting,* tells MultiMate what to delete. You can choose from several methods of marking text.

First, you can use any of the cursor-movement functions to move the cursor to the end of the text to be deleted. You can move the cursor ahead a single character, for example, with the right arrow key, or you can move it ahead many pages with the GO TO function, F1. You can delete any amount of a document you wish. You merely move the cursor to the last character of the text block to be erased.

If you mark too much text, you can back the cursor up, unmarking the text, or press ESC to cancel the procedure and start over. You can mark text only when the cursor is going toward the document's end. You can't delete by sending the cursor from the bottom of a page to the top, for example.

MultiMate has a special function, called *search-ahead,* that can automatically mark sections of text for you. During the marking procedure, you can press any character or formatting key, and MultiMate searches ahead through the document until the first identical character is found. If you type a period, MultiMate looks ahead and marks all text up to the first period it encounters. If you type another period, it searches ahead for the next period. Thus, by telling MultiMate a specific character to look for, you can tell MultiMate to search ahead and mark a specific section of text.

To delete three words, for example, you might press the space bar three times. Because MultiMate sees a word as any group of characters followed by a space, it will mark the next three words in the text. With MultiMate, paragraphs end with carriage returns, so if you tell the program to look for the next carriage return (you press ENTER), MultiMate will mark a paragraph. You can mark as little or as much text as you like, depending on the characters you ask MultiMate to find.

When it comes to marking text for deletion, you have numerous ways to do the same thing. (We'll discuss a few more in chapter 16.) Which way you use is simply a matter of discovering the method that works best for you. With a little practice, you'll soon become adept at marking blocks of text quickly, and you'll find MultiMate uses these same text-marking procedures in other editing functions—such as moving text from one place to another—so you have learned more than just how to delete text.

Inevitably, sometime during a deletion procedure, you'll make a mistake and press the wrong key. MultiMate may then race off searching for a character it will never find—dangerously marking all the rest of your document for deletion. If you find MultiMate madly marking page after page for the "big sleep"—calmly press ESC. MultiMate immediately cancels the deletion process.

SUMMARY

You can move the cursor with the keys shown in figure 5.6. You can insert text using the procedure shown in figure 5.7. To delete text, use the procedure shown in figure 5.8.

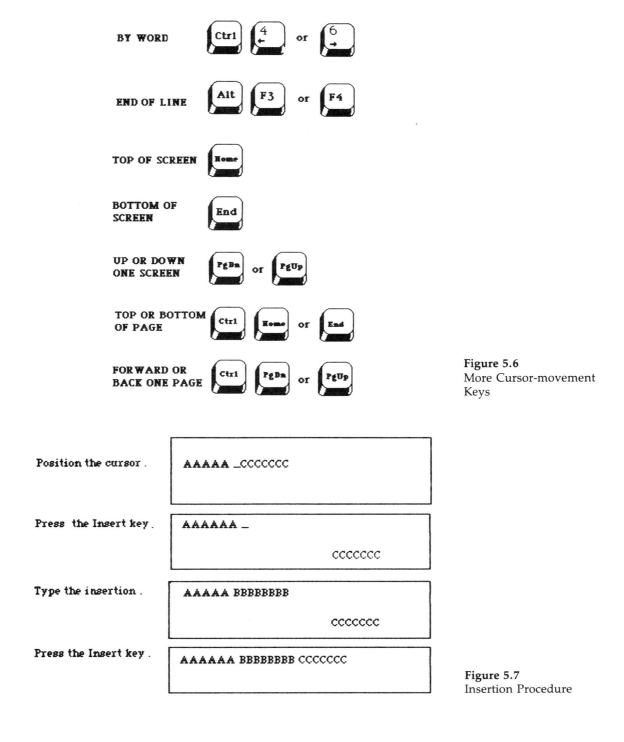

Figure 5.6
More Cursor-movement Keys

Figure 5.7
Insertion Procedure

Position the cursor .

Press the Delete key .

Mark the text to be deleted .

Press the Delete key .

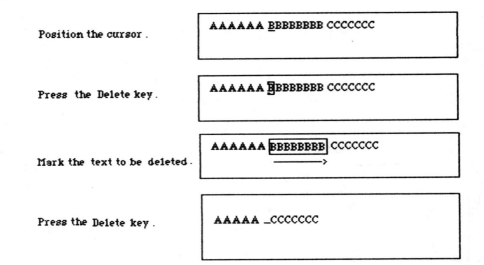

Figure 5.8
Deletion Procedure

Chapter 6

PUTTING TEXT WHERE IT BELONGS

Preparation

> Your computer should be turned on and the MultiMate main menu should be on the screen. Your exercise disk should be in drive B, and it should contain the documents called LETTER and COPY. Create the COPY document according to the instructions in appendix C.

One blessing of word processing is that you rarely have to retype text. Once you've typed it, you can copy text to other places in a document. You can also move text from one place to another and rearrange the sequence of information.

You might move a letter's last paragraph up to become the first one, for example. You can even copy text from one document and put it in another. You might steal a paragraph or two from a recent report and put it in a business letter without retyping anything.

With MultiMate, copying text means duplicating it in another place in the document. The copy procedure has several steps. First you press the COPY key, F8, to initiate the procedure. Next you tell MultiMate how much text to copy by marking it. You're familiar with marking text blocks from the deletion procedure. You can copy all or any part of a document.

After marking the text to be copied, you must tell MultiMate where to put the copy. You do that by moving the cursor to where the duplicate text is to appear. Finally, you tell MultiMate to finish the procedure by pressing F8—a copy is made instantly.

Moving text and copying it are similar procedures, but the result is different. When you move text, it disappears from its original location and pops up in another. The move procedure begins with a press of the MOVE key, F7. After that, you mark the text and complete the procedure almost exactly as you do for copying.

Both the move and the copy procedures affect text within a document. If you want to copy something from one document into another, you must perform an external copy. An external copy involves an added step—you must tell MultiMate from which document to copy. Outside of this, an external copy is similar to the regular copy procedure.

After learning the copy, move, and external copy procedures, you'll have an opportunity to practice the editing procedures you've learned so far as you edit the original LETTER document.

DUPLICATING TEXT

Objective: Copying Text to a New Location

The copy procedure provides a little keyboard abracadabra. To perform a copy, you position the cursor under the first character to be copied and press F8, the COPY key. You then move the cursor to the last character of the text to be duplicated. You can mark the text using the cursor-movement functions or the search-ahead capability that you learned so far.

With the text marked, you press F8 again. MultiMate asks you where to duplicate it. You move the cursor to a new location. You can copy text to any location in a document (except within the text to be copied).

You press F8 a final time, and MultiMate duplicates the text for you.

In the next exercise, you'll learn how to edit page 1 of the COPY document to look like figure 6.1.

Procedure

1. From the main menu, select "Edit an Old Document" by typing "1" and pressing ENTER.

2. Type the document name, "COPY", and press ENTER. Be sure the drive specification indicates the drive holding the exercise disk.

3. Press F10 at the Document Summary screen.

4. On page 1 of COPY, move the cursor under the tab marker on line 3, column 23.

5. To copy this line, press F8. The message "Copy What?" appears

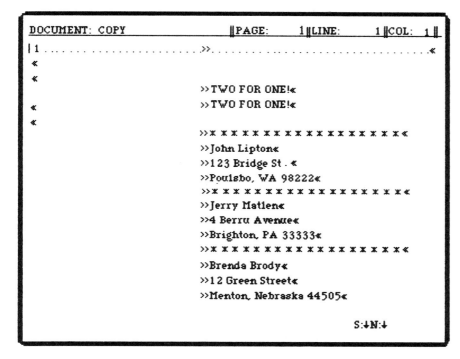

Figure 6.1
Edited Page of COPY Document

in the screen's top right corner. MultiMate is asking you to mark the amount of text to be copied.

6. To mark the whole line, press ENTER. This uses the search-ahead capability to mark text up to the carriage-return marker at the end of the line.

7. Press F8. The message "To Where?" appears on screen. After you mark the text, MultiMate asks where it is to be copied to. You next move the cursor to a new location.

8. Move the cursor under the carriage-return marker on line 4, column 1. This is where the text will appear.

9. Press F8 a final time to complete the copy. *Voilà!* Two typed lines for the effort of one. To get a little more practice, try copying the row of asterisks several times.

10. Move the cursor under the tab marker on line 7, column 23.

11. Press F8. If you make a mistake, you can press ESC to cancel the procedure and start over.

12. Press ENTER to mark the line.

13. Press F8. Now you must move the cursor to a new position.

14. Move the cursor under the tab marker on line 11, column 23, and press F8. Although you're copying only single lines, you can copy as much text as you wish by marking larger amounts. Try copying the line of asterisks one more time.

15. With the cursor under the tab marker in line 11, column 23 (the row of asterisks), press F8.

16. Move the cursor to the end of the line under the carriage-return marker.

17. Press F8.

18. Move the cursor under the tab marker on line 15, column 23, and press F8. Your page should now look like figure 6.1.

19. Press F1, type "2", and press ENTER to move to page 2.

Explanation

The general copying procedure is as follows:

1. Press F8.

2. Mark the text.

3. Press F8.

4. Move the cursor to a new position.

5. Press F8.

Notice that you press the COPY key, F8, at the beginning, middle, and end of the procedure. Pressing the same key repeatedly makes the procedure easy to remember.

You begin by positioning the cursor on the first character to be copied. You press F8 to initiate the procedure. Next, you tell MultiMate how much text to copy. You do that by marking the text using the same methods you learned in the deletion procedure. You can simply move the cursor to the end of the text, use the searcl.-ahead function, or use one of the text-marking function-key combinations. Text marked for copying becomes highlighted. If you mark too much text, you can simply move the cursor backward to unmark it.

With the text block marked, you press F8 to move to the next step. Now you must indicate where the copy is to be made. You move the cursor to a new site in the text. The copy will appear at the cursor's location when you press F8 a final time.

You cannot interrupt the procedure to edit the text. You must carry out the whole sequence of steps in one continuous procedure. If you make a mistake, you can cancel the procedure at any time by pressing ESC. The text returns to its original state.

Copying sections of text from one part of a document to another can be tricky. You must often decide whether to include screen markers, such as tab or carriage-return markers, in the marked text or whether to include beginning or ending spaces. If you copy a word, for example, you sometimes want to copy the preceding or trailing spaces around it to a new position as well. Then, when the word arrives in the new location, it doesn't run together with surrounding words (because it's separated by spaces brought with it).

Likewise, when you copied the line of asterisks in the exercise, you included the tab and carriage-return markers in the marked text. When the new copied text appeared several lines below, it was formatted correctly with its own tab and carriage-return markers. If you hadn't included the tab marker in the marked text, the copied line would not have been tabbed over as all the other lines were.

You must decide which formatting markers must be included in the marked portion of text. If you copy text into a page that has a different format line, the resulting copy may appear reformatted incorrectly. You may have to do some formatting by inserting or deleting screen markers, such as tab stops and carriage returns, or even by adjusting the format line.

When you copy several pages of a document, MultiMate also copies the format lines that appear at the top of each page after the first one. When the copy is complete, the text will appear as originally formatted. The first page of a copy, however, will not take the original format line with it unless you tell it to do so.

When you copy two or three words from one page to another, you don't need to worry about differences in format lines. If you are copying a specially formatted text section consisting of columns of numbers, however, you'll want the format line in the new location to match the original. (Otherwise your columns of numbers may be scrambled.) You can also copy a text's format line and take it with the text to a new location. After pressing F8 the first time, you simply press the FORMAT key, F9; when the copy appears, its original format line will appear over it.

All this talk of transferring format lines may seem to be a lot of detail now. You may see its usefulness, however, the first time you copy a text block that appears bizarrely formatted in a new location.

The next exercise, which tries out the move procedure, should be simple now that you know how to copy.

TRANSFERRING TEXT

Objective: Moving Text to a New Location

With the move procedure, you pick up a text block and plunk it down in a new place. You might use it to quickly transpose words or transfer pages from one place to another.

The move procedure is begun by pressing the MOVE key, F7. You perform the same procedure as you did when copying text, except that you press the MOVE key instead of the COPY key. After pressing F7, you mark the text, press F7 again, move the cursor to a new location, and press F7 a final time. Again, you can move any amount of text you wish forward or backward in a document.

Try using the move procedure to edit the second page of COPY to look like figure 6.2.

Procedure

1. On page two of the COPY document, move the cursor under the space just before the first *B* on line 3, column 34.

2. To move the *B*s in front of the *C*s, press F7 to initiate a move. The message "Move What?" appears at the screen's top right corner. MultiMate is asking you to mark the text to be moved.

3. Mark the *B*s by moving the cursor to line 3, column 39. Just use the right arrow to move the cursor to the right.

4. Press F7. The message "To Where?" appears. You must now move the cursor to the place where the text is to appear. Let's put the *B*s in front of the *C*s.

5. Move the cursor to the first space before the *C*s in line 3, column 28.

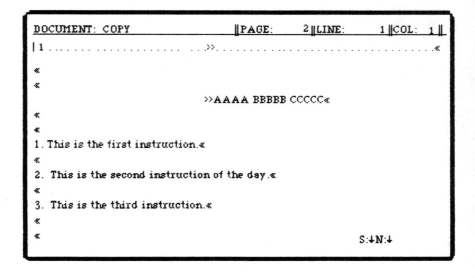

Figure 6.2
Edited Second Page of COPY Document

6. Press F7. The *B*s jump in front of the *C*s. You've now completed a simple move procedure. Now try moving a little more text—a whole line. Let's put the three numbered instructions in the proper order.

7. Move the cursor under the "1" on line 11, column 1.

8. Press F7 to initiate the move procedure.

9. To mark the entire line, press ENTER. MultiMate's search-ahead capability marks the entire line up to and including the carriage-return marker.

10. Press F7. When "To Where?" appears, you move the cursor to where the first instruction should appear.

11. Move the cursor under the carriage-return marker on line 6, column 1.

12. Press F7 to complete the move. Your screen should now look like figure 6.2. You can move small or large blocks of text with this procedure; the only difference is in the amount of text you mark.

The general move procedure is as follows: **Explanation**

1. Press F7.

2. Mark the text.

3. Press F7.

4. Move the cursor to a new position.

5. Press F7.

Notice that you press the MOVE key, F7, at the beginning, middle, and end of the procedure. This is the only difference between the move procedure and the COPY procedure that you just learned.

You begin by positioning the cursor on the first character to be moved. You press F7 to initiate the procedure. Next you tell MultiMate how much text to move. You can simply move the cursor to the end of the text or use the search-ahead function. Text marked for moving becomes highlighted. If you mark too much text, you can simply move the cursor backward to unmark it.

With the text block marked, you press F7 to proceed to the next step. You must now indicate where the text is to be located by moving the cursor to a new site. The text will appear at the cursor's location when you press F7 a final time. The marked text block disappears from the original position, and the text that is left behind is reformatted automatically.

You cannot interrupt the procedure to edit the text. You must carry out the whole sequence of steps in one continuous procedure. If you make a mistake, you can cancel the procedure at any time by pressing ESC. The text returns to its original state.

As with the copy procedure, you may need to practice the move procedure to learn how much text to mark. Most often you will want to include formatting markers within the marked text. If every page in a document has the same format line, your text will be moved and will appear formatted correctly. The text's formatting may be thrown off, however, if the format line in the new site is different from that of the text's original location.

As with copy, you can press the FORMAT key, F9, just after initiating the move procedure to move the original format line with the marked text to another location. This assures that specially formatted text blocks arrive properly formatted.

COPYING TEXT BETWEEN DOCUMENTS

Objective: Using External Copy to Copy Text from Other Documents

Good words never go stale. Any text you've typed with MultiMate can be reused in other documents. You can copy text from another document into the one you're presently editing. You start out by moving the cursor to where you want the copied text to appear.

With the external-copy procedure, you must begin by telling MultiMate which document contains the text you wish to copy. You press SHIFT F8, specify the drive location and document name, and press F10.

The specified document's first page appears on screen. Using the normal cursor-movement functions, you move the cursor to the beginning of the text to be copied. You press SHIFT and F8 to begin marking the text. You move the cursor to the end of the text block and press SHIFT F8 a last time. MultiMate copies the marked block to the original document and you can continue editing.

To practice the external-copy procedure, try copying the address from the LETTER document into the third page of COPY. Your third page will look like figure 6.3 when done.

Procedure

1. To move the cursor to page 3, press F1, type "3", and press ENTER.

2. Move the cursor down to line 8, column 1. You're going to copy the address to this location.

3. To initiate the external copy, hold down SHIFT and press F8. A message telling you the procedure's name appears; it also has places for you to specify a drive and document name.

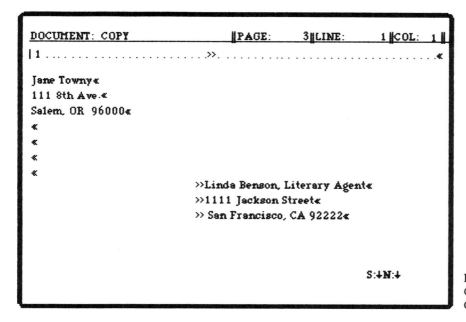

```
DOCUMENT: COPY                    ‖PAGE:      3‖LINE:      1‖COL:  1‖
│1 . . . . . . . . . . . . . . . . . . . .≫. . . . . . . . . . . . . . . . . . . . .≪

Jane Towny≪
111 8th Ave.≪
Salem. OR  96000≪
   ≪
   ≪
   ≪
   ≪
                        ≫Linda Benson. Literary Agent≪
                        ≫1111 Jackson Street≪
                        ≫ San Francisco, CA 92222≪




                                           S:↓N:↓
```

Figure 6.3
Completed Third Page of
COPY Document

4. To specify the drive, press the left arrow key and type "B". (Your prompt may already show "B", in which case you can skip this step. You want drive B because that is where the LETTER document is located. If you're using a hard disk you must specify the C drive.)

5. To move the cursor to the document name prompt, press TAB and type "LETTER".

6. With the name of the document specified, press F10. Page 1 of LETTER appears on screen. The message "START COPY WHERE?" appears on screen (see figure 6.4). You must now move the cursor to the beginning of the text to be copied.

7. To copy the address, move the cursor down to line 5, column 1, under the "L" of "Linda". The copy will start here.

8. Press SHIFT F8 and, with the arrow keys, move the cursor to line 7, column 24, under the carriage-return marker. Your text is now marked.

9. Press SHIFT F8 a final time. The COPY document appears on screen with the copied address on page 3.

10. To finish formatting the screen to print the information for an envelope, press the plus key and then press TAB to insert a tab

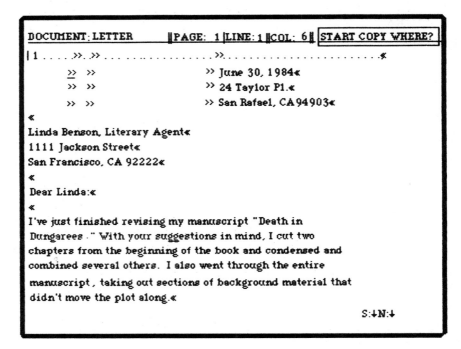

```
┌─────────────────────────────────────────────────────────────────────┐
│ DOCUMENT: LETTER        ‖PAGE: 1‖LINE: 1‖COL: 6‖ START COPY WHERE?    │
│ |1 . . . . .». .» . . . . . . . . . . . . . . . . .». . . . . . . . . . . . . . . . . . . . .«
│          »  »                      » June 30, 1984«
│          »  »                      » 24 Taylor Pl.«
│          »  »                      » San Rafael, CA 94903«
│ «
│ Linda Benson, Literary Agent«
│ 1111 Jackson Street«
│ San Francisco, CA 92222«
│ «
│ Dear Linda:«
│ «
│ I've just finished revising my manuscript "Death in
│ Dungarees." With your suggestions in mind, I cut two
│ chapters from the beginning of the book and condensed and
│ combined several others. I also went through the entire
│ manuscript, taking out sections of background material that
│ didn't move the plot along.«
│                                                       S:↓N:↓
└─────────────────────────────────────────────────────────────────────┘
```

Figure 6.4
"Start Copy Where?"
Prompt

under the first line of the address.

11. Move the cursor down one line under the first 1 of "1111 Jackson Street" and insert another tab by pressing the plus key and then pressing TAB.

12. Tab the last line over by moving the cursor under the *S* of "San Francisco" and press the plus key and then TAB. You now have formatted addresses to print an envelope.

13. Press F10 to stop editing and save this document.

Explanation

The general procedure for an external copy is as follows:

1. Position the cursor where the text is to appear in your document.

2. Press SHIFT F8.

3. Specify the document's name and drive location.

4. Press F10.

5. Move the cursor to the beginning of the text to be copied.

6. Press SHIFT F8.

7.   Mark the text.

8.   Press SHIFT F8.

Although more steps are involved, you probably see the similarity between this procedure and the copy procedure. Visually, the process looks something like figure 6.5.

    Most of the external-copy procedure involves designating the text

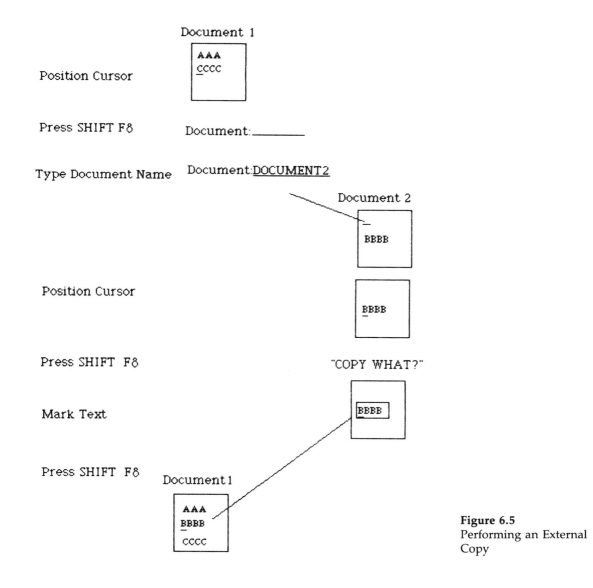

Figure 6.5
Performing an External
Copy

to be copied. Notice that you press the same key combination, SHIFT F8, repeatedly during the procedure, which simplifies remembering which keys to press.

This procedure does not in any way change the document from which the text is being copied. You merely duplicate a section of its text in the document you are currently editing. You can copy many pages of a document, if you wish; the only limit is that you must have room on disk to hold both the original document and the copied text.

The external-copy procedure literally makes your word-processing documents a library of text from which you can draw information. You should get in the habit of never typing text that you can copy. Once you're used to the procedure, you can quickly patch documents together with often-used sections of text where possible. (MultiMate has even faster methods of inserting boilerplate text and creating form letters that you'll learn later.)

During the procedure, you can press ESC at any time to cancel an external copy. The original document will be redisplayed where editing left off and neither document will be affected.

Congratulations! You've learned a good many of MultiMate's editing procedures. The next exercise will give you a chance to practice editing and consolidate your new knowledge.

EDITING PRACTICE

Objective: Review of MultiMate's Editing Procedures

For practice, try editing the LETTER document to look like figure 6.6. Only general instructions will be provided here; you should be able to handle the details of the procedure yourself. Remember, if you're in doubt, MultiMate often displays messages during its editing procedures that guide you. In addition, you can always press ESC to cancel a procedure.

Also remember that you can press SHIFT F1 to use MultiMate's Help facility at any time.

Procedure

1. From the main menu, load the LETTER document.

2. Once you have page 1 of LETTER on the editing screen, try changing the format line as follows:
   Press F9.
   Put a new tab at column 32 (move the cursor and press TAB).
   Space over the tab on column 37.
   Change the right margin to column 55 by locating the cursor there and pressing ENTER.
   Press F9.

   Notice how the text took on the shape of the new specifications.

```
DOCUMENT:LETTER          ‖PAGE:      1 ‖LINE:      1‖COL:   1‖
|1 . . . . .>>.>> . . . . . . . . . . . .>>. . . . . . . . . . . . . . . . . . . . . .✄
         >>  >>              >> June 30, 1984«
         >>  >>              >> 24 Taylor Pl.«
         >>  >>              >> San Rafael, CA 94903«
«
Linda Benson«
 Benson Literary Agency«
1111 Jackson Street«
San Francisco, CA  92222«
«
Dear Linda:«
«
I've just finished revising my manuscript "Death in
Dungarees ." With your suggestions in mind, I cut two
chapters from the beginning of the book and condensed and
combined several others. «
  «
I feel the book is strengthened considerably thanks to
your reading.«
  «
 I have also done the following:«
 «
     >>1.->Clarified who killed whom and put some
           additional material at the end so that
           Jamal's situation is more clearly resolved.«
  «
     >>2.->Translated the excerpts I lifted from Camus'
           books to make them more accessible to the
  «        reader.«
     >>3.->Wrote a brief foreword that sets the book in
           a historical context.«
  «
  «
                   <->Thank you!«
  «
     >>  >>                        >>Sincerely,«
  «
  «
     >>  >>                        >>Bill Green«
                                           S:↓N:↓
```

Figure 6.6
Edited LETTER
Document

3. Erase "Literary Agent" after Linda Benson's name on line 5. Don't erase the carriage return at the end of the line, however.

4. Insert "Benson Literary Agency" on line 6:

   Position the cursor on line 6, column 1.
   Press INS.
   Type "Benson Literary Agency".
   Press ENTER to end the line.
   Press INS.

5. Delete the sentence beginning "I also went . . ." on line 15, column 31. Position the cursor, press DEL, type a period, and press DEL again.

6. Move the sentence beginning "I feel the book is strengthened . . ." up to line 11. To do so, follow these steps:

   Position the cursor at line 30, column 1.
   Press F7, the MOVE key.
   Mark the sentence by pressing ENTER.
   Press F7.
   Move the cursor under the carriage-return marker on line 11, column 1.
   Press F7.
   Press the plus key to insert a space.
   Press ENTER to insert a carriage-return marker.

7. Next, try creating text formatted to print on an envelope on page 2. You can do that by copying the addresses from page 1 to page 2. Then you can reformat the copied text. Follow these steps:

   With the cursor on line 1, column 6 of page 1, press F8, the COPY key.
   Mark the address text down to line 9, column 1.
   Press F8.
   Press F1, type "2", and press ENTER.
   Press F8.

8. Next, edit the address text to create an envelope:

   Erase the date line ("June 30 . . .") and insert "Bill Green" and a carriage return.
   Erase the tab markers in front of the remaining two lines of the return address.
   Insert five blank lines. With the cursor on line 4, column 1, press INS, press ENTER five times, and press INS again.
   Finally, insert tab markers in front of the remaining address lines to move them to the right. Use the INS key to insert three tab markers before each line.

9. Save the document by pressing F10.

10. Experiment with printing the document at different settings for the left and top margins. Select "Print Document Utility" from the main menu to initiate the printing procedure.

MultiMate performs a little word-processing sleight-of-hand with the move and copy procedures. You can easily rearrange and copy any text you wish from place to place and even from document to document. Figure 6.7 illustrates the steps in the COPY and MOVE procedures.

The external-copy procedure uses the steps shown in figure 6.8.

SUMMARY

Copy Procedure

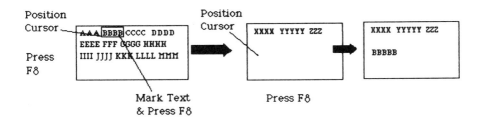

Move Procedure

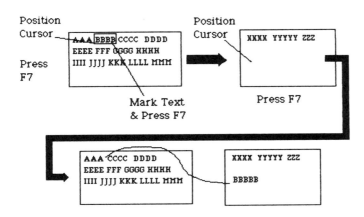

Figure 6.7
Copy and Move
Procedures

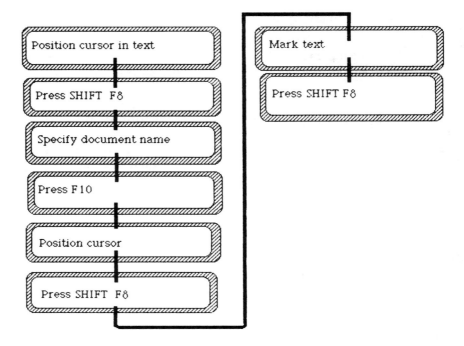

Figure 6.8
External-copy Procedure

Chapter 7

SEARCHING FOR THE LOST WORD

Preparation

Your computer should be turned on and the MultiMate main menu should be on the screen. Your exercise disk should be in drive B and should contain the document SEARCH. Create the SEARCH document according to the instructions in appendix D.

MultiMate is a speed reader par excellence. You can tell it to read through a document until it sees a specific word, phrase, or perhaps sentence and then show you the text's location. This ability to sift through a document uses MultiMate's search function.

Suppose you have typed a fifty-page document. Somewhere within that document is a stretch of text that needs editing. You're not exactly sure where it is, however. You do know that a specific word or phrase is used in that text. Rather than paging through and reading the document, you can ask MultiMate to scan the document for that specific word or phrase.

You specify the word or words (actually any group of characters will do) that are associated with a text passage, and MultiMate zooms through your document page after page hunting for it. When it finds the phrase, MultiMate stops and displays the text on the screen. MultiMate can search from a document's beginning to its end and show you each place a specific word or character group is located.

The search function is useful for more than just locating text. You can edit the document and even delete text with it. If you've ever typed a long document only to discover that you've misspelled a word consistently dozens of times, MultiMate has a great surprise for you. It can go through an entire text and one by one rake out the misspelled words and replace them with any other word or words you choose. The process is called *search and replace.*

Not only can you search for a word or phrase and replace it with another, you can also quickly edit the format of a document by searching for screen markers and automatically deleting or replacing them. The next exercise takes a look at MultiMate's search and replace functions to see how they apply to editing.

SEARCHING FOR TEXT

Objective: Locating Text in a Document

You initiate the search function by first positioning the cursor somewhere before the text to be found (MultiMate only searches in one direction, from the document's beginning toward the end). Next, you press F6, the SEARCH key.

MultiMate asks you what to search for. You type the search criteria, a word or phrase up to 46 characters long. With the search criteria specified, you press F6 again and MultiMate begins looking through the document. If it finds text that matches your criteria, MultiMate stops and displays the text. You can then either stop and edit, or continue searching for other instances of the criteria.

To learn how the search function works, try out a search or two in the SEARCH document seen in figure 7.1.

Procedure

1. From the main menu, select "Edit an Old Document" by typing "1" and pressing ENTER.

2. Type the document name "SEARCH". Check that the drive specification is correct and then press ENTER.

3. Press F10 to skip from the Document Summary screen to the editing screen. On page 1, try searching for the word "boy".

4. To initiate the search, press F6. The message "Search For" appears. MultiMate is asking you what to search for.

5. Type "boy". If you make a typing mistake, you can backspace and type over, insert, or delete single characters with the INS and DEL keys.

6. With the search criteria specified, press F6 to begin the search. Notice how the cursor jumps to the first occurrence of "boy" in the text.

7. To continue the search, press F6 again. MultiMate finds the next

```
┌─────────────────────────────────────────────────────────┐
│ DOCUMENT: SEARCH      ║PAGE: 1║LINE:   1║COL:   1║ SEARCH MODE│
│ | 1 . . ≫ . . . ≫ . . . ≫ . . . . . . . . . . . . ≫ . . . . . . . . . . . . . . . . . . . ◄ │
│                                                           │
│ XXXXXXXXXX XXXXXXXXXX XXXXXXXXXX XXXXXXXXXX XXXXXXXXXX     │
│ XXXXXXXXXX XXXXXXXXXX XXXXXXXXXX XXXXXXXXXX XXXXXXXXXX     │
│ XXXXXXXXXX boy XXXXXX XXXXXXXXXX XXXXXXXXXX XXXXXXXXXX     │
│ XXXXXXXXXX XXXXXXXXXX X boy XXXX XXXXXXXXXX XXXXXXXXXX     │
│ XXXXXXXXXX XXXXXXXXXX XXXXXXXXXX XXXXXXXXXX XXXXXXXXXX     │
│ XXXXXXXXXX XXXXXXXXXX XXXXXXXXXX XXXXXXXXXX XXXXXXXXXX     │
│ XXXXXXXXXX XXXXXXXXXX XXXXXXXXXX XXXXXXXXXX XXXXXXXXXX     │
│ XXXXXXXXXX XXXXXXXXXX XXXXXXXXXX XXXXXXXXXX XXXXXXXXXX     │
│ XXXXXXXXXX xx boy xxx XXXXXXXXXX XXXXXXXXXX XXXXXXXXXX     │
│ XXXXXXXXXX XXXXXXXXXX XXXXXXXXXX XXXXXXXXXX XXXXXXXXXX     │
│ XXXXXXXXXX XXXXXXXXXX XXXXXXXXXX XXXXXXXXXX XXXXXXXXXX     │
│ XXXXXXXXXX XXXXXXXXXX XXXXXXXXXX XXXXXXXXXX XXXXXXXXXX     │
│ XXXXXXXXXX XXXXXXXXXX xx boy xxx XXXXXXXXXX XXXXXXXXXX     │
│ XXXXXXXXXX XXXXXXXXXX XXXXXXXXXX XXXXXXXXXX XXXXXXXXXX     │
│ XXXXXXXXXX XXXXXXXXXX XXXXXXXXXX XXXXXXXXXX XXXXXXXXXX     │
│ XXXXXXXXXX XXXXXXXXXX XXXXXXXXXX XXXXXXXXXX XXXXXXXXXX     │
│ XXXXXXXXXX XXXXXXXXXX XXXXXXXXXX XXXXXXXXXX XXXXXXXXXX     │
│ XXXXXXXXXX XXXXXXXXXX XXXXXXXXXX XXXXXXXXXX XXXXXXXXXX     │
│ XXXXXXXXXX XXXXXXXXXX XXXXXXXXXX XXXXXXXXXX XXXXXXXXXX     │
│ XXXXXXXXXX XXXXXXXXXX XXXXXXXXXX XXXXXXXXXX XXXXXXXXXX     │
│ XXXXXXXXXX x Boyer xxx XXXXXXXXXX XXXXXXXXXX XXXXXXXXXX    │
│ XXXXXXXXXX XXXXXXXXXX XXXXXXXXXX              S:↓N:↓       │
└─────────────────────────────────────────────────────────┘
```

Figure 7.1
Page 1 of SEARCH
Document

occurrence of "boy". Each time you press F6 the search continues. To cancel the search press ESC.

8. Continue the search: press F6 three times. Notice that the cursor stopped on the word "Boyer". This happened because the word "boy" is included in the word "Boyer".

9. Type "B" to cancel the search. You can cancel a search by pressing any key. Normally, you could continue searching this way through an entire document.

10. Press CTRL HOME to move the cursor to the top of the page.

No words are ever lost with MultiMate.

Explanation

To search an entire document, you place the cursor at the top of page 1. You can position the cursor anywhere within a document, however, and the search will start from that point and go toward the document's end.

To locate a section of text, you must specify a search criteria that is unique, a word or phrase that probably occurs only in the text you're looking for. Naturally, if you search for a single word like "the", the search will probably stop frequently and not be much help. Searching for a word or several words, such as a title or subheading, can speed the search to the desired destination.

MultiMate looks rather blindly through a document. If you specify a search for the word "man", for example, the search might also turn up the words "many", "woman", and "Oman", because they contain the word "man". If you search for a rarely used word or phrase, such as "xylophone", however, it's unlikely the search will stop on any but this particular word.

To locate your search criteria as a whole word only, not as part of another word, type the search criteria with a space before and after the word. If you are searching for "man", for example, and you don't want to locate "woman", press the space bar, type "man", and then press the space bar again. MultiMate will then look for your criteria exactly as you spelled it, spaces and all. Because most words are surrounded by spaces, MultiMate will locate only "man" as a whole word. (It wouldn't find "man", however, if it was the last word in a sentence ending in a period, because MultiMate is looking for the word ending with a space.) You must be careful to tell MultiMate exactly what you're looking for.

MultiMate looks for the words or phrase (or even punctuation or screen markers) just as you specify them at the "Search For" prompt. You mustn't leave any extra characters on the line after specifying your criteria, because MultiMate will look for your criteria exactly as spelled—including the extra characters. Be sure to delete any unwanted characters, even spaces, at the "Search For" prompt.

MultiMate will ignore whether a word is spelled with upper- or lower-case letters unless you specify otherwise. If you tell MultiMate to search for "boy", it will also find "Boy", "bOy", or even "BOY" in your text. You can search for words using the exact upper- and lower-case spellings, however; this is called a case-specific search.

After pressing F6, you type the search criteria using the upper- and lower-case letters exactly as they are in the word you want found. You then press ALT G to specify a case-specific search. If you specified "Boy", for example, MultiMate would locate only that exact character group, ignoring "boy", which doesn't start with a capital letter.

You can type any pattern of letters, punctuation, or screen markers at the "Search For" prompt and MultiMate will look for them. You can even search for a format line. To search for a format line, you press F6 then F9, the FORMAT key, instead of typing search criteria. MultiMate will search ahead for the first format line it finds.

Sometimes in a long document, you may realize MultiMate is never going to find the criteria you specified, and so you want it to stop looking. Pressing ESC halts the search, leaving the cursor where the search left off. If MultiMate locates a matching character group in the text and stops to display it, any key you press will stop the search. You can edit the text and then continue searching for the same criteria again by pressing F6 twice.

Now that you've got the idea of searching for a pattern of characters, you're ready to try searching for one pattern and replacing it with another group of characters.

To search for a word or phrase and replace it with another, you first press SHIFT F6. MultiMate lets you choose to replace text automatically throughout a document or to replace text selectively. When you want to change every occurrence of a character group without stopping throughout a document, you select a *global* replace. If you want MultiMate to stop and allow you to decide whether to replace specific instances of a character group, you select a *discretionary* search.

After selecting a global or discretionary search, MultiMate asks you for the group of characters to search for. Just as with the search function, you type a group of characters to be located in the text. You press F6 and then type a replacement for the group of characters. Wherever the search criteria is located, this new group of characters will appear. Finally, you press F6 again and the search and replace function takes off.

In the following search-and-replace exercise, you'll change the SEARCH document's first page to look like figure 7.2.

REPLACING TEXT

Objective:
**Automatically
Searching for and
Replacing Character
Groups**

Procedure

1. With the cursor at the top of page 1, press SHIFT F6. You will see the message "Replace Mode" at the top of the screen. At the screen's bottom, you have three choices: "Global", "Discretionary", and "Abort". The discretionary search and replace stops the search each time the specified phrase is found and lets you decide if a replacement is to be made.

2. Type "2" to select "Discretionary". A "Replace What" prompt appears at the screen's bottom. MultiMate is asking what it should search for.

3. Type "boy" and press F6. MultiMate now knows it should find the word boy. A "Replace With" prompt appears. Here you designate what MultiMate should substitute for the word "boy".

4. Type "girl". MultiMate will now change every "boy" in the text to the word "girl".

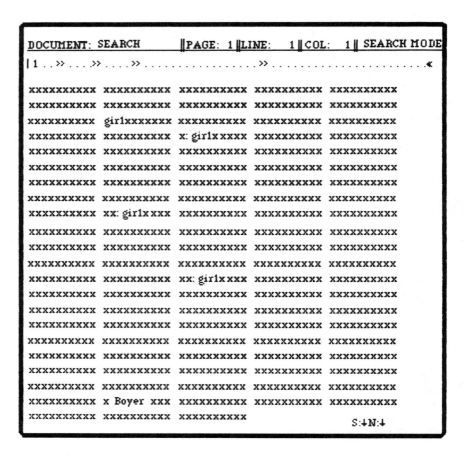

Figure 7.2
SEARCH after First
Search and Replace

5. Press F6 to start the search-and-replace function. After finding the first "boy" in the text, MultiMate displays the message "Replace?". The program is asking you if it should make the replacement. You can type "Y" for "yes," "N" for "no," or any key to stop the search-and-replace function.

6. Type "Y". The word "boy" is replaced with "girl" and MultiMate finds the next instance of "boy". You can now decide to replace it or not.

7. Type "Y".

8. Continue typing "Y" until the search finds the word "Boyer" at the screen's bottom. You don't want to substitute "girl" for "Boyer", so let's skip this replacement.

9. Type "N". MultiMate moves ahead with the search, continuing

on to the last page (page 2), where the search-and-replace function stops.

10. To return to page 1, press F1, type "1", and press ENTER. Now try a global search and replace.

11. Press SHIFT F6 to start the search-and-replace function.

12. Type "1" to select "Global".

13. At the "Replace What" prompt, type "girl" and press F6.

14. At the "Replace With" prompt, type "Boyer" and press F6. MultiMate shoots off, changing every instance of "girl" in the text to "Boyer" and continuing until it reaches the end of page 2.

15. Press F1, type "1", and press ENTER. You are again on page 1 and can see the results of the global replace. You can also delete text with the search-and-replace function.

16. With the cursor at the top of page 1, press SHIFT F6.

17. Select "Global" by typing "1".

18. Type "Boyer" and press F6. Let's delete every "Boyer" from the text.

19. Press the DEL key until all the characters are deleted from the "Replace With" prompt and press F6. Watch as MultiMate deletes every "Boyer" automatically.

20. When the search-and-replace process stops on page 2, press F1, type "1", and press ENTER to return to page 1 to view the changes.

The general steps of the search-and-replace functions are as follows: **Explanation**

1. Press SHIFT F6.

2. Select a "Global" or "Discretionary" replace function. (Select "Abort" to cancel the function.)

3. Type the character group MultiMate is to find.

4. Press F6.

5. Type the character group MultiMate is to use as a replacement.

6. Press F6.

7. If you are doing a discretionary replacement, type "Y" to make the replacement or "N" to skip it each time MultiMate finds your search criteria. You can press ESC at any time to stop the process.

When you select a global search and replace, MultiMate runs through your document making changes without stopping. Every time it finds a character group that matches your search criteria, it makes the replacement automatically. This can be good and bad.

With a global replace, you don't have to make any decisions and replacements are made at top speed. If you typed a three-page letter, misspelling a client's name consistently throughout, a global replace can quickly remedy the problem.

Sometimes MultiMate may make improper replacements, however. Suppose you are replacing a word throughout the text. In the middle of the sentence the word is lower-case, but if it occurs at the beginning of a sentence it is, of course, capitalized. If you tell MultiMate to replace the word with another lower-case word globally, sentences that begin with your search criteria will be inappropriately replaced with a lower-case word. Thus, automatic replacements may not always be accurate.

You can get around making inappropriate replacements by selecting a discretionary replacement process. A discretionary replacement is slower, because you must approve every replacement before it is made. Every time MultiMate finds an instance of your search criteria, it stops and asks if it should replace it or not. You respond to this question by typing "Y" for "yes" or "N" for "no" to skip the replacement and continue on. Pressing any other key stops the discretionary replace process.

After deciding upon a global or discretionary search-and-replace function, you specify the character group to be found. You can specify a group of characters (words, phrases, punctuation, or screen markers) up to 46 characters long. If you are looking for a specific configuration of upper- and lower-case letters, you can press ALT G to perform a case-specific search. MultiMate will find only those character groups that match your search criteria exactly as you typed it, including the use of upper- and lower-case characters.

Another useful option of search and replace lets you search for and change format lines throughout a document. With a fifty-page document, deciding to change the right margin means going to each page and adjusting the format line by hand. You can automate the process by pressing F9 instead of typing the search criteria. You can then create the format line you wish to use throughout the document and press F10. MultiMate will make the format line changes for you. You can also do this kind of format-line adjustment using a discretionary replacement, which helps you guard against changing specially formatted pages.

Used creatively, search and replace can save you a good deal of editing time. If you're typing a long document that uses the phrase "Transcontinental Railroad" repeatedly, you might just type a short abbreviation for the phrase, such as "TCRR", instead of typing the entire phrase each time. When the document's done, you can globally replace every "TCRR" with "Transcontinental Railroad" and avoid typing those 25 characters again and again. (MultiMate also has a special function called *library* that is actually better suited for substituting long phrases with little typing effort. You'll learn about the library function later.)

The next exercise gives you a little more practice with the search-and-replace function.

Besides changing words and phrases, you can also use the search-and-replace function to change a page's format. Instead of typing letter characters as the search criteria, you can use format markers, such as tab or carriage-return markers, and substitute them with other formatting markers. For example, try reformatting page 2 of SEARCH to look like figure 7.3.

EDITING WITH SEARCH AND REPLACE

Objective: Changing Page Format with Search and Replace

1. Press F1, type "2", and pres ENTER to go to page 2.

Procedure

2. With the cursor at the page's top, press SHIFT F6 to start the search-and-replace procedure. Start by reformatting the four instructions so that they are tabbed over two places instead of three.

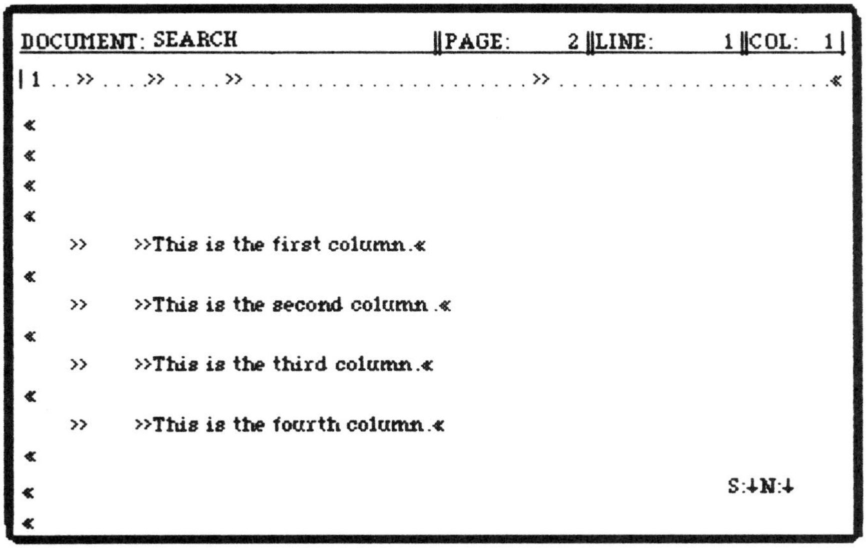

```
DOCUMENT: SEARCH              ‖PAGE:    2 ‖LINE:      1 ‖COL:  1│
│1 . . ≫ . . . . ≫ . . . . . ≫ . . . . . . . . . . . . . . . . ≫ . . . . . . . . . . . . . . . . . . ≪
 ≪
 ≪
 ≪
 ≪
     ≫     ≫This is the first column.≪
 ≪
     ≫     ≫This is the second column .≪
 ≪
     ≫     ≫This is the third column.≪
 ≪
     ≫     ≫This is the fourth column .≪
 ≪
 ≪                                              S:↓N:↓
 ≪
```

Figure 7.3
Reformatted Second Page of SEARCH

3. Type "1" to select "Global".

4. Press TAB three times at the "Replace What" prompt. Use the DEL key to delete any extra letters that may appear on the line.

5. Press F6.

6. Press TAB twice at the "Replace With" prompt.

7. Press F6. Watch as MultiMate reformats the instructions.

8. Press HOME to move the cursor to the screen's top. Now try separating each line with a carriage return. To do that you'll have MultiMate put two carriage-return markers wherever it finds one.

9. Press SHIFT F6.

10. Type "1" to select "Global".

11. Press ENTER at the "Replace What" prompt and press the DEL key until all other characters are erased.

12. Press F6.

13. Press ENTER twice at the "Replace With" prompt.

14. Press F6. Watch as MultiMate reformats the page.

15. Press F10 to save this document.

Explanation

Search and replace can help you make formatting changes throughout a document. If you decide upon a formatting change, you might be able to do the reformatting automatically. You need only identify a unique set of formatting markers associated with the formatting problem. Using that sequence of markers as the search criteria, you can substitute another set of markers that reformats the document the way you want.

To use format markers as search criteria, you press the keys that normally produce the markers on screen. At the "Replace What" prompt, you can press ENTER to create a carriage-return marker, TAB to produce a tab marker, etc. You can also create replacement strings of markers the same way at the "Replace With" prompt.

When faced with a repetitive editing task, such as erasing tab marker after tab marker, you should consider using search and replace; it might be able to help.

SUMMARY

Searching for text follows a procedure similar to that shown in figure 7.4. You can also search for and replace text. You can do this using a nonstop global substitution process or using the discretionary process, which enables you to decide when specific replacements are made. The search-and-replace procedure is illustrated in figure 7.5.

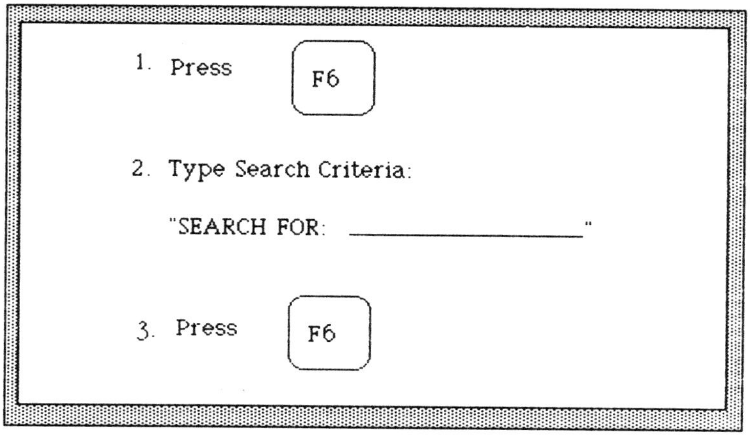

1. Press [F6]

2. Type Search Criteria:

   "SEARCH FOR: _____ "

3. Press [F6]

Figure 7.4
Search Procedure

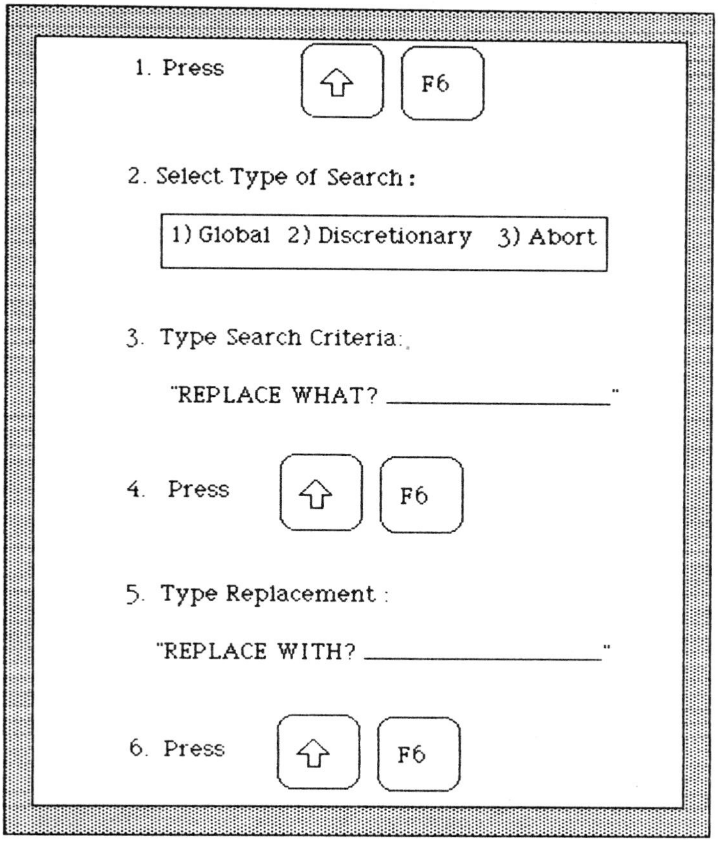

1. Press [⇧] [F6]

2. Select Type of Search:

   | 1) Global 2) Discretionary   3) Abort |

3. Type Search Criteria:

   "REPLACE WHAT? _____ "

4. Press [⇧] [F6]

5. Type Replacement :

   "REPLACE WITH? _____ "

6. Press [⇧] [F6]

Figure 7.5
Search-and-replace
Procedure

Chapter 8

SETTING UP
A NEW PAGE

Preparation

> Your computer should be turned on and the MultiMate main menu should be on the screen. Your exercise disk should be in drive B and should contain the document called SEARCH, which you used in the last chapter.

Up to now, you've used a format line at the screen's top to control page lay-out. You can also create complicated page lay-outs by inserting additional format lines within the page.

For example, midway down a page you might use another format line to reset margins and tab stops for columns of numbers. Or you might format the page to accommodate an illustration to be pasted into the page after printing. By inserting format lines in different positions within a page, you can alter the shape of the text any way you desire. Inserting (and deleting) format lines is as easy as a key press or two.

As you insert and delete blocks of text, pages naturally become too short or too long. You can adjust page length across several pages by dividing and combining pages on the screen. If one page has 60 lines and the next has 40, you might move ten lines from one to produce two pages of 50 lines each. Dividing and combining text across page boundaries is simple with MultiMate.

After editing a fifty-page document, however, you might not

want to adjust lines between individual pages. Manually dividing and combining pages can have an accordion effect: If one page is too long, you can take ten lines from it and add them to the next page— but then that page may be too long. You might end up readjusting the length of every page.

MultiMate takes care of this problem automatically. It has a re-pagination process that adjusts every page of a document to a desired page length, all with little effort on your part. Electronically, MultiMate goes through an entire document, counting lines per page, and moving lines so that each page is a set length.

You can also protect specially formatted pages from being divided up during repagination. If you have special tables of numbers, for example, you might not want any of those tables to start on one page and end on another. You can stop MultiMate from arbitrarily dividing a page during repagination by inserting "Required Page Breaks".

In this chapter, you'll knock the previous chapter's SEARCH document into a variety of shapes as you practice advanced formatting.

What if halfway down a page you want the right margin to change from 60 columns to 40? You can make this formatting change by inserting an additional format line, as shown in figure 8.1.

ALTERING PAGE LAY-OUT

Objective: Inserting and Deleting Additional Format Lines

To insert a format line, you position the cursor where the format change is to occur. You press ALT F9 to insert a format line like the one at the top of the page. You can now edit this format line. You reset tabs by pressing the TAB key where a tab stop is to appear and space over tab stops you want to delete. To change the line length, you position the cursor and press ENTER. You press F9 a final time, and the new format line is in place.

Pressing ESC at any time during the format line's creation cancels the procedure and causes it to disappear. If you should change your mind later, you can also delete format lines by pressing DEL, F9, and DEL a final time.

Let's insert two additional format lines in the SEARCH document to make it look like figure 8.1, then we'll delete the format lines again.

1. From the main menu, type "1" and press ENTER to select "Edit an Old Document".   **Procedure**

2. To specify the document's name, type "SEARCH" and press ENTER. (Check that the drive specification is correct.)

3. Press F10 at the Document Summary screen.

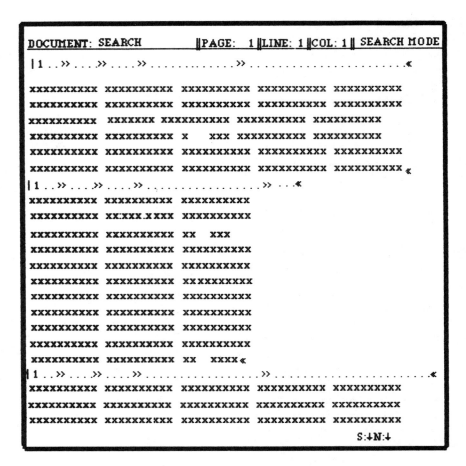

Figure 8.1
SEARCH with Additional
Format Lines

4. When the editing screen appears, move the cursor down to line 7, column 1.

5. To insert a format line at this point, hold down the ALT key and press F9. A new format line appears at the cursor position. Now you can edit the format line. Try changing the line length to forty columns.

6. With the right arrow key, move the cursor to column 40 and press ENTER. The line length is now forty columns.

7. To finish creating the format line, press F9. Notice how the text below the new format line reformats. Let's insert another format line for practice.

8. Move the cursor to line 18, column 1.

9. Hold down ALT and press F9. Leave this format line just as it is.

10. Press F9. You now have a format change in the middle of the page, and the format goes back to the original after the last format line you inserted. You might insert as many format lines with different specifications in a page as you wish. Let's try deleting the format lines.

11. Position the cursor on line 7, column 1. You need only put the cursor somewhere under the format line to delete it. There is no special position from which to start a deletion.

12. Press DEL, press F9, then press DEL a final time. The format line above line 7 disappears. You cannot delete the top format line, however. MultiMate always needs the top one. Let's delete the other inserted format line.

13. Move the cursor to line 14, column 1.

14. Press DEL, then F9, then DEL. The format line disappears. Notice that MultiMate inserted carriage-return markers above each of the inserted format lines at line 6, column 56 and line 13, column 31. This was necessary to make the change in format.

Explanation

To insert a format line within a page, you first position the cursor where the new format line is to appear. You have several choices about the kind of format line to be inserted. If you just want to insert the same format line as seen at the top of a page, you hold down the ALT key and press F9. You can edit this format line if you want.

If you edit the format line, all the text that falls beneath it will follow the new format line's specifications. To revert to the original format again farther down the page, you can insert another format line.

Instead of pressing ALT F9, you can also press CTRL F9 to insert a format line that is set up like MultiMate's original format line—the one that is used whenever you create a new document. You can also press SHIFT F9, which inserts a format line just like the one most recently used. Knowing how to insert these different format lines may save you a little time. You really only need to remember, however, that ALT F9 inserts a format line that you can easily edit as you wish.

Once a format line appears in the page, you set up line spacing, tab stops, and line length. Using format lines, for example, you can alternate between single and double spacing throughout a page. Although MultiMate displays only single-spaced text on screen, during printing the page will come out with the spacing set by your format lines.

Deleting an unwanted format line is easy. You move the cursor somewhere underneath the format line, press DEL, press F9 (the FORMAT key), and press DEL. The format line disappears. If a format line is included in a block of text marked for deletion, it will be deleted from the screen as well.

By now you may have noticed that F9 is the key used to change and insert format lines. Combinations of F9 and SHIFT, CTRL, and ALT all involve format-line procedures. Whenever you want to do something involving a format line, think F9.

MANUALLY ADJUSTING PAGE LENGTH

Objective: Dividing and Combining Pages to Adjust Page Length

If a page becomes too long, you can divide it into two parts, a little like sawing off the end of a board. Rather magically, you can also attach the text you cut off onto the next page with a seamless fit.

To divide a page, you position the cursor where the division is to occur and press F2, the PAGE BREAK key. The text below the cursor will be split off as a page of its own, as illustrated in figure 8.2.

To combine two pages, you move the cursor to the last character of the page to which your text will be appended. (Remember, press CTRL END to jump to page end.) With the cursor positioned, you press SHIFT F2; the following page will be appended to the one currently visible on the screen.

The following exercise will give you practice in dividing and combining pages with the SEARCH document.

Procedure

1. With page 1 of the SEARCH document on the screen, move the cursor to line 6, column 56, under the carriage-return marker. Let's divide the page here.

2. Press F2. Notice that you are now on page 2 of the document; everything below the cursor when you pressed F2 was split off as page 2. Let's divide page 2.

3. Position the cursor at line 8, column 31, under the carriage-return marker. (You can divide a page anywhere you wish. The carriage-return marker is used here only because it's easy to find.)

4. Press F2. You're now on page 3. You have divided the document's first page into three pages. The document is now four pages long. Move from page to page to see the four pages of this document.

5. Press F1, type "1", and press ENTER. Examine all four pages. Go to step six and return to page 1 when done.

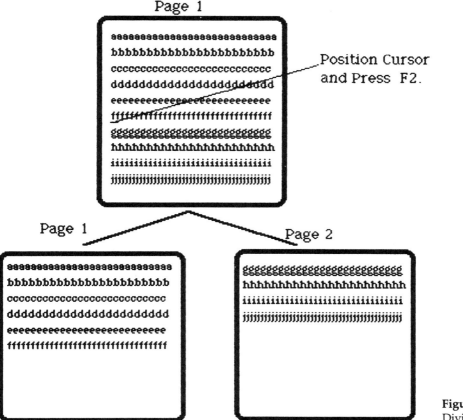

Figure 8.2
Dividing Pages

6. Press F1, type "1", and press ENTER. Next, combine all four pages into two again. On page 1, you must move the cursor to the last character.

7. Hold down CTRL and press END. Now combine page 1 with page 2.

8. Holding down SHIFT, press F2. See how page 2 moved up and combined with page 1? Let's continue and combine this page with the next one.

9. Holding down CTRL, press END to move to the bottom of the page.

10. Holding down SHIFT, press F2. You've now recombined all the

text that was originally on page 1. The document is now only two pages long. Check to see, if you like.

Explanation

To divide a page, you position the cursor where the text is to be divided (anywhere within a page), and press F2. MultiMate cuts off the text below the cursor and makes it a page of its own. You might divide a page that is 70 lines long into one that has 50 lines and another that has only 20 lines, for example. You might then combine the shorter 20-line page with the following page.

Another way to adjust the number of lines per page is to MOVE a block of text from one page to another. You position the cursor, press F7, the MOVE key, mark the text to be moved, and then position the cursor at the top of the next page. Both methods have the same result.

Sometimes you need to combine two short pages together. To do so, first move the cursor to a page's bottom (that is, to its last character) and press SHIFT F2. You'll see an error message if the cursor isn't all the way at the page's bottom. The following page is then added to the one you're on. Figure 8.3 illustrates page combining.

Naturally, because MultiMate can handle only pages that have a maximum 156 lines, you can't combine two pages if the resulting page would be longer than this limit. MultiMate stops you, telling you the pages can't be combined.

Notice that all the page functions use F2, the PAGE key.

Although adjusting single pages manually this way is useful for a quick fix, MultiMate provides a much faster method of adjusting the page length of a multipage document. The next section looks at the repagination procedure.

ADJUSTING THE PAGE LENGTH FOR AN ENTIRE DOCUMENT

Objective: Using MultiMate's Repagination Procedure

Repagination means adjusting the number of lines that make up each page of a document. For instance, with a multiple-page document, you might want each page to have 48 lines. During editing, however, you often insert and delete lines that can make some pages shorter than 48 lines and others much longer. You must go back through each page, count the lines and make any necessary adjustments. With long documents, adjusting lines per page manually is a slavish and tedious task at best.

MultiMate can do it for you automatically. You need only position the cursor on the page where repagination is to start, press CTRL F2, tell MultiMate how many lines are to be on each page, and press ENTER. MultiMate madly buzzes off cutting your pages into proper lengths.

In the next exercise, you'll repaginate the SEARCH document

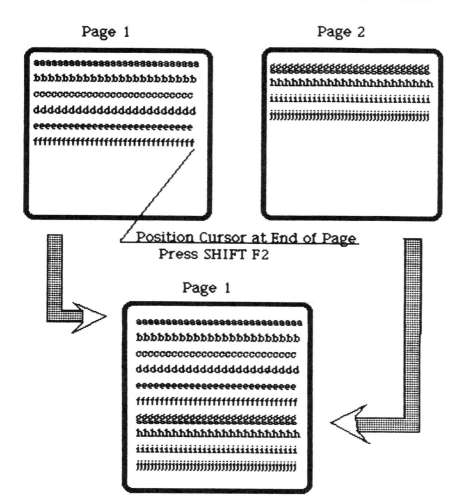

Figure 8.3
Combining Pages

several times. The first time, you'll divide the document's remaining two pages into four pages that are each ten lines long, the first page of which can be seen in figure 8.4.

1. Move the cursor to the top of page 1 of SEARCH by pressing   **Procedure**
    CTRL HOME.

2. Holding down CTRL, press F2. At the top right corner of the
    screen "Repaginate Mode" appears, and the prompt "Enter Lines
    Per Page" appears at the screen's bottom. MultiMate is asking
    how many lines should appear on a page.

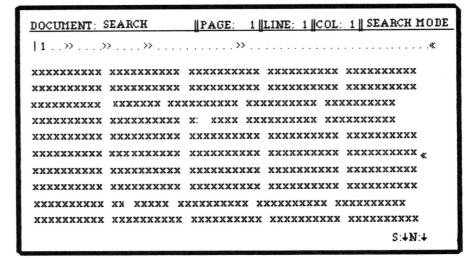

Figure 8.4
Page 1 of SEARCH after
Repagination

3. Type "10" and press ENTER. MultiMate begins repaginating and displays a sign asking you to wait until it's done.

4. When MultiMate has finished, with the F1 key, move the cursor to each of the document's four pages to see the results of repagination.

5. Press F1, type "1", and press ENTER to return to page 1.

6. Now repaginate the document again, but this time make the page length 48 lines. Holding down CTRL, press F2, type "48", and press ENTER. Wait until MultiMate has finished repaginating. When it's done, move the cursor to the bottom of the page to see that the four-page document is now one page.

Explanation

You can repaginate all or part of a document. MultiMate repaginates from the cursor's position all the way to the document's end. After positioning the cursor, you press CTRL F2, type the number of lines per page, and press ENTER. MultiMate does the rest.

You can encounter problems, however. First, you must have enough disk space to hold every page of the newly repaginated document. If you repaginate a document that is 60 lines per page into a document that is 10 lines per page, for example, the document will have six times as many pages and may not fit onto the current disk. You may have to move the document to another disk or otherwise divide it up if you encounter such a problem.

During repagination, every page is usually given the same number of lines. If you allow it to, however, MultiMate may make a few judgment calls on where a page breaks. When you first create a document, you set a parameter on the Modify Document Defaults screen that says "Allow Widows and Orphans?" A widow is the first line of a paragraph stranded at the bottom of a page, separated from the rest of the paragraph on the following page. An orphan is the last line of a paragraph that appears by itself at the top of a page. Some people prefer not to have single lines stranded on a page this way.

If you set the "Allow Widows and Orphans" prompt to "N" for "no", MultiMate will make sure no widow or orphan lines occur during editing. It will either end the page early or allow an extra line or two to prevent widow and orphan lines. Otherwise, MultiMate will repaginate according to the number of lines per page you specified, without regard for how text divides across pages.

Suppose you have a ten-page document and you want the first five pages to be 48 lines per page and the last five to be 60 lines per page. You must repaginate the document twice to accomplish this. With the cursor at the document's beginning, you repaginate the entire document at 48 lines per page. You then move the cursor to page 5 and repaginate again at 60 lines per page. Thus, working from front to back, you can automatically repaginate different portions of a document to different page lengths.

Of course, you may have special pages, such as those showing tables or columns of numbers, that you do not want repaginated (that is, divided across pages). Next you'll see how you can protect a page from the repagination process.

A required page break is a screen marker that tells MultiMate it must end the page at that spot. If you have a page of text, say a table of numbers, that you want to be printed in its entirety on one page (not divided across pages), you can use required page breaks to prevent the table from being broken up. You might think of a required page break as a fence that you put on either side of a text block to prevent other text from trespassing.

PROTECTING PAGES FROM BEING REPAGINATED

Objective: Setting Up Pages with Required Page Breaks

To insert a required page break, you position the cursor where the page is to end. Holding down ALT, press "B" (for "break"). The page divides, leaving a screen marker like the one seen at the bottom of figure 8.5.

Try inserting a required page break in the SEARCH document and then repaginating to see how it affects page division.

1. Move the cursor to line 23, column 1. This is where you'll insert the required page break.

Procedure

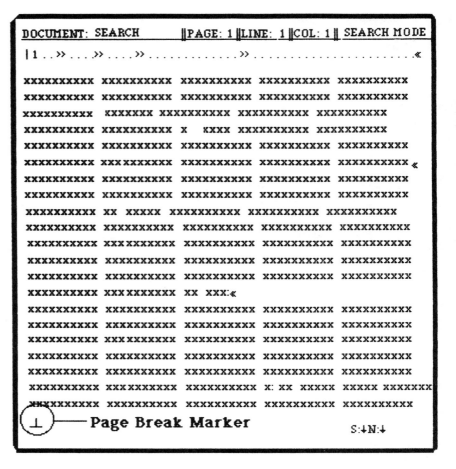

Figure 8.5
Page 1 of SEARCH with
Required Page Break

2. To insert a required page break, hold down ALT and press "B". Notice that the bottom half of the document is now on page 2. If you repaginate the document, MultiMate will be unable to add the two pages together. The required page break forces MultiMate to start a new page.

3. To prepare for repaginating the document, press F1, type "1", and press ENTER to move the cursor to page 1. Let's try to combine both pages into one big page again.

4. Holding down CTRL, press F2.

5. Type "48" and press ENTER to specify 48 lines per page. When the repagination procedure is done, notice that MultiMate honored the required page break and did not combine the two

pages. If this had been a longer document, all subsequent pages would have been repaginated normally.

6.   Press F10 to save the document.

Explanation

To protect text from being repaginated, you put a required page break at the bottom of both the preceding page and the page you wish to protect. As shown in figure 8.6, each required page break forces MultiMate to begin a new page regardless of the number of lines per page.

You might use a required page break to make sure a page ends where you want it to, or to fence in a text block that should appear all on one page.

To eliminate a required page break, you move the cursor under it and delete it. During repagination, that page will no longer be required to end at that spot.

SUMMARY

You can create as elaborate a page format as you wish by inserting format lines within a page. These format lines can change the formatting specification as often as you need. To insert a format line:

1.   Position the cursor where the format line is to appear.

2.   Press   ALT F9   to insert a format line identical to the one at the page's top.

         SHIFT F9   to insert a format line like that most recently used in the document.

         CTRL F9   to insert a format line like the original default format line with which MultiMate always begins a document.

Page 1   Page 2   Page 3

Required page breaks stop page 2 from combining with pages 1 and 3.

Figure 8.6
Function of Required Page Breaks

3. Edit the format line if necessary.

4. Press F9.

You can divide and combine pages using the keys shown in figure 8.7.

Finally, required page breaks can protect text from being inappropriately repaginated. You insert a required page break by holding down ALT and pressing "B".

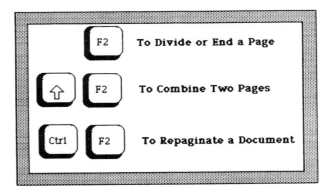

Figure 8.7
Keys for Adjusting Page
Length

Chapter 9

UPS AND DOWNS
OF EDITING

Preparation

> Your computer should be turned on and the MultiMate main menu should be on the screen. Your exercise disk should be in drive B and should contain the document called COLUMN. Refer to appendix E for instructions on how to create the COLUMN document.

One tedious job with a typewriter is typing properly aligned numbers in columns. Forget that tedium; MultiMate has a special tab function, called Dectab, that automatically aligns numbers and text vertically. The first exercise in this chapter will teach you to use MultiMate's Dectab feature.

Financial documents often require you to type columnar information. The information is organized going up and down the page, perhaps in several columns of numbers. Up to now, you've learned how MultiMate copies, moves, inserts, and deletes text. These editing procedures usually have you marking text *across* the page. What happens when you need to delete a column of numbers going down the page?

Figure 9.1 shows three columns of numbers. Pretend you want to delete just the middle column. If you use MultiMate's normal method of deletion, the other two columns will also be marked for deletion during the marking procedure (as shown in the figure).

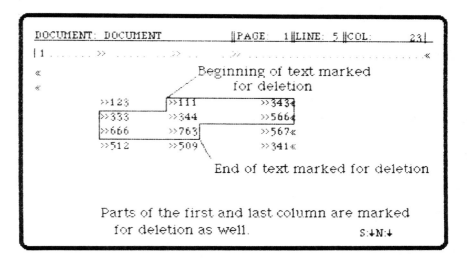

Figure 9.1
Deleting a Column

MultiMate marks a whole line across the page before it begins marking lines below. You therefore can't successfully just delete one column of numbers using this method. You'd have to individually delete each number of a column to preserve the neighboring number columns.

MultiMate can handle columnar information wonderfully, however. With three columns of numbers on screen, you might delete just the middle column, move one column in front of another, copy a column, or insert space vertically on the page. MultiMate uses special editing procedures to handle columnar information; to access these procedures, select column mode.

This chapter will give you a taste of editing financial documents that consist mainly of columns of numbers. You'll delete, copy, and move columns and insert extra space vertically in a document. MultiMate can even total rows and columns of numbers for you, saving you the burden of checking your addition.

When you are editing columns, you'll use the same basic steps as you used to delete, copy, and move text, except that the text you'll be marking is vertically oriented. Although you won't be a column-editing expert by the chapter's end, you will know how to perform simple column editing. You can refine these skills on your own. Knowing you can edit in a columnar fashion can also save you time when you are editing normal text documents as well. Simply keep an eye out for times when a vertically oriented procedure would be more effective than a horizontally oriented one.

You'll start out by creating a document with columns of numbers and then try out column-editing procedures.

To type columns of numbers (or text), you begin by setting tab stops in the format line where columns are to occur. During the actual typing of a number, instead of pressing the TAB key, however, you press SHIFT F4, the Dectab key. The cursor jumps to the tab stop and puts a Dectab marker on screen. As you type the number, it will move to the left across the screen.

After typing a number, you can press Dectab again to tab to the next column or press ENTER to end the line. You can erase Dectab markers just as you can tab or indent markers.

Try typing the columns of numbers and text you see in figure 9.2. The small squares appearing before the numbers (and column labels) are Dectab markers.

1. Type "1" and press ENTER to select "Edit an Old Document".

2. Type the document name, "COLUMN", and press ENTER. (Be sure the drive specification is correct.)

3. Press F10 to bypass the Document Summary screen.

4. Move the cursor down to line 11, column 1. Here's where you'll type the labels for the four column headings. Rather than using tabs, however, you'll line up the labels with Dectabs.

AUTOMATICALLY ALIGNING COLUMNS

Objective: Aligning Numbers and Text with Dectabs

Procedure

```
DOCUMENT: COLUMN           ‖PAGE:     1 ‖LINE:       1‖COL:   1 |
| 1 . . . . . . . . . . . . . . . .>> . . . . . . . . .>> . . . . . . . . . . .>> . . . . . . . . . .>>. . . .«
John Talbot, Director«
Dashing Dishes, Inc.«
123 Green Street«
San Francisco, CA 94999«
«
Dear John:«
«
Here are the monthly sales for the quarter.  You'll see from
these that I '11 need a pay raise shortly.  Just kidding.«
«
             □JANUARY   □FEBRUARY      □MARCH        □TOTAL «
«
Barnes       □$123,000  □$150,000    □$160,000     □$433,000«
Jackson      □$25,000   □$75,000     □$125,000     □$225,000«
Baily        □$120,000  □$122,000    □$133,000     □$375,000«
Monthly Total      □          □           □             □«
«
«                                                    S:↓N:↓
```

Figure 9.2
COLUMN Document with Number Columns

5. Holding down SHIFT, press F4. The cursor tabs over and a Dectab marker appears.

6. Type "JANUARY". Notice how the word moves from the right to the left across the screen. That's the secret to how the Dectabs feature aligns numbers correctly. To move the cursor to the right, you will press SHIFT and F4 again.

7. Holding down SHIFT, press F4.

8. Type "FEBRUARY".

9. Holding down SHIFT, press F4.

10. Type "MARCH".

11. Holding down SHIFT, press F4 and type "TOTAL".

12. Press ENTER twice to end the line and skip down one line.

13. Type "Barnes". Next, you want to begin typing the first number column.

14. Holding down SHIFT, press F4. Now type "$123,000".

15. Holding down SHIFT, press F4; type "$150,000".

16. Holding down SHIFT, press F4; type "$160,000".

17. Holding down SHIFT, press F4; type "$433,000" and press ENTER to end the line.

18. Type the "Jackson" and "Baily" figures seen in figure 9.2. Remember to use SHIFT F4 before each figure. Notice how they align automatically?

19. At line 16, column 1, type "Monthly Total". You're going to do something special on this line later. For now, just put four Dectab markers on the line as pictured.

20. To put the four Dectab markers on the line, hold down SHIFT and press F4 four times. Press ENTER. By now, you get the idea behind using Dectabs to type columns.

Explanation

You might think of Dectabs as book ends. They hold columns of numbers upright. If you accidentally take out one or two Dectabs, you may find your numbers slouching in a disorganized pile. You can straighten up figures into a properly aligned column by sticking the book ends (Dectabs) back into place, just as you can insert and delete other screen markers.

The secret to typing columns of numbers successfully is in carefully setting up a format line. As with a typewriter, you set tab stops where columns are to appear. With MultiMate's Dectab function, however, the tab stops must mark where numbers (such as those in the exercise) should *end*. Compare the column positions with the format line's tab stops in figure 9.2 to see how tab stops must be set where numbers are expected to end.

You must also allow enough space between the tab settings to hold the largest number of the column. If a number is too large to fit between columns, the Dectab function stops working.

After you press SHIFT F4, the cursor jumps ahead to a tab stop. As you type a number, $500 for·example, it is entered in this direction:

Thus, as you type columns with Dectabs, the numbers all end in the same place, at the tab-stop locations.

Numbers that have decimal places (such as $5.00 or 59.8 degrees) act slightly differently when aligned with Dectabs. These numbers line up on the dividing period, or decimal point. This type of automatic alignment on a decimal point gave the Dectab its name (it stands for "decimal tab"). If you typed a column of three numbers with decimal figures, they would align as the following numbers do:

|1................................... ≫ ....≪
                      □122222.000
                      □1.000050
                      □100.5

When you are setting up a format line for columns of these types of numbers, you should locate tab stops where the numbers' decimal points are to appear.

You may remember from the Modify Document Defaults screen that figures can line up on commas or on periods (decimal points) when you use the Dectab function. You make this selection at the Modify Document Defaults screen when you first create a document.

All column-editing procedures begin by switching to column mode. To do so, hold down SHIFT and press F3.

Once in column mode, you press the editing key you'd normally use to initiate an editing procedure. To delete columns, for example, you press DEL, the DELETE key.

To delete text from a column, place the cursor in a column's top corner and move it sideways to mark the column's width. After marking column width, you move the cursor down to the last line to be deleted from the column.

DELETING COLUMNS

Objective: Using Column Delete to Erase Text

With the column marked, you press DEL to complete the procedure. The marked columnar text disappears and any text to the right slides over to take its place.

You can cancel a column delete by pressing ESC.

Try deleting two columns from the COLUMN document to make it look like figure 9.3.

Procedure

1. Move the cursor under the dollar sign on line 13, column 52. You'll delete this column first. You must start a deletion with the cursor in the column's top left corner. You're going to delete just the numbers, leaving the Dectab markers, which you'll need for row addition later in this chapter.
2. Holding down SHIFT, press F3. The message "Column Mode" appears in the screen's top right corner. The next key you press will tell MultiMate what kind of column editing you wish to perform.
3. Press DEL. The message "Column Delete" appears. At the screen's bottom, MultiMate tells you to mark the text by first moving the cursor to the right, then down.

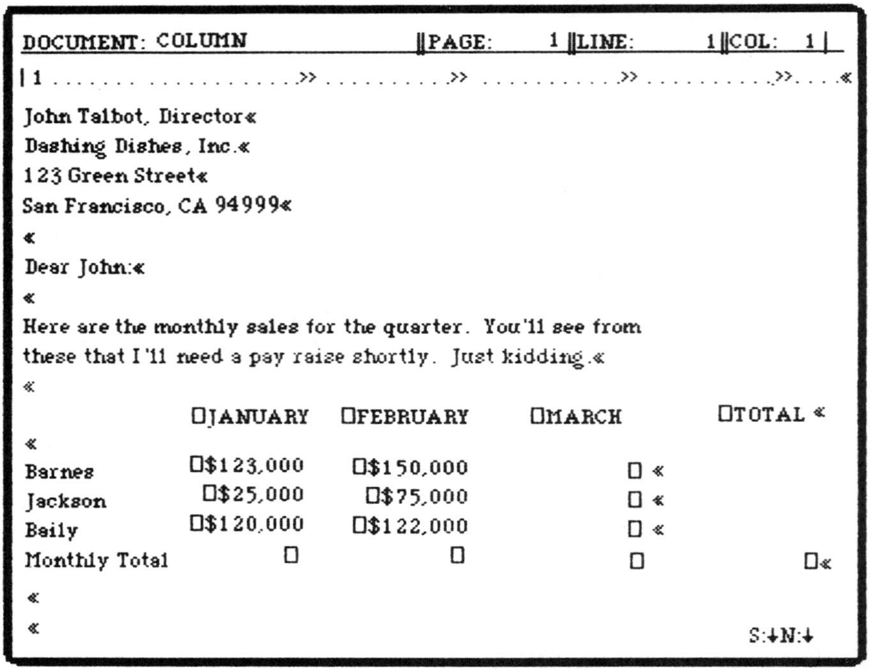

```
DOCUMENT: COLUMN                ║PAGE:    1 ║LINE:      1║COL:  1 |
| 1 . . . . . . . . . . . . . . .>> . . . . . . . . .>> . . . . . . . . . . .>> . . . . . . . . . .>>. . . «
John Talbot, Director«
Dashing Dishes, Inc.«
123 Green Street«
San Francisco, CA 94999«
«
Dear John:«
«
Here are the monthly sales for the quarter.  You'll see from
these that I'll need a pay raise shortly.  Just kidding.«
«
               □JANUARY    □FEBRUARY      □MARCH          □TOTAL «
«
Barnes         □$123,000    □$150,000             □ «
Jackson         □$25,000     □$75,000             □ «
Baily          □$120,000    □$122,000             □ «
Monthly Total          □            □             □              □«
«
«                                                           S:↓N:↓
```

Figure 9.3
COLUMN Document with Two Columns Deleted

4. Move the cursor right to line 13, column 59. Notice that the characters get brighter as you mark them. Don't mark the carriage-return markers, because you need them to end the lines and keep the columns from mixing up.

5. Move the cursor down to line 15, column 59. You've now marked the column for deletion. Notice that the other columns were not marked.

6. Press DEL. The marked column disappears. For practice, delete the MARCH column as well.

7. Move the cursor to line 13, column 39, under the Dectab marker.

8. Holding down SHIFT, press F3 to start column mode.

9. Press DEL to initiate a column delete.

10. Move the cursor to the right to line 13, column 47.

11. Move the cursor down to line 15, column 47.

12. Press DEL. The second column disappears.

Column delete follows this general procedure: **Explanation**

1. Position the cursor in the upper corner of the text to be deleted.

2. Press SHIFT F3 to enter column mode.

3. Press DEL.

4. Mark the text.

5. Press DEL.

You can delete as much text as you wish with column delete. You can delete columns running the entire width of a page or delete a single string of characters down the page. With column delete, for example, you might "vacuum up" format markers, such as tab markers, running down the page to bring about some quick reformatting. You can't delete beyond the page you're on, however.

The main difference between column delete and the normal deletion procedure is in marking text. With column delete, you mark the column width and then the length of the text to be deleted. To mark text, you use the left, right, and down arrow keys. If you mark too much text, you can simply back up the cursor to unmark it. The column marked for deletion becomes highlighted on screen, and no text on either side of the marked block will be deleted.

It may take a little practice to get the feel of how column delete works. Marking the column can be tricky if numbers are of different sizes. Figure 9.4 shows a common problem with column delete. In this figure, some of the numbers are wider than the one at the column's top. Thus, you can't quite mark all of the numbers in a straight up and down column. To take care of this problem, you can begin the deletion on the right side of the column (where the numbers all line up evenly) and move the cursor to the left when marking the column width until the longest number is included entirely in the marked area. Then the entire column can be successfully marked and deleted.

You must also consider whether you want to delete the format markers surrounding the column. Deleting the carriage-return markers ending each line of a column can disastrously disorganize all your columns. If you're deleting a column of text to replace it with another, you may wish to leave the Dectab markers (which format the column to be deleted) in place. With the Dectabs left behind, you can use them as targets, moving the cursor under them to insert other numbers later. Other times, however, you may need to delete both text and format markers.

You should probably create a document and try out several kinds of column deletions for practice. Although the instructions here have taught you to start a column deletion in the top left corner of the column, you could start it in the top right corner and mark text by pressing the left arrow key first.

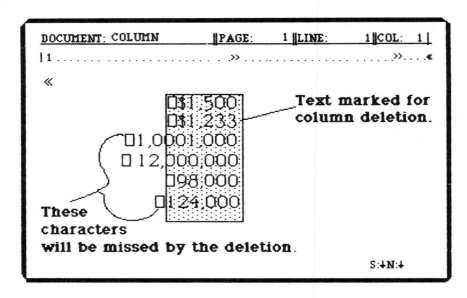

Figure 9.4
Deleting an Uneven
Column of Numbers

Let's juggle some figures. You can reposition columns within a page. With three columns on screen, for example, you might move the first column to become the third column. Column move is similar to the move procedure; in fact, it uses the same key, F7.

First, position the cursor and, holding down SHIFT, press F3 to enter column mode. Next, press the MOVE key, F7. You mark the column as you did in the column-delete procedure. You press F7 and the column disappears.

Move the cursor to a new site and press F7 a final time. The marked column jumps to the new position. You can press ESC to cancel a column move at any time.

Try editing the COLUMN document so that it looks like figure 9.5. You'll move the first column to become the second.

1. Move the cursor to line 13, column 15 under the Dectab marker. You'll move January's figures to the February column.

2. Holding down SHIFT, press F3 to initiate column mode.

3. Press F7 to initiate column move. The message "Column Move" appears at the screen's top. Next, you mark the column.

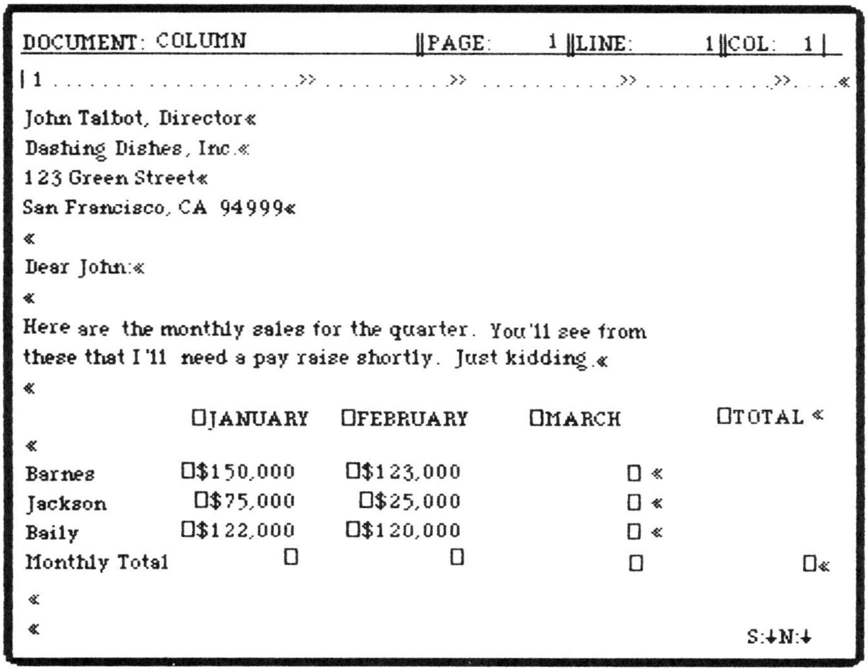

MOVING COLUMNS

Objective: Using Column Move to Switch Column Positions

Procedure

```
DOCUMENT: COLUMN              ║PAGE:     1 ║LINE:      1║COL:   1 │
│ 1 . . . . . . . . . . . . .>> . . . . . .>> . . . . . . . .>> . . . . . . .>>. . . .«
John Talbot, Director«
Dashing Dishes, Inc.«
123 Green Street«
San Francisco, CA 94999«
«
Dear John:«
«
Here are the monthly sales for the quarter. You'll see from
these that I'll need a pay raise shortly. Just kidding.«
«
              □JANUARY   □FEBRUARY    □MARCH       □TOTAL «
«
Barnes        □$150,000  □$123,000         □ «
Jackson       □$75,000   □$25,000          □ «
Baily         □$122,000  □$120,000         □ «
Monthly Total       □          □          □         □«
«
«                                              S:↓N:↓
```

Figure 9.5
COLUMN Document after Column Move

4. Move the cursor right to line 13, column 23.

5. Move the cursor down to line 15, column 23.

6. Press F7. The column disappears, the second column slides over, and the message "To Where?" appears. Next, you move the cursor to the top left corner of where the column should appear.

7. In this case, move the cursor to line 13, column 35 under the Dectab marker. The column will be inserted just before this column of Dectab markers.

8. Press F7. The column reappears as the second column; the column of numbers that was there slides over to the left.

Explanation

Column move enables you to pick up a text column and drop it in another position. You can't move a column beyond the page you're on. The general procedure is as follows:

1. Position the cursor at the column's top corner (left or right).

2. Press SHIFT F3 to enter column mode.

3. Press F7 to initiate a column move.

4. Mark the column.

5. Press F7.

6. Move the cursor to the top left corner of where the column should appear.

7. Press F7.

You can move a column anywhere on the page, but be sure the format line is set up to handle the column in the new position. The easiest column moves are made laterally, as you did in the exercise—simply switching column positions. If you moved a column down the page, ignoring the fact that it lacks ending carriage returns (or Dectabs) as book ends on the right side, you'd see the column "unformat" dramatically. What was a vertical column would become a horizontal line of figures.

The hardest decision during a column move is picking out the column's new location. Most often, you'll move the cursor under a screen marker (Dectab or carriage-return marker). Remember that the column will appear *before* the marker. If you wanted to move the first column of the exercise so that it becomes the last column, you'd position the cursor directly under the carriage-return marker that ends line 13. When the moved column appeared, the figures would end with carriage returns.

You should probably try out various column moves in a practice document to get the hang of it.

You can duplicate text columns with the column-copy procedure, which is almost identical to column move. You'll copy the first column of the COLUMN document to become a third column, as shown in figure 9.6.

To perform a column copy, you position the cursor and press SHIFT F3 to enter column mode. You then press the COPY key, F8. You mark the text to be copied, press F8, move the cursor to a new location, and press F8 a final time. A duplicate of the column appears at the cursor position. You can cancel the procedure with ESC at any time.

COPYING COLUMNS TO NEW POSITIONS

Objective: Using Column Copy to Duplicate Columns

1. To copy the first column, move the cursor under the Dectab marker on line 13, column 15.

2. Holding down SHIFT, press F3 to initiate column mode.

3. Press F8 to initiate column copy. The message "Column Copy"

Procedure

```
DOCUMENT: COLUMN                    ||PAGE:     1 ||LINE:      1||COL:   1 |
| 1 . . . . . . . . . . . . . . . .>> . . . . . . . . .>> . . . . . . . . .>> . . . . . . . . .>>. . . .«

John Talbot, Director«
Dashing Dishes, Inc.«
123 Green Street«
San Francisco, CA 94999«
«
Dear John:«
«
Here are the monthly sales for the quarter. You'll see from
these that I'll need a pay raise shortly. Just kidding.«
«
              □JANUARY   □FEBRUARY    □MARCH        □TOTAL «
«
Barnes        □$150,000  □$123,000    □$150,000        □ «
Jackson       □$75,000   □$25,000     □$75,000         □ «
Baily         □$122,000  □$120,000    □$122,000        □ «
Monthly Total     □          □            □            □«
«
«                                                  S:↓N:↓
```

Figure 9.6
COLUMN Document after Column Copy

appears at the screen's top. Next, you mark the text to be copied.

4. Move the cursor right to line 13, column 23, under the last number of the column.

5. Move the cursor down to line 15, column 23. The column is now marked.

6. Press F8. The message "To Where?" appears. You now move the cursor to where the copy is to appear.

7. Move the cursor to line 13, column 47 under the Dectab. You must position the cursor at the upper left corner of where the copy should be located.

8. Press F8. The first column is duplicated.

Explanation

Like column move, you can copy a column anywhere within a page, but not beyond it. You can copy a column that is as wide and long as you wish.

The general procedure is as follows:

1. Position the cursor at the column's top corner (right or left).

2. Press SHIFT F3 to enter column mode.

3. Press F8 to initiate a column copy.

4. Mark the column.

5. Press F8.

6. Move the cursor to the top left corner of where the column should appear.

7. Press F8.

It's usually best to copy the formatting markers with the text to a new location. It is more likely to format correctly on arrival. If you copy a column to a distant corner of the page, you also want to make sure that a format line will produce the correct results there. As you may remember, you can insert multiple format lines in a page. You can therefore set up a page to produce columns of text and figures in various positions.

Again, your main concern during a column copy is that you select the correct cursor position where the copy is to appear. It's easy to press F8 a final time only to discover the copied column missed the mark. Remember that the copy appears *before* the cursor position. You'll want to practice the column copy procedure on your own.

INSERTING COLUMNS OF SPACE

Objective: Using Column Insert to Insert Columns of Blank Spaces

When you press the plus key several times, it inserts blank spaces horizontally across the screen. Column insert inserts blocks of spaces vertically.

First, enter column mode by pressing SHIFT F3. Then press INS, for column insert. You type the number of blanks to be inserted across and another number for how many rows down should have blanks inserted in them. You press INS a final time, and the blanks appear in the text.

In the COLUMN document, try inserting some blanks in front of the column of names at the left margin. When you are finished, the COLUMN document will look like figure 9.7. Notice that all three names (Barnes, Jackson, and Baily) have been indented two spaces from the left margin. Blanks were inserted before all three names in one procedure, column insert.

Procedure

1. Move the cursor to line 13, column 1. You're going to insert a column of two blank spaces down the left margin. These spaces will push the names to the right.
2. Holding down SHIFT, press F3.
3. Press INS. The message "Column Insert" appears at the screen's

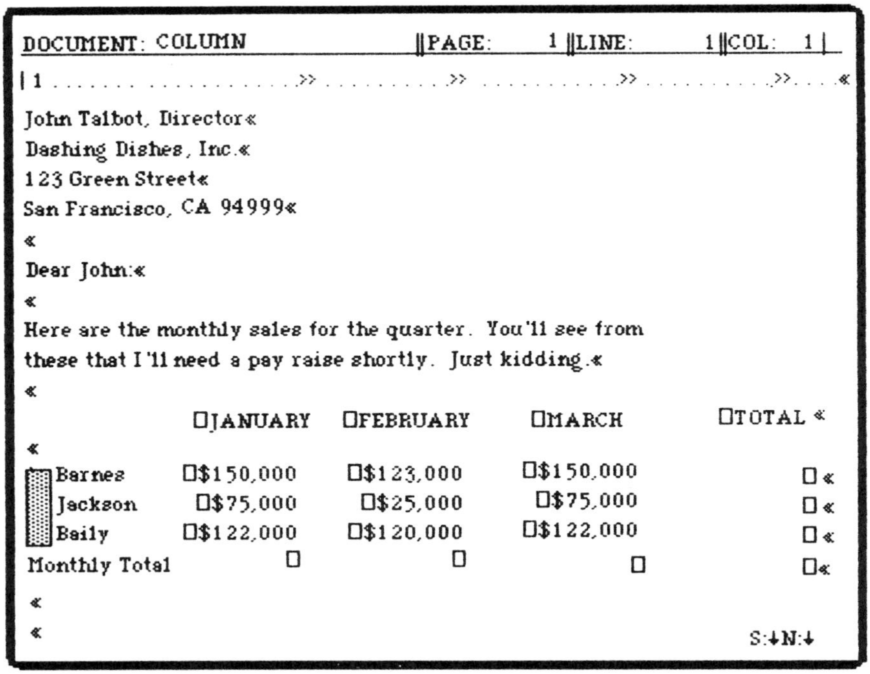

DOCUMENT: COLUMN ‖PAGE: 1 ‖LINE: 1‖COL: 1|

|1 . . . .>> . . . .>> . . . .>> . . . .>>. . . .«

John Talbot, Director«
Dashing Dishes, Inc.«
123 Green Street«
San Francisco, CA 94999«
«
Dear John:«
«
Here are the monthly sales for the quarter. You'll see from
these that I'll need a pay raise shortly. Just kidding.«
«

	□JANUARY	□FEBRUARY	□MARCH	□TOTAL «
«				
Barnes	□$150,000	□$123,000	□$150,000	□«
Jackson	□$75,000	□$25,000	□$75,000	□«
Baily	□$122,000	□$120,000	□$122,000	□«
Monthly Total	□	□	□	□«

«
« S:↓N:↓

Figure 9.7
COLUMN Document with Indented Names

top. At the bottom, MultiMate asks you to specify the number of spaces (columns) to be inserted and the number of lines down the insert should go.

4. To insert two spaces, type "02" at the "# of Columns" prompt. Next, tell MultiMate how many lines down (from the cursor position) the blank spaces should extend.

5. Press ENTER to move the cursor to the "# of Lines" prompt and type "03". Two spaces will be inserted before each of the three lines.

6. Press F10 to complete the procedure. Notice the insertion of a column, two spaces wide, before each name in lines 13 through 15.

Explanation

Using column insert is a little like driving a spike of blank space down into text. Although the column you inserted in the exercise was only two spaces wide and three lines long, you can insert as large a column as you wish.

Column insertion is most useful for reformatting by inserting columns of space to move columnar information left or right. You might use it to insert a margin of blank spaces and then type text into that margin.

The general procedure for column insert is as follows:

1. Position the cursor at the top left corner of the location in which the column is to appear.

2. Press SHIFT F3 to enter column mode.

3. Press INS to initiate column insert.

4. Type a number corresponding to the number of spaces across to be inserted and press ENTER.

5. Type a number corresponding to the number of lines down from the cursor that should be preceded by spaces.

6. Press F10 to complete the procedure.

Column insert has limited applications. You will most likely use it when you need to add a space or two down an entire column, as you did in the exercise. You can also use it to push columns left or right by inserting blocks of space to move them over. Most often, however, you'll want to adjust column position by changing tab stops on the format line.

Inserting a column of space in normally formatted text, say a paragraph, can be as frustrating as trying to dig a hole in mud. As soon as you insert the space you want, the paragraph reformats, adjusting every line and swamping over the inserted space. In fact, you can use any of the column-editing functions, such as column delete, move, or copy, on normal text. The results will be so awful, however, that you'll want just to erase the whole mess.

TOTALING UP NUMBERS

Objective: Using MultiMate's Column and Row Addition to Total Numbers

If you're disinclined to add up long columns or rows of numbers (or maybe just not so hot at it), you can let MultiMate do the ciphering for you.

Rows of numbers formatted with Dectabs can be totaled if you press CTRL F3. You first place the cursor under a Dectab where the total is to appear at the end of the row. After you press CTRL F3, MultiMate looks across the screen, adds up all the numbers, and places the total at the Dectab marker.

You can also automatically tally a column of figures. You place the cursor under a Dectab where the total is to appear and press CTRL F4. MultiMate calculates and displays the total almost instantly. Try adding the rows and columns in the COLUMN document to make it look like figure 9.8.

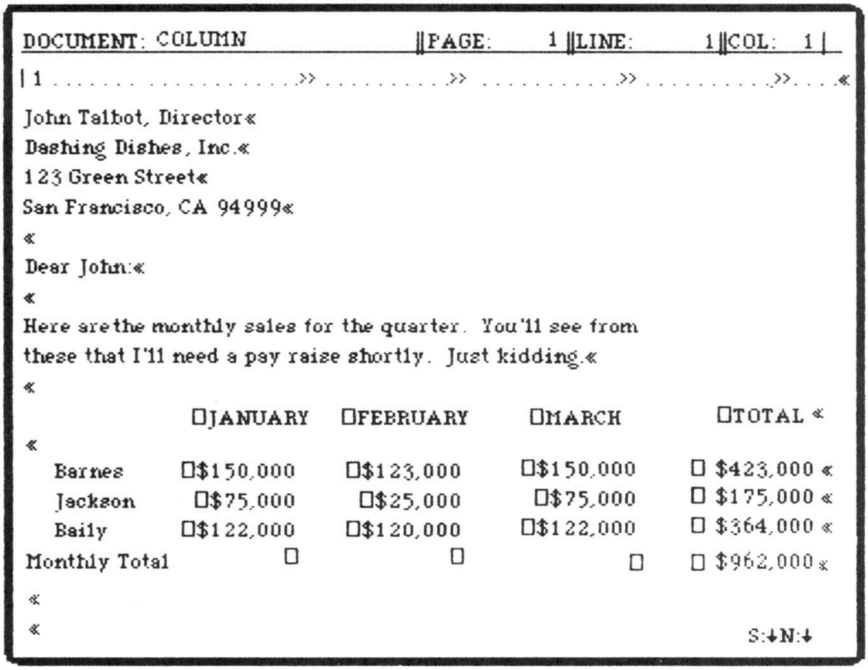
DOCUMENT: COLUMN ‖PAGE: 1 ‖LINE: 1 ‖COL: 1 |

| 1 . . . .>> . . . .>> . . . .>> . . . .>>. . . «

John Talbot, Director«

Dashing Dishes, Inc.«

123 Green Street«

San Francisco, CA 94999«

«

Dear John:«

«

Here are the monthly sales for the quarter. You'll see from these that I'll need a pay raise shortly. Just kidding.«

«

	JANUARY	FEBRUARY	MARCH	TOTAL «
Barnes	$150,000	$123,000	$150,000	$423,000 «
Jackson	$75,000	$25,000	$75,000	$175,000 «
Baily	$122,000	$120,000	$122,000	$364,000 «
Monthly Total				$962,000 «

«

« S:↓N:↓

Figure 9.8
COLUMN Document with Totals

Procedure

1. Move the cursor to line 13, column 59, under the Dectab. The cursor *must* be directly under the Dectab. MultiMate will not total a row unless the cursor is under a Dectab where it can place the results. Tell MultiMate to add up this row.

2. Holding down CTRL, press F3. Instantly, the total $423,000 appears.

3. Move the cursor to line 14, column 59. Add this row, too.

4. Holding down CTRL, press F3. Now add up the "Baily" row of figures.

5. Move the cursor under the Dectab at line 15, column 59.

6. Holding down CTRL, press F3. Now that you've added up rows, try adding the columns for January, February, and March.

7. Move the cursor to line 16, column 23, under the Dectab. You must have a Dectab at a column's bottom where the sum can be placed.

8. Holding down CTRL, press F4. The column-addition function displays $347,000 as the total.

9. Move the cursor under the Dectab at line 16, column 35.

10. Holding down CTRL, press F4. The column-addition function displays $268,000 as the total.

11. Move the cursor under the Dectab at line 16, column 47.

12. Holding down CTRL, press F4. The column-addition function displays $347,000 as the total.

13. Move the cursor under the Dectab at line 16, column 59.

14. Holding down CTRL, press F4. The column-addition function displays $962,000 as the total. Try experimenting with column and row addition. Change some of the figures and then have MultiMate recalculate the totals.

Explanation

No more taking your shoes off to do some heavy arithmetic. MultiMate's row- and column-addition functions are excellent ways of checking for typographical errors in financial documents. If you know the totals you should get, you can ask MultiMate to tally the figures and check the answer. If the answer differs from the expected amount, you know that at least one figure in the document is inaccurate.

MultiMate can only add numbers; it can't multiply or divide them.

If you wish to subtract numbers, you mark them with a hyphen either before or after the number or put parentheses around the number. Numbers marked this way are seen as negative numbers and are subtracted from the total.

MultiMate can add as many numbers as fit on a line or column of one page. You can't add figures across page boundaries.

Before totaling a row or column, you must place a Dectab at the end of the figures to hold the total. You move the cursor under the Dectab and, holding down CTRL, press F3 to total rows or F4 to total columns. If a number already appears at the Dectab's location, you don't have to erase it. MultiMate will replace the number with the new total automatically.

If you use dollar signs, commas, or decimal points, these marks will appear in the total as well.

If you have two columns stacked on top of each other, as shown in figure 9.9, you must put a format line between the columns. Otherwise, MultiMate will add both columns as one long column, and the total for the bottom column will be wrong.

SUMMARY

You've seen how Dectabs (SHIFT F4) can be used to align columns of figures automatically. You must, of course, set up a format line with tab stops spaced for your columns.

You've also learned column delete, as shown in figure 9.10. You can move and copy columns as well, using the procedure shown in figure 9.11. Occasionally, you may need to insert space before or

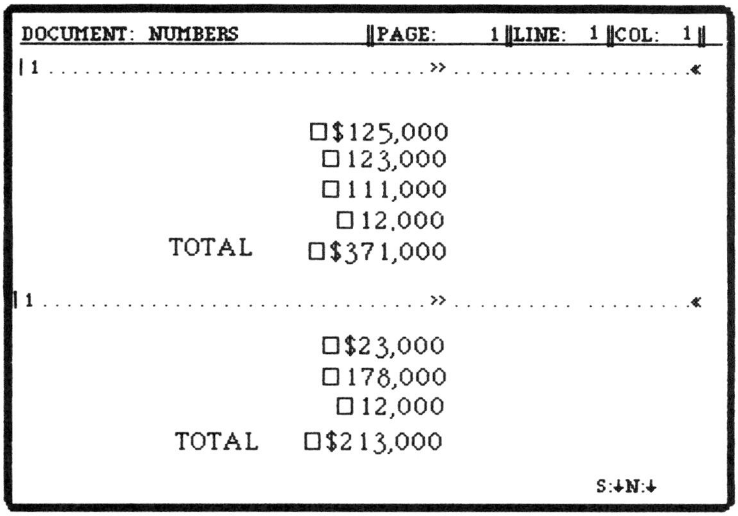

Figure 9.9
Dividing Columns with
Format Lines

within columns. MultiMate's column-insert procedure is used as shown in figure 9.12.

MultiMate can save your brain cells some processing time with its automatic addition functions, pictured in figure 9.13.

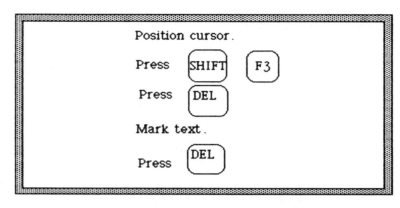

Figure 9.10
Column Delete

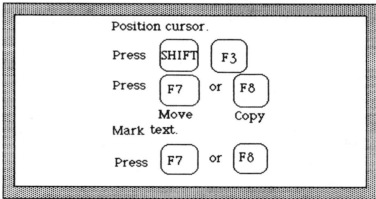

Figure 9.11
Column Move and Copy

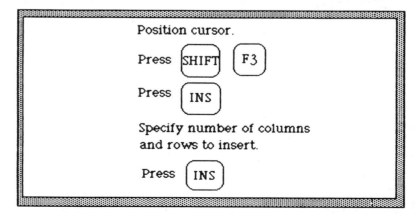

Figure 9.12
Column Insertions

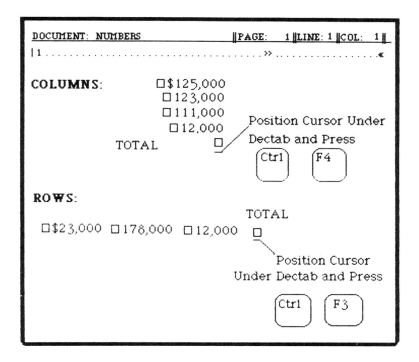

Figure 9.13
Column and Row
Addition

Chapter 10

HEADING UP A DOCUMENT AND UTILITIES

Preparation

Preparation

Your computer should be turned on and the MultiMate main menu should be on the screen. Your exercise disk should be in drive B and should contain the document called HEADER. Refer to appendix F for instructions on how to create HEADER.

You'll also be printing the HEADER document several times. You need to turn on your printer and have it loaded with either continuous form or single-sheet typing paper.

MultiMate is good for solving long-document headaches. Multiple-page documents, such as long reports, often require headings or titles that appear at the top or bottom of every page. For example, a company name and report title might appear at the top of each page and a page number at the bottom. With a typewriter, you'd have to type these lines fifty times for a fifty-page document—just one more typing burden. With MultiMate you type them once and the program remembers and prints them appropriately on every page.

Repeating titles that appear at the top of a page are called *headers* (or *headings*). Titles that appear at the bottom of a page are called *footers* (or *footings*). Figure 10.1 shows an example of headers and footers appearing in a several-page document. MultiMate's header and footer capabilities make it easy to set up a document with repeating titles, and you'll learn to use them on a short two-page document in this chapter.

Another headache with long documents is typing page numbers. If you move, copy, delete, or insert a page, page numbers are liable to be thrown off for all pages after that. You don't have to fool with renumbering pages, however. MultiMate can automatically count and number pages for you. Automatic page numbering is done as part of the header and footer set up, which you'll also learn shortly.

You've been working hard learning to create documents—now you'll get a chance to destroy one. Once recorded on disk, documents sometimes need to be copied, deleted, or perhaps given new names. You use special functions, called *utilities,* to perform document-handling procedures. Rather than working *in* a document, these utilities allow you to work *on* it as a whole.

MultiMate provides other utilities for viewing or printing Document Summary screens (as references to document contents) or searching for a specific document whose exact name you perhaps can't remember. You'll try out a few of MultiMate's utilities found under the main menu's "Document Handling Utilities", the sixth option.

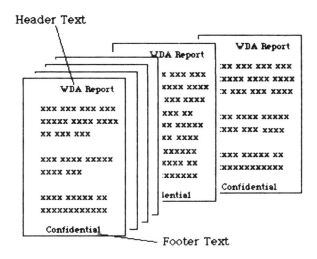

Figure 10.1
Examples of Headers and Footers

CREATING REPEATING TITLES AT THE TOP OF EVERY PAGE

Objective: Creating Headers in Multiple-page Documents

Let's create the header text seen in figure 10.2. This header will print the titles "FINANCIAL REPORT" and "ABC COMPANY" on every page of the document. You can create headers with any text you wish, up to five lines long. MultiMate will swiftly print a header on page after page, without your having to lift a finger.

To create a header, you begin a page with a special header marker. You hold down the ALT key and type "H" at the page's top. You type the text to appear on each page, formatting it just as you want it printed. For example, if you want the header centered, you center it on the screen.

After typing the header text, you end it with another header screen marker by typing ALT H again. During printing, MultiMate knows that everything between the two header markers should appear on every page.

In the next exercise, you'll create a simple header on the two-page HEADER document. You'll print this document to see how headers work.

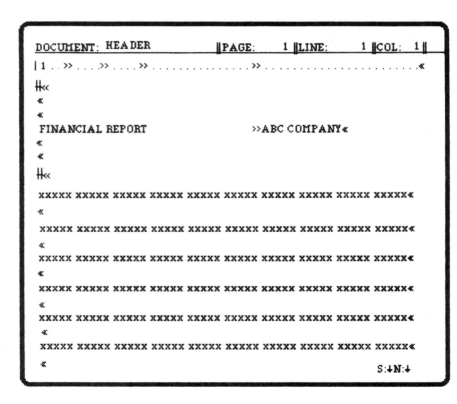

Figure 10.2
HEADER Document with Header

1. Type "1" and press ENTER to select "Edit an Old Document"   **Procedure** from the main menu.

2. Type "HEADER" as the document name and press ENTER. (Check that the drive specification correctly designates the site of the exercise disk.)

3. Type your name as the author of the HEADER document and press F10 at the Document Summary screen. When the editing screen appears, you begin creating the header.

4. With the cursor located at line 1, column 1, press INS. Because there's already text on screen, you'll insert the header at the page's top.

5. Holding down ALT, type "H". The header marker appears. You must always end this marker with a carriage return so that it appears as its own line.

6. Press ENTER. Any text you type now will be repeated on every page of the document. Let's skip down two lines from the page's top and type a single header line.

7. Press ENTER twice and type "FINANCIAL REPORT".

8. Press TAB and type "ABC COMPANY"; press ENTER. There should be two blank lines between this header and the text, so let's skip down two lines before finishing the header.

9. Press ENTER twice and, holding down ALT, type "H"; press ENTER. You've now ended the header text with the mandatory header marker and carriage return. Everything that appears between the two markers will be printed on every page of the document.

10. Press INS to leave the insert mode and then press F10 to save the document. Let's print the document.

11. Type "3" and press ENTER to select "Print Document Utility" from the main menu.

12. Press ENTER to accept the document name HEADER at the Document Specification screen.

13. Set the print menu as shown in figure 10.3. If you're using continuous-form computer paper, set "Pause between pages" to "N" for "no." If you're using separate sheets of typing paper, set this option to "Y" for "yes." The "Printer Action Table" option should list the print driver for your type of printer.

```
        Print Parameters for Document    B:HEADER

Start print at page number    001    Lines per inch: 6 / 8              6
Stop print after page number  002    Justification: N / Y / M(icro)    N
Left margin                    010    Proportional Spacing: N / Y       N
Top margin                     000    Char translate/width table    _____
Pause between pages: N / Y      N     Header/footer first page number  001
Draft print: N / Y              N     Number of original copies        001
Default pitch (4=10 cpi)        4     Document page length             066
Printer Action Table  Your Printer    Sheet Feeder Action Table  Your Feeder
Sheet Feeder Bin Numbers (0/1/2/3): First page: 0 Middle: 0 Last page:  0
P(arallel) / S(erial) / L(ist) / A(uxiliary) / F(ile)                   ?
                                      Device Number                    001

Print document summary screen: N/Y N Print printer parameters :    N/Y N
Background / Foreground:       B/F B Remove queue entry when done:Y/N Y
Current Time is:    00:00:00    Delay Print until Time is: 00:00:00
Current Date is:    00/00/0000  Delay Print until Date is: 00/00/0000
Press F1 for Printers, F2 for Sheet Feeders - only the first 16 are displayed
        Press F10 to Continue,  Press ESC to Abort              S:↓ N:↓
```

Figure 10.3
Print Menu for HEADER

14. With the print menu set up, press F10. If the printer pauses between pages, set up the second page of the document in the printer and press ESC.

Explanation

You can dress up a document's top with headers as you like. Just remember to start and end the header text with the header screen marker and a carriage return. You type a header just as you want it to appear on paper. That includes placing blank lines above or below the header text, if desired.

A header's first line corresponds to the first line printed on a page. If you want header text to appear two lines from the page's top, you might begin the header with two carriage returns (to skip down two lines). You might then type text, as you did in the exercise. You can indent, center, or perhaps use a special format line to format text as you wish.

To create two blank lines after the header text, you might follow the text with two carriage returns as well. You end the header with the header marker and another carriage return. Instead of typing the exercise's single line of header text, you might just as easily create five lines of text.

The header you created in the exercise was a full five lines long (four blank lines and one line of text: the two header marker lines don't count). If you need more space at the top of the page, you can set the top margin with the print menu before printing.

Setting the print menu's "Top margin" option to 3, for example, starts out each page with three blank lines, after whch the header text prints (including any blank lines you included in it). The bigger the number you set for the top margin at the print menu, the farther down on the page the header text is pushed.

Header text is added to the total number of lines per page. If a document's first and second page are 50 lines each, they both print 55 lines long if you add a five-line header to page 1. On the screen, page 2 of your document may display only 50 lines, but during printing the five-line header is added to it. As you type a document, you must allow for additional header lines being added to each page later.

If you type a document with 62 lines per page, for example, and then add a five-line header, each page will print with 67 lines—too many for the standard 66-line typing sheet. Header text lengthens the size of every page, not just the page it's typed on.

You can start printing headers anywhere in a document. They don't have to start on a document's first page. You can also use several different headers in a document of many pages. One header might start on page 2 and a different one begin on page 4, for instance. To change header text, you simply create a new header on the page where the change is to occur. Wherever a new header appears in the document, it's printed from that page onward.

You can also stop printing headers. To "turn off" header text, you create a header without any text in it. You just enter two header markers at the top of a page. The header would look like this:

```
DOCUMENT: DOCUMENT NAME     PAGE   LINE   COL:
|1..........≫......≫ ...............................................≪
⫲≪
⫲≪
```

After MultiMate reads this header during printing, it knows you don't want a header anymore. From that page onward, no header is printed.

Besides changing header text, you can use two different headers at once. You can set up different headers to appear on alternating pages. For example, you might print a document with one header on odd pages and another on even. To make MultiMate "switch hit" between headers, you create a different header on two consecutive pages. During printing, MultiMate will alternate the headers until it encounters a new header (or one that turns headers off).

With the concept of headers grasped, you've learned quite a bit about footers as well. Creating footers is almost identical to the header procedures, except that different screen markers are used and footer text is typed at a page's bottom.

CREATING REPEATING TITLES AT THE BOTTOM OF EVERY PAGE

Objective: Creating Footers in Multiple-page Documents

You create footers almost exactly as you create headers. Instead of beginning and ending a footer with ALT H, however, you press ALT F ("F" for "footer").

First you position the cursor on a page's bottom line. To have a footer appear on line 55 of every page, you must create the footer on line 55. Press ALT F and press ENTER. Type the footer text, up to five lines, end the footer with ALT F, and press ENTER again.

In the HEADER document, try creating the footer you see in figure 10.4.

Procedure

1. Type "1" and press ENTER to select "Edit an Old Document" from the main menu.

2. Type "HEADER" as the document name and press ENTER. (Check that the drive specification correctly designates the site of the exercise disk.)

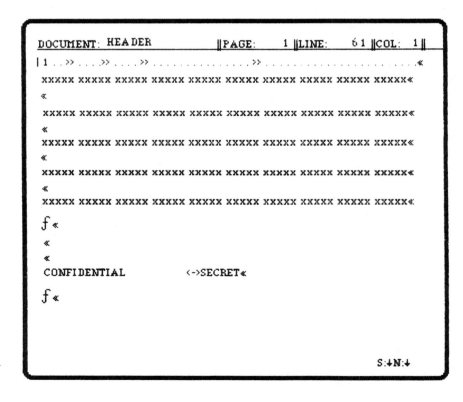

Figure 10.4
HEADER Document with Footer

3. Press F10 at the Document Summary screen. When the editing screen appears, you begin creating the footer.

4. With the cursor located at line 55, column 1, hold down ALT, type "F", and press ENTER. The footer screen marker appears. You must always end this marker with a carriage return so that it appears as its own line.

5. Press ENTER twice and type "CONFIDENTIAL".

6. Press F3, type "SECRET", and press ENTER.

7. Holding down ALT, type "F", and press ENTER. You've now ended the footer text with the mandatory marker and carriage return. Everything that appears between the two markers will be printed on every page of the document. Next you'll print it to see how it works.

8. Press F10 to save the document.

9. Type "3" and press ENTER to select "Print Document Utility" from the main menu.

10. Press ENTER to accept the document name "HEADER" at the Document Specification screen.

11. Set the print menu as shown in figure 10.3. If you're using continuous-form computer paper, set "Pause between pages" to "N" for "no." If you're using separate sheets of typing paper, set this option to "Y" for "yes." The "Printer Action Table" option should list the print driver for your type of printer.

12. With the print menu set up, press F10. If the printer pauses between pages, set up the second page of the document in the printer and press ESC.

When creating a footer, your main decision is choosing the line on which it should be typed. You can create footers at the bottom of any page. The line number on which you create a footer is important. If the footer is to appear on line 60 of every page, for example, the first footer marker must be placed on line 60.

    If a page is short, less than the expected 60 lines, say, MultiMate will space down the page until it reaches the appropriate line for the footer and print it. Footers will appear in the same place on every page.

    If a page is longer than expected, however, such that the printer can't print the footer on the specified line, it won't be printed until the page is finished. After the last text line prints, MultiMate then

Explanation

adds the footer below it. If the page is too long, MultiMate may print the footer right off the paper's end. In this case, you need to reduce the number of text lines appearing on that page.

On what line should you place the footer? Ask yourself how many lines the longest page of the document has. Then create the footer to fit below the last line of the longest page. You may need to space down using carriage-return markers to create a footer low enough on the page.

You must take into account one more complicating factor, however. Are any lines of header text (which are sometimes out of sight) being added to the document's pages? You must fit the footer underneath *all* the text, including the header, if any. If a header adds six lines to every page, and pages have a maximum of 54 lines, you'll want to create a footer at line 60 or below.

If you ignore the header and create a footer at line 54, you might end up with footers printed at various bottom margins, bobbing up and down like the wooden heads of carousel horses. Or worse, the extra lines of the header may consistently shove the footer off the bottom of the paper—which is called "thin-air printing" (and worse terms, of course).

As with header text, you can use as many different footers throughout a document as you wish. You simply create new footers on pages where they should first appear. To stop a footer from printing, you create a new footer without text (two footer markers alone at a page's bottom).

MultiMate also prints alternating footers, just as it can alternating headers. You create different footers on two consecutive pages, and MultiMate will print using one, then the other.

AUTOMATICALLY NUMBERING PAGES

Objective: Setting up Headers and Footers for Automatic Page Numbering

MultiMate can count pages and print page numbers for you. Automatic page numbering is linked with the creating of headers and footers. If you place a special symbol, a pound sign (#), in header or footer text, MultiMate prints the current page number where the symbol appears.

MultiMate can print page numbers at the top or bottom of a page. You merely imbed the symbol within a header or footer. MultiMate then prints each page with its corresponding page number. Figure 10.5 shows a header set up for automatic page numbering.

You may want MultiMate to start numbering pages with a specific number—say you're printing a book's second chapter and the first page of chapter two should be numbered 55. You specify the number MultiMate should start numbering with at the "Header/footer first page number" option of the print menu.

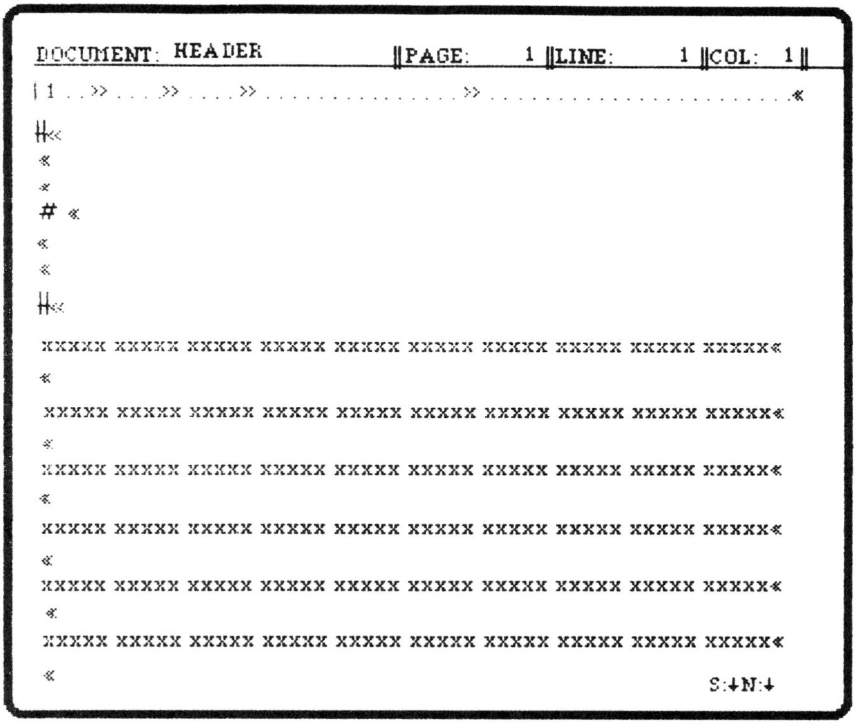

```
DOCUMENT: HEADER              ‖PAGE:    1 ‖LINE:     1 ‖COL:   1 ‖
| 1 . . >> . . . . >> . . . . >> . . . . . . . . . . >> . . . . . . . . . . . . . . . . . . . . .«
‖«
 «
 «
# «
 «
 «
‖«

xxxxx xxxxx xxxxx xxxxx xxxxx xxxxx xxxxx xxxxx xxxxx xxxxx«
 «
xxxxx xxxxx xxxxx xxxxx xxxxx xxxxx xxxxx xxxxx xxxxx xxxxx«
 «
xxxxx xxxxx xxxxx xxxxx xxxxx xxxxx xxxxx xxxxx xxxxx xxxxx«
 «
xxxxx xxxxx xxxxx xxxxx xxxxx xxxxx xxxxx xxxxx xxxxx xxxxx«
 «
xxxxx xxxxx xxxxx xxxxx xxxxx xxxxx xxxxx xxxxx xxxxx xxxxx«
 «
xxxxx xxxxx xxxxx xxxxx xxxxx xxxxx xxxxx xxxxx xxxxx xxxxx«
 «                                                   S:↓N:↓
```

Figure 10.5
Header Set for Automatic
Page Numbering

Although the HEADER document is short, try numbering its two pages anyway.

Procedure

1. Type "1" and press ENTER to select "Edit an Old Document" from the main menu.

2. Type "HEADER" as the document name and press ENTER. (Check that the drive specification correctly designates the site of the exercise disk.)

3. Press F10 at the Document Summary screen. When the editing screen appears, you begin editing the header.

4. Move the cursor to line 4, under the "A" of "ABC COMPANY". Let's erase this part of the header.

5. Press DEL, move the cursor to the "Y" of "Company", and press DEL. Next, let's insert the pound sign to invoke page numbering.

6. To insert the pound sign, press INS; holding down SHIFT, type "3" (to get the "#" sign), and press INS.

7. Press F10 to save the document. Let's print the document.

8. Type "3" and press ENTER to select "Print Document Utility" from the main menu.

9. Press ENTER to accept the document name "HEADER" at the Document Specification screen.

10. Set the print menu as shown in figure 10.3. If you're using continuous-form computer paper, set "Pause between pages" to "N" for "no." If you're using separate sheets of typing paper, set this option to "Y" for "yes." The "Printer Action Table" option should list the print driver for your type of printer.

11. With the print menu set up, press F10. If the printer pauses between pages, set up the second page of the document in the printer and press ESC. When printing's done, let's try automatic page numbering with a different twist.

12. Type "1" and press ENTER to select "Edit an Old Document" from the main menu.

13. Type "HEADER" as the document name and press ENTER.

14. Press F10 at the Document Summary screen. When the editing screen appears, you'll change the document to make page numbers appear in the footer text.

15. Move the cursor to line 4, column 36 under the pound sign (#), and press the minus key to erase it.

16. Move the cursor down to line 57, under the "S" of "SECRET". You'll erase the word "SECRET" and type "Page" followed by a pound sign.

17. Press DEL, move the cursor under the "T" of "SECRET", and press DEL.

18. Press INS, type "Page #", and press INS. Now the footer will print the word "Page" followed by a page number. Let's print the document.

19. Press F10 to save the document.

20. Type "3" and press ENTER to select "Print Document Utility" from the main menu.

21. Press ENTER to accept the document name "HEADER" at the Document Specification screen.

22. Set the print menu as shown in figure 10.3. If you're using continuous-form computer paper, set "Pause between pages" to "N" for "no." If you're using separate sheets of typing paper, set this option to "Y" for "yes." The "Printer Action Table" option

should list the print driver for your type of printer. This time, you'll set the first page to start numbering with 30.

23. In the print menu, move the cursor to the "Header/footer first page number" option and type "030". The first page will now be numbered 30, and all pages will be numbered consecutively after that.

24. With the print menu set up, press F10. If the printer pauses between pages, set up the second page of the document in the printer and press ESC.

Once you've created a header or footer, automatic page numbering is a snap to set up. You imbed the pound symbol in a header or footer at the position where the number is to print. MultiMate takes care of the rest.

Explanation

You can dress up page numbering in a variety of forms. For instance, page numbers might look like the following:

In Header or Footer	On Paper
#	1
PAGE #	PAGE 1
- # -	- 1 -
(#)	(1)
-(#)-	-(1)-
Chapter 1:#	Chapter 1:1

You can specify a number that should be used as the first page number with the "Header/footer first page number" option of the print menu. If you specify a number for the first page, all following pages are numbered from that number up. After telling MultiMate to begin numbering with 32, for example, you might just print the document's fifth page; it will be printed with the correct page number—36. Once MultiMate knows you want page numbering and knows which number to start with, it keeps your page numbers straight.

To stop page numbering part of the way through a document, you create another header or footer without the pound sign.

Occasionally, you must perform a few word-processing chores. If you run out of space on a disk, you may have to copy documents to other disks or delete unwanted documents. You might also rename a document to make its contents easy to remember. These tasks are performed with the "Document Handling Utilities", option 6 of the main menu.

WORKING WITH DOCUMENTS ON DISK

Objective: Using Utilities to Copy, Rename, and Delete Documents

After selecting "Document Handling Utilities", you will see a menu (see figure 10.6). You'll find that performing the copy, move,

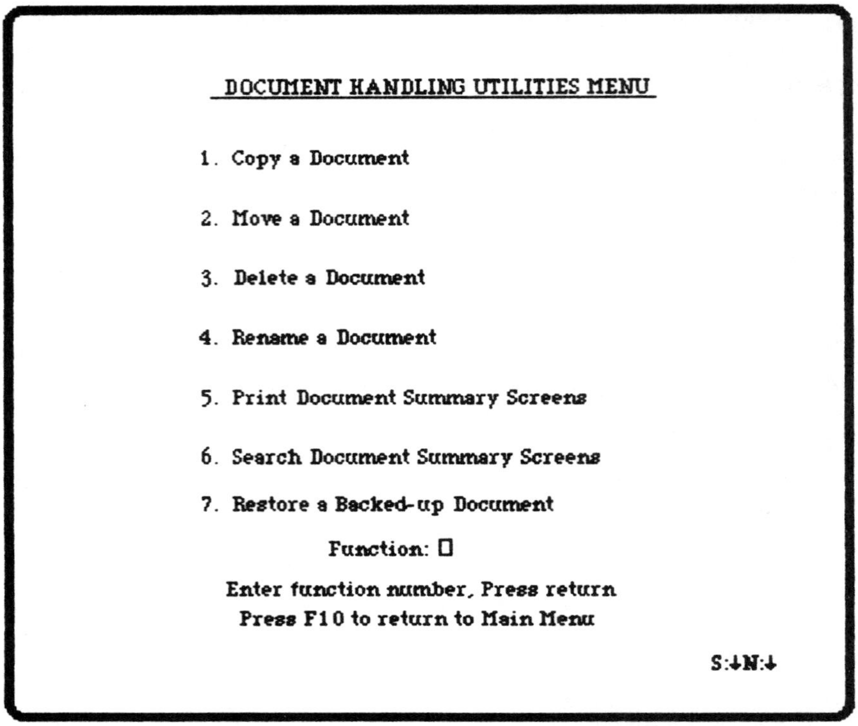

```
     DOCUMENT HANDLING UTILITIES MENU

     1. Copy a Document

     2. Move a Document

     3. Delete a Document

     4. Rename a Document

     5. Print Document Summary Screens

     6. Search Document Summary Screens

     7. Restore a Backed-up Document

              Function: □

        Enter function number, Press return
        Press F10 to return to Main Menu

                                          S:↓N:↓
```

Figure 10.6
Document Handling
Utilities Menu

rename, and delete functions is similar to completing the Document Specification screen. You mainly specify drive specifications and document names.

In the next exercise, you'll try out these procedures on the HEADER document.

Procedure

1. Type "6" and press ENTER to select "Document Handling Utilities" from the main menu. Let's first make a copy of HEADER on the exercise disk.

2. Type "1" and press ENTER to select "Copy a Document". You'll see several prompts asking you where to find the document to be copied (the "From" side) and where to place the new copy (the "To" side). First let's specify the document you want copied.

3. Type "HEADER" at the "Document" prompt (the one on the left). Check that the "Drive" prompt displays the letter of the drive holding the exercise disk. If it doesn't, press SHIFT TAB and type the correct letter.

4. Press ENTER to move the cursor to the "Copy To"/"Drive" prompt. Type the letter of the drive holding the exercise disk.

5. Press ENTER to move the cursor to the "Document" prompt and type "HEADER2". You've now told MultiMate to make a copy of HEADER and give it the name HEADER2. If you were copying to a different disk, you could use the same document name.

6. Press F10. MultiMate asks you to insert the correct disks in the drive, if necessary. Because the disks are already in the drive, you can continue.

7. Press F10. MultiMate copies HEADER. When the process is complete, MultiMate displays a completion message at the screen's bottom.

8. Press the space bar. Notice that HEADER2 is now listed in the directory. Next, get out of the copy option and delete a document.

9. Press ESC. The document handling utilities menu reappears. Let's select "Delete a Document".

10. Type "3" and press ENTER. MultiMate displays a screen that enables you to designate the name and drive location of the document to be deleted. Let's delete HEADER.

11. Type "HEADER" as the document name to be deleted. Change the drive specification, if necessary, so that it refers to the drive holding the exercise disk.

12. Press F10. Notice the message MultiMate displays. MultiMate asks you to insert the required disk, if necessary.

13. Press F10. MultiMate rubs out your document and comes back to tell you the operation is complete.

14. Press the space bar. (Actually, pressing any key would do.) Notice that HEADER is no longer listed in the directory. Next, rename HEADER2 as HEADER again.

15. Press ESC to return to the document handling utilities menu.

16. Type "4" and press ENTER to select "Rename a Document". By now, it should seem fairly evident how you rename HEADER2 to HEADER.

17. Type "HEADER2" as the document name (on the "Rename From" side). Check that the drive specification is correct.

18. Press ENTER and type "HEADER", which will be HEADER2's new name.

19. Press F10 twice. The document is renamed.

20. Press the space bar. Look at the directory to see that only HEADER

is now listed there.

21. Press ESC to return to the document handling utilities menu.

Explanation

Copying, renaming, and deleting documents mainly involves specifying drive locations and document names. Copying a document produces a duplicate on another disk (or on the same disk, if you assign the copy a different name). Deleting a document erases it from the disk, making more room available for other documents. Renaming a document simply changes the name of an existing document.

The move procedure, which you didn't try out here, is nearly identical to the copy procedure. It takes the document off one disk and puts it on another. If you need to make space available on disk, you might use this utility to transfer documents onto other disks.

During all of these procedures, MultiMate displays a directory of the documents on the default disk. You can see documents residing on other disks by pressing the PGDN key (you must place the disk in a disk drive, of course).

Let's talk about a word processing disaster. The number one disaster in word processing is accidentally deleting or otherwise ruining a document. One procedure hurriedly performed, a finger stumble, and a document vanishes. Hours of work irrecoverably lost. *Don't let this happen to you.*

Always make copies of important documents (preferably on separate disks). Because the copy procedure is simple, use it often. People experienced with word processors usually organize their disks so that they can easily make back-up copies of documents. You might copy the document you're working on as often as every ten minutes. Some people back up a document just after finishing it. How often you back up copies depends on how much text you can risk losing. If you make a back-up copy every half hour, the most work you'll ever lose is a half hour's worth. Of course, most of us learn this lesson the hard way. . . .

SEARCHING FOR THE LOST DOCUMENT

Objective: Using Utilities to Review Document Summary Screens and Search for Documents

Document Summary screens provide information about a document's contents. You might print these screens on paper as a catalog of documents or you might quickly review Document Summary screens as you look for a particular document. You can do both using the utility "Print Document Summary Screens" from the document handling utilities menu.

You might want to locate a document that was created on a specific date or had a certain author, for example. You can search for a document based on any information recorded in the Document

Summary screen. If you're looking for a document with a certain author, you can use "Search Document Summary Screens", the last option of the document handling utilities menu, to provide you with a list of documents by that author. You might also locate documents by operator, addressee, keyword, or even information stored in the comments lines.

When you first initiate the "Print Document Summary Screens" or "Search Document Summary Screen" options, you will see a screen similar to figure 10.7. This screen is used to tell MultiMate which disk to use and whether information should be printed or displayed on screen for viewing only.

Next, you'll review some Document Summary screens; then you'll conduct a search for a document that has your name as the author.

Procedure

1. Type "5" and press ENTER to select "Print Document Summary Screens" from the document handling utilities menu. A screen appears asking you to specify if you wish to print the Document Summary screens or view them on screen. You must also tell MultiMate which drive holds the disk you wish to use.
2. Press the down arrow key and type "S" for "screen". Change

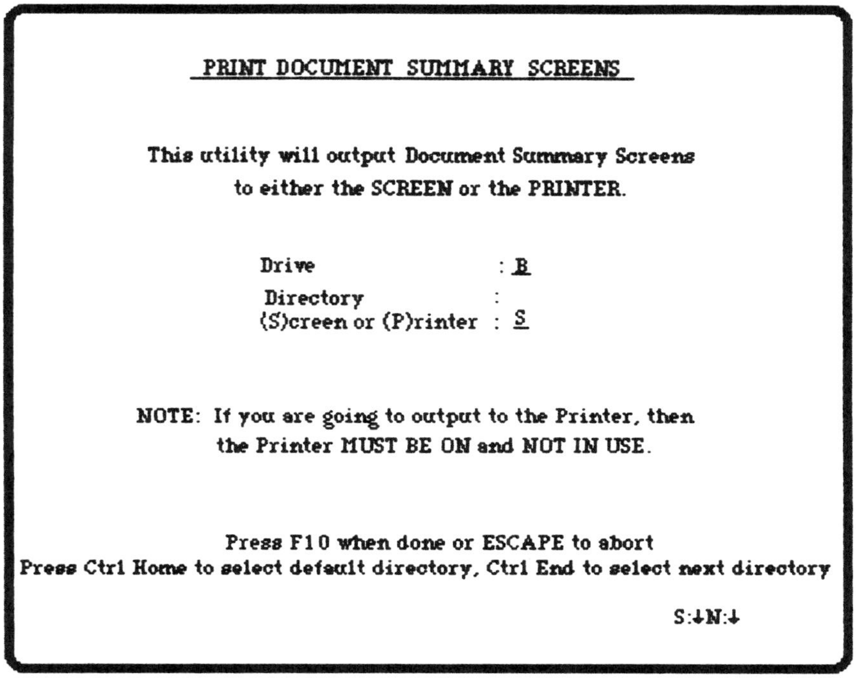

PRINT DOCUMENT SUMMARY SCREENS

This utility will output Document Summary Screens
to either the SCREEN or the PRINTER.

Drive : B
Directory :
(S)creen or (P)rinter : S

NOTE: If you are going to output to the Printer, then
the Printer MUST BE ON and NOT IN USE.

Press F10 when done or ESCAPE to abort
Press Ctrl Home to select default directory, Ctrl End to select next directory

S:↓N:↓

Figure 10.7
Print Document Summary Screens

the drive specification to the drive holding the exercise disk, if necessary. Next, tell MultiMate to start displaying Document Summary screens.

3. Press F10. The first Document Summary screen appears.

4. Press the space bar (or any other key) to see the next screen (if another document exists). You might review all the Document Summary screens on disk this way. MultiMate can also print them, two per page, if you select "P" for "print" at the initial screen. Let's try searching for a document now.

5. Press ESC to return to the document handling utilities menu.

6. Type "6" and press ENTER to select "Search Document Summary Screens". Again, you see a screen asking you which drive to use and whether the information is to be printed or displayed on screen.

7. Press the down arrow key and type "S" for "screen". Check that the "Drive" prompt indicates the drive holding the exercise disk.

8. Press F10. A blank Document Summary screen appears. You use this screen to tell MultiMate what you're looking for. If you're looking for a document by a certain author, you type the author's name in the author line.

9. Type your name on the author line and press F10. MultiMate searches the disk for all documents with that author. A list of documents by that author appears on screen. HEADER should be among them, because you placed your name in the Document Summary screen as author.

10. Press ESC twice to return to the main menu.

Explanation

With sometimes-cryptic eight-letter names, documents can be difficult to distinguish. The "Print Document Summary Screens" utility can help you with the problem. You can print the Document Summary screens for every document on disk or review them one after the other on screen.

Begin by telling MultiMate which drive holds the disk you wish to use and whether you wish to display or print the document summaries. If you print them, MultiMate will print two per page. Because documents are often updated, printed Document Summary screens tend to go out of date, however. Often quickly stepping through a review of a disk's document summaries can locate the desired document.

If you can't find a document, you can use "Search Document Summary Screens" to search for it. Once you tell MultiMate what to look for, it can display or print a list of documents that it found during its search. You tell MultiMate what to look for by completing the blank document-summary screen that is displayed during the procedure.

You can search for a document by name, author, addressee, or operator. If you've recorded special keywords associated with certain documents, you can use these keywords as search criteria. You can also search for a document based upon information recorded in the comment line. Simply type the word or phrase that you're looking for on the blank comment line, and MultiMate will do its best to locate documents whose comment lines contain that word or phrase. You can even search for documents that have a certain creation or modification date.

You can base your search on any information recorded in a document summary (except information such as total page length and keystrokes used). You can fill in one or several lines of information, depending on how much you know about the document. The more information MultiMate has, the higher the chance it will locate the exact document you desire.

During the search, MultiMate looks for any documents with information matching that you supplied. If one or more documents have matching information, MultiMate displays a list of document names on screen (or prints the list if you specified printing). You can examine the documents named in the list for the one you're searching for.

You can cancel both the "Print Document Summary Screens" and "Search Document Summary Screens" utilities by pressing ESC.

Header and footer text is set up as illustrated in figure 10.8. You can invoke automatic page numbering by putting a pound sign (#) within a header or footer. You can start page numbering on a specific page number with the "Header/Footer first page number" prompt of the print menu.

The "Document Handling Utilities" (see figure 10.6) enable you to copy, move, delete, and rename documents. You can also print Document Summary screens and use information stored in them to search for specific documents.

SUMMARY

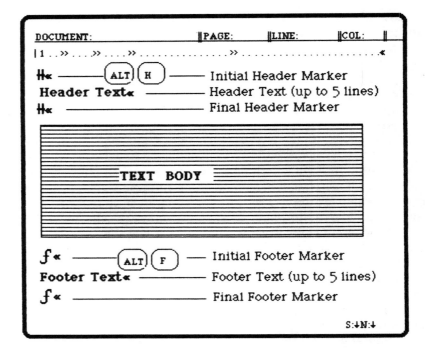

Figure 10.8
Header and Footer Text
Set-up

Chapter 11

USING THE LIBRARY

> Your computer should be turned on and the MultiMate main menu should be on the screen. Your exercise disk should be in drive B.

MultiMate's library is not a quiet place for reading. It's a magician's library where you open books and white doves flurry out and where pages magically fill themselves with text like stock exchange panels.

MultiMate's library function can save you loads of typing. Like a good scribe, the library function will write out words, phrases, paragraphs, and pages on the screen so that you don't have to type them.

Suppose you type the same billing notice, with small variations, many times every day. You can create the standard notice in a library document. When you need to fill out a bill, you press a few keys and MultiMate displays the notice on screen for you. You make the few required changes and the bill is done. With the library function, in an hour you might create a hundred billing notices, compared with the dozen or so you might create without the library function.

If you compose contracts or leasing agreements using standard clauses, you can store the clauses in a library document. With a library of clauses at your fingertips, you can compose contracts by inserting clause after clause in a document with only a key press or two. You might use MultiMate's library to compose documents that use "boiler-plate" text passages.

In a legal or other professional setting, you might find yourself typing the same specialized vocabulary repeatedly. Haven't you ever wished that you could press a single key and have the typewriter type long words, such as *responsibility, San Francisco,* or even *Sincerely Yours*? You can teach MultiMate a specialized vocabulary by storing often-repeated (or just difficult-to-type) words and phrases in a library. With such a library document, you can press a key or two and type whole words and phrases instead of a single character at a time.

CREATING LIBRARY DOCUMENTS

Objective: Creating a New Library Document for Use during Editing

In this section, you'll start by creating a library document and then you'll use it to create a letter. Creating a library document is similar to creating regular text documents.

First, you select "Create a New Document" to create a library document. You give it a document name as you do all documents. At the Document Summary screen, however, you treat a library document differently. Instead of filling in the Document Summary screen, press F5.

MultiMate asks you for a code for the first library entry. Type up to three characters as the code and press ENTER. MultiMate then displays an editing screen in which you can type the text to be inserted. You can edit and format the text as you would any word-processing text.

Once the entry is complete, you press F2 to create the next entry. MultiMate asks you for the next code; after you type it and press ENTER, the editing screen appears for the entry's text. Continue in this manner until you've created all your library entries. When you are done, press F10 to save the library document.

In this exercise you'll create a library with a first entry as seen in figure 11.1.

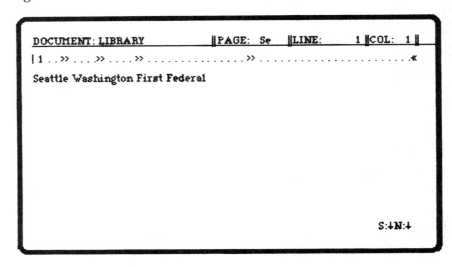

Figure 11.1
LIBRARY Document with First Entry

1. Type "2" and press ENTER to select "Create a New Document" **Procedure**
   from the main menu.

2. Type "LIBRARY" as the document name and press ENTER. When
   the Document Summary screen appears, you must tell MultiMate
   that this is a library document, not a regular word-processing
   text. Instead of filling out the Document Summary screen, you'll
   press F5.

3. Press F5. MultiMate displays the message "Library Entry Name?".
   The program is asking you to supply the code for the first entry.
   You can type any one, two, or three characters you like.

4. Type "Se" and press ENTER. Be sure to use a capital *S* and a
   lower case *e*. (This is the code for the first entry. Each entry will
   have an easy-to-remember code.) After you press ENTER, a blank
   editing screen appears for the text entry.

5. Type "Seattle Washington First Federal". This is the first entry.
   To create another one, you press F2 to start a new page.

6. Press F2.

7. Type "in" and press ENTER.

8. Type "investments" as the second entry.

9. Press F2.

10. Type "cd" and press ENTER.

11. Type "Certificates of Deposit" as the third entry.

12. Press F2.

13. Type "tb" and press ENTER.

14. Type "Treasury Bills" as the fourth entry.

15. Press F2.

16. Type "mm" and press ENTER.

17. Type "Money Market Accounts" as the fifth entry.

18. Press F2.

19. Type "lin" and press ENTER.

20. Type "Low Interest Housing Loans" as the sixth entry.

21. Press F2.

22. Type "add" and press ENTER.

23. Ending each line with a carriage return, type the following address:

    John North
    123 West Green
    San Francisco, CA 94111

    Press ENTER twice to create two blank lines after the address.

24. Press F2.

25. Type "ad2" and press ENTER.

26. Ending each line with a carriage return, type the following address:

    Bill Bates
    235 Jack London Square
    Oakland, CA 92111

    and press ENTER twice to put two blank lines after the address.

27. Press F2.

28. Type "Sin" and press ENTER.

29. Press TAB twice and type "Sincerely,".

30. Press ENTER three times.

31. Press TAB twice and type "John North". Press ENTER.

32. Press TAB twice and type "Vice President of Finance". Press ENTER. The library document is now finished.

33. Press F10 to save the document. The main menu returns to the screen.

Explanation

Except for the twist of supplying codes, creating a library document is similar to creating a regular document. To create a library document, select "Create a New Document" from the main menu and type a document name at the Document Specification screen. Press F5 at the Document Summary screen instead of filling it out. Next you'll be asked to supply an entry code, which can be any one, two, or three characters.

You create a library document page by page. You can have only one entry per page, and entries can't be longer than a page. In fact, if you try to insert in your text a library entry that will make the page longer than MultiMate can hold, MultiMate will produce an error message.

You type and format entries as you wish them to appear on screen. If an entry requires special tab stops or margins, you must insert an additional format line in or above an entry. You shouldn't simply change the format line at the page's top. An entry's top format line does not transfer to another document with the library text. If you insert a format line in an entry, however, it will be transferred with the entry text.

After typing a library entry, press F2, the Page Break key, to create the next entry. You are asked to supply another code. You begin each page by supplying a code this way; the code characters are used to invoke the library entry later. Try to select codes that are easy to remember. One-, two-, and three-letter codes can be cryptic and easy to forget. You can differentiate between upper- and lowercase letters, which can help you assign distinctive codes. For example, you might use "A" to stand for Alaska and "a" to stand for "airline".

You can edit or add new library entries to the library document later. To do so, select "Edit an Old Document" from the main menu and specify the library document's name at the Document Specification screen. MultiMate displays the first page of the library.

When you edit a library document, almost all editing procedures work the same as with a regular document. One editing procedure that works differently, however, is the Go To page function. Because library entries have codes instead of page numbers, you press F1, the GO TO key, and specify an entry's code to display the entry on screen. All other cursor-movement functions work as they normally do.

To add new entries to an existing library document, you position the cursor at the bottom of a library's page and press F2. You'll be asked to specify a code and a new entry as you did when originally creating the document. You can add as many new entries to an old library document as can be held on disk.

The next exercise uses the new library document that you just created to create a letter.

EFFICIENT TYPING WITH THE LIBRARY FUNCTION

Objective: Inserting Often-used Vocabulary with the Library Function

Library documents help you type text. While word-processing, you first tell MultiMate the name of the library document you wish to use. This is called "attaching" the library to the document you're currently editing. You attach a library document by pressing SHIFT F5, typing the library document's name (and a drive specification, if necessary) and pressing ENTER.

Your library is ready for use. To insert a word, phrase, or text passage, you press F5 and type the code that is associated with the text that you want to insert in the document. When you press ENTER, the designated text will appear on the screen.

Try typing the letter you see in figure 11.2. You'll use the library document you just created to insert commonly used terms. Although the words you'll be inserting in the letter are banking terms, they might be any vocabulary that is routinely used in your line of work.

You'll begin by creating a regular text document called BANK-ING. You'll then attach the LIBRARY document you just created. As you type the letter, you'll periodically use the library function to insert words and phrases. Notice the amount of typing you can save yourself.

Procedure

1. Type "2" and press ENTER to select "Create a New Document" from the main menu.

2. Type "BANKING" and press ENTER to specify a document name. (Check that the drive specification designates the exercise disk.)

3. Press F10 at the Document Summary screen.

```
DOCUMENT: BANKING            ‖PAGE:    1 ‖LINE:      1 ‖COL:   1‖
 |1 . . . . . .≫ . . . . . . . . . . . . . . . . . . ≫ . . . . . . . . . . . . . . . . . . . . . . .≪
John North≪
123 West Green≪
San Francisco, CA 94111≪
≪
≪
Bill Bates≪
235 Jack London Square≪
Oakland, CA 92111≪
≪
≪
Dear Bill:≪
≪
We at Seattle Washington First Federal are intensifying our
efforts to increase investments, Certificates of Deposit,
Money Market Accounts, Low Interest Housing Loans, and
Treasury Bills. Sales representatives will reach their
goals or reenlist in the Seattle Washington First Federal
training program.≪
≪
         ≫                    ≫Sincerely,≪
≪                                            S:↓N:↓
≪
```

Figure 11.2
BANKING Letter

4. Press F10 at the Modify Document Defaults screen.

5. Press F9 to start setting the format line. Set the format line with a tab stop at column 10 and column 35 and a right margin of 60. (No other tab stops should appear on the format line. Space over them to erase them.)

6. Press F9 to complete setting the format line. Next, let's attach LIBRARY for use.

7. Holding down SHIFT, press F5.

8. Type "LIBRARY" and press F10 to attach the library. (The drive specification should designate the exercise disk.) The message "Library Attachment Successful" will appear. Now you can begin typing the letter. First, you'll use the library to put the sender's address at the letter's top.

9. Press F5, type the code "add", and press ENTER. (Be sure to use lower-case letters "add".) John North's address appears. Now, enter the recipient's address.

10. Press F5, type the code "ad2", and press ENTER. Bill Bate's address appears.

11. Type "Dear Bill:".

12. Press ENTER twice and type "We at" and press the space bar. The next phrase is "Seattle Washington First Federal", a long phrase that you'll let the library type for you.

13. Press F5, type the code "Se", and press ENTER. (Be sure to use a capital S as you did when creating the library document.)

14. Press the space bar and type "are intensifying our efforts to increase". Next comes a string of commonly used banking terms that you'll insert using the library.

15. Press the space bar, press F5, and then type "in". Press ENTER. The word "investments" appears on the screen.

16. Type a comma and one space.

17. Press F5, type "cd", and press ENTER. The phrase "Certificates of Deposit" appears on the screen.

18. Type a comma and one space.

19. Press F5, type "mm", and press ENTER. The phrase "Money Market Accounts" appears on the screen.

20. Type a comma and one space.

21. Press F5, type "lin", and press ENTER. The phrase "Low Interest Housing Loans" appears on the screen.

22. Type a comma, press the space bar, and type "and". Press the space bar again.

23. Press F5, type "tb", and press ENTER. The phrase "Treasury Bills" appears on the screen.

24. Type a period to end the sentence and press the space bar twice.

25. Type "Sales representatives will reach their goals or reenlist in the" and press the space bar.

26. Press F5, type "Se", and press ENTER. The phrase "Seattle Washington First Federal" appears on the screen.

27. Finish the paragraph by pressing the space bar once and typing "training program." and press ENTER twice. Let's end the letter with the closing from the library.

28. Press F5, type "Sin", and press ENTER. The "Sincerely" closing appears on the screen, properly formatted. Examine the letter to judge how much work the library function can save you.

29. To save the letter on disk, press F10.

Explanation

Now do you believe in the magic? You can insert up to a page of text in a document with just a few key presses. The nature of the text—whether it's a memo heading, a contract clause, or simple words and phrases—is up to you.

No particular size limits exist for the number of entries a single library document can hold. A library can be as large as the space available on disk. You can also create as many library documents as you want. You can't create a single entry longer than one page, however.

Before you can use a library document, you must "attach" it to the current document. Holding down SHIFT, press F5. Specify the library document name and drive and press ENTER. If you press SHIFT F1 instead of typing a document name, MultiMate displays a directory of documents available on the default disk. You might use this feature if you have several library documents from which to choose and you've temporarily forgotten their names. (You also can view a disk directory this way during an external copy—copying text between two different documents.)

Once a library document is "attached", you can insert any of its entries, in any order, in a document. You tell MultiMate which entry by typing a short code, up to three characters long. You associate codes with library entries as you create a library document. Library entries appear at the cursor position. They are inserted in the text, harmlessly pushing surrounding text aside without erasing it.

A code might be a single letter—such as "a" to insert the word "arbitrary"—or three letters—such as "mem" to insert a memo heading. If you have many entries, these short codes may be difficult to remember. After pressing F5, you can see which codes are used by the library if you press SHIFT F1 instead of specifying a code. A list of the library's codes appears on screen. After spotting the code you need, you can type that code and press ENTER to insert the entry.

You must use the exact code for an entry. If the code is a capital A and you type a lower-case a, MultiMate will not find the correct entry. The characters you type must exactly match the library code.

You have access to a library's entries for as long as you are editing the current document. If you save the document, returning to the main menu, the library entries are no longer available. If you begin editing another document, you have to attach the library again. You can also switch from one library to another by simply attaching a new one. You can access only one library at a time.

By now, you've noticed how easy it is to pack text with commonly used terms. Your LIBRARY document saved you close to 50 percent of the typing that would normally have been required to produce the document. Carefully planned libraries (and remembering to use them) can greatly speed document production.

Library documents aren't made of cement. Because they are easy to create, you might quickly throw one together before starting out any multipaged document. You can update and add entries to a library document as you work, making your word processing ever more efficient. You can always erase the library when a document is done if the library doesn't apply to other documents you might create.

Keep an eye out for opportunities to use the library function creatively. You should think about creating a library document any time you expect to type text repeatedly.

To create a library document, follow the steps illustrated in figure 11.3. To use a library document, follow the procedure shown in figure 11.4.   **SUMMARY**

1. Select "Create A New Document"

2. Type library document name
   and press ENTER.

3. At the Document Summary Screen
   press F5.

4. Type a library entry code
   and press ENTER.

5. Type a library entry and press
   F2.

6. Type more entries, repeating
   steps 4 and 5.

7. When all entries are typed,
   press F10.

Figure 11.3
Creating a Library
Document

1. To attach a library document to
   a document that you are editing,
   press SHIFT and F5.

2. Type the library document name
   and press F10.

3. To call a library entry into the
   document that you are editing,
   press F5.

4. Type the code for the desired
   entry and press ENTER.

Figure 11.4
Using a Library
Document

Chapter 12

PRINTING PERSONALIZED FORM LETTERS

Preparation

Your computer should be turned on and the MultiMate main menu should be on the screen. Your exercise disk should be in drive B.

Because no one is immune to junk mail, you've probably received letters from a friendly computer. These letters (for example, those informing you that you're indeed *almost* a winner in the annual sweepstakes) are standard forms, yet the computer specifically mentions your name several times in the text. Perhaps thousands of letters were mailed just like it, all with different names in them.

Have you ever wondered how such a letter is produced? The computer is supplied with a list of names and a specially coded form letter. As the form letter is printed repeatedly, the computer switches a new name into the text with each printing. The resulting letter appears somewhat personalized.

MultiMate can produce mass mailings of personalized form letters as well. With a little work and MultiMate, you too can clog America's mailboxes!

Besides producing junk mail, MultiMate's mass-mailing capability is invaluable for tasks such as producing numerous billing notices, sending standard form letters to large club memberships, or even sending holiday notes to all your friends and relatives.

You simply create a standard form and a list of recipients' names and addresses. Both the form and the list are coded so that MultiMate can transfer the list's information into the form during printing. In effect, you merge two documents (the form and the list of addresses) to produce multiple copies of individually addressed form letters. Producing this kind of mass mailing is called *merge-printing*.

Although merge printing is typically used to produce form letters, you can also use it to print envelopes, mailing lists, and memos and to insert other types of information (besides names and addresses) in documents that are printed repeatedly.

In this chapter, you'll learn how to set up MultiMate documents for mass mailings. You'll put together a coded form letter and a short coded list of names from the beginning and then merge-print them.

SETTING UP A CUSTOMER LIST FOR MASS MAILINGS

Objective: Creating a Merge Data Document

To create a merge data document, you'll first type a set of merge codes. A typical merge code looks like the following:

⊢ADDRESS⊢

It is created by holding down ALT and typing "M". A merge symbol (⊢) appears on screen. Next, you type a code name of up to twelve characters. A code name might be any combination of characters you choose. It's a good idea, however, to have the code name represent the information to be transferred with it. After typing a code name, you finish the merge code with a merge symbol and carriage return.

On the line below the merge code, you type the text to be transferred. You might type a single word or several paragraphs. You must end the text with a merge symbol and a carriage return. You create a merge code for each piece of information to be printed in the form letter.

In the following exercise, you'll create a three-page merge data document called MERGDATA with the merge codes shown in figure 12.1.

Procedure

1. Type "2" and press ENTER to select "Create a New Document" from the main menu.

2. Type "MERGDATA" and press ENTER at the Document Specification screen. (Check that the "Drive" prompt designates the drive holding the exercise disk.)

3. Press F10 at the Document Summary screen.

4. Press F10 at the Modify Document Defaults screen. A blank editing screen appears. Let's begin by typing our first merge code.

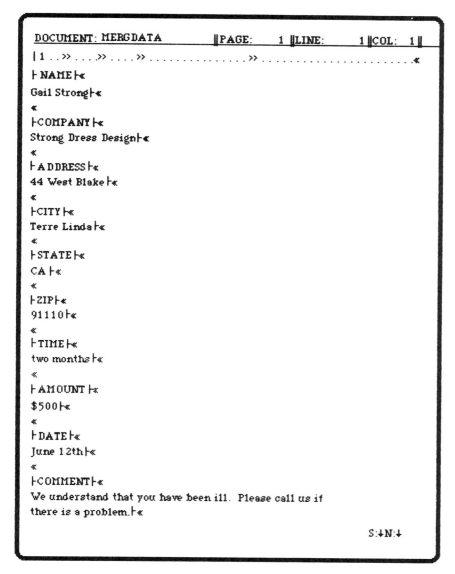

Figure 12.1
MERGDATA Document
and Merge Codes

5. Holding down ALT, type "M". The merge symbol appears on screen. A merge code must start and end with this symbol.

6. Type "NAME". This is the name of your code. You might type any sort of code you please, using up to twelve characters. Because this code will transfer client names, the word "NAME" is used to make it easy to remember.

7. Hold down ALT and type "M"; press ENTER. You've now completed the first merge code. On line two, you might type a customer name, ending it with a merge symbol and a carriage return. In this exercise, however, you'll set up your merge codes before typing in customer information.

8. With the cursor on line two, column 1, hold down ALT and type "M"; press ENTER twice. Later you'll insert customer information here. The next code transfers a company name into the form letters, so it might be named COMPANY.

9. Hold down ALT and type "M"; type "COMPANY".

10. Hold down ALT and type "M"; press ENTER.

11. Hold down ALT and type "M"; press ENTER twice. Later you'll insert company names on line 5 before the single merge symbol. The next merge code transfers a street address to the form letter, so it's named ADDRESS.

12. Hold down ALT and type "M"; type "ADDRESS".

13. Hold down ALT and type "M"; press ENTER.

14. Hold down ALT and type "M"; press ENTER twice. Later you'll insert a street address on line 8 before the single merge symbol. The next merge code transfers a city's name to the form letter, so it's named CITY.

15. Hold down ALT and type "M"; type "CITY".

16. Hold down ALT and type "M"; press ENTER.

17. Hold down ALT and type "M"; press ENTER twice. By now you've got the hang of creating merge codes. Create two more that transfer state and zip code information.

18. Hold down ALT and type "M"; type "STATE".

19. Hold down ALT and type "M"; press ENTER.

20. Hold down ALT and type "M"; press ENTER twice.

21. Hold down ALT and type "M"; type "ZIP".

22. Hold down ALT and type "M"; press ENTER.

23. Hold down ALT and type "M"; press ENTER twice. The form letter that you'll create in the next section will tell delinquent tenants how far in arrears they are in rent. You'll use a merge code here to transfer information regarding how many months' rent is due. This merge code is named TIME. Later, when you

print the form letters, you'll see that more than just address information can be transferred to a form letter.

24. Hold down ALT and type "M"; type "TIME".

25. Hold down ALT and type "M"; press ENTER.

26. Hold down ALT and type "M"; press ENTER twice. Each letter will also tell the renter precisely how much money they owe. This information will be transferred with a merge code named AMOUNT.

27. Hold down ALT and type "M"; type "AMOUNT".

28. Hold down ALT and type "M"; press ENTER.

29. Hold down ALT and type "M"; press ENTER twice. Each letter will also tell the renter when payment is due. This information will be transferred with a merge code named DATE.

30. Hold down ALT and type "M"; type "DATE".

31. Hold down ALT and type "M"; press ENTER.

32. Hold down ALT and type "M"; press ENTER twice. The last merge code will transfer a short note or comment to the form letter. This information will be transferred with a merge code named COMMENT.

33. Hold down ALT and type "M"; type "COMMENT".

34. Hold down ALT and type "M"; press ENTER.

35. Hold down ALT and type "M"; press ENTER. You've now successfully typed all the merge codes you need for the mailing list. From now on you can simply copy them to other pages as needed. The mailing list you'll create later will hold only three customer addresses, so the codes need to be copied to only two other pages. First, create two blank pages in the merge data document.

36. Press END to move the cursor to the page's bottom and press F2. A new blank page appears as page 2 of the merge data document.

37. Press F2 to create a third page. Next, copy the merge codes from page 1 to pages 2 and 3.

38. Press F1, type "1", and press ENTER. The cursor moves to page 1.

39. With the cursor on line 1, column 1, press F8 to initiate a copy procedure.

40. Holding down CTRL, press END to mark the entire page.

41. Press F8.

42. Holding down CTRL, press PGDN. The cursor jumps to page 2.

43. Press F8. The merge codes appear on page 2.

44. With the cursor on line 1, column 1 of page 2, press F8.

45. Holding down CTRL, press END to mark the entire page.

46. Press F8.

47. Holding down CTRL, press PGDN. The cursor jumps to page 3.

48. Press F8. The merge codes appear on page 3. You are ready to start typing the names, addresses, and other rental information of the mailing list.

49. Press F1, type "1", and press ENTER.

50. Move the cursor to line 2, column 1. The first name on the list is "Gail Strong".

51. Press INS, type "Gail Strong", and press INS. Gail's company name is Strong Dress Design. This information is recorded under the COMPANY merge code.

52. Move the cursor to line 5, column 1.

53. Press INS, type "Strong Dress Design", and press INS. In a similar manner, insert the rest of Gail Strong's address information.

54. Move the cursor to line 8, column 1.

55. Press INS, type "44 West Blake", and press INS.

56. Move the cursor to line 11, column 1.

57. Press INS, type "Terre Linda", and press INS.

58. Move the cursor to line 14, column 1.

59. Press INS, type "CA", and press INS.

60. Move the cursor to line 11, column 1.

61. Press INS, type "91110" and press INS. According to your records, Gail Strong is two months behind in rent. Put that time interval under the TIME merge code.

62. Move the cursor to line 20, column 1.

63. Press INS, type "two months", and press INS. Gail Strong owes $500 back rent. Put that amount under the AMOUNT merge code.

64. Move the cursor to line 23, column 1.

65. Press INS, type "$500", and press INS. The back rent should be paid by June 12th. We'll put that date under the DATE merge code.

66. Move the cursor to line 26, column 1.

67. Press INS, type "June 12th", and press INS. Last, you want to include a short comment in Gail's letter. You'll type a short sentence or two under the COMMENT merge code.

68. Move the cursor to line 29, column 1.

69. Press INS and type "We understand that you have been ill. Please call us if there is a problem." Press ENTER and then INS. You've now completed the first page of the merge data document. Your screen should look like figure 12.1. As you can see, initially creating a mailing list document takes a little work. Fortunately, once you've created it, you can use it over and over again.

70. Press F1, type "2", and press ENTER. To hasten completion of the merge data document, insert the information you see in figure 12.2 in page 2. Make sure that you don't accidentally erase merge symbols.

71. With page 2 complete, press F1, type "3", and press ENTER. Insert the information you see in figure 12.3 in page 3.

72. With page 3 completed, press F10 to save the document.

Explanation

When you first create a merge data document to hold a mailing list, remember that you'll be using the list for many different purposes. The same merge data document can be used to print letters, envelopes, labels, etc. If you code a primary document to print form letters, the merge data document can supply information in the letters. If the primary document is formatted to address envelopes, the same merge data document supplies information for envelopes—without altering the merge data document at all.

You begin a merge data document by deciding what kinds of information will be included in it. If you're only going to print address labels, you need only create a merge code for each part of an address. For letters, such as a rental notice, you might also create codes that transfer information such as the amount of rent and date due, and even special comments. The number and kinds of merge codes used

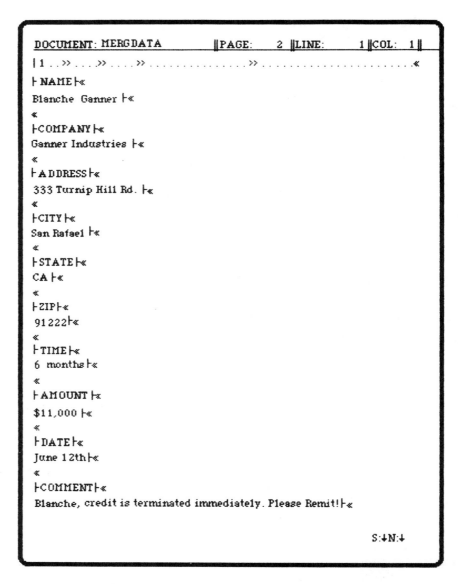

Figure 12.2
Page 2 of MERGDATA
Document

is up to you; the only limit is the number of codes you can fit on one page.

Because you'll likely be using the same merge data document for different purposes, it's best to make sure that the list contains all the information you'll want to use later. After a long merge data document is completed, adding even a single new merge code and information to it can mean a lot of work. If the merge data document

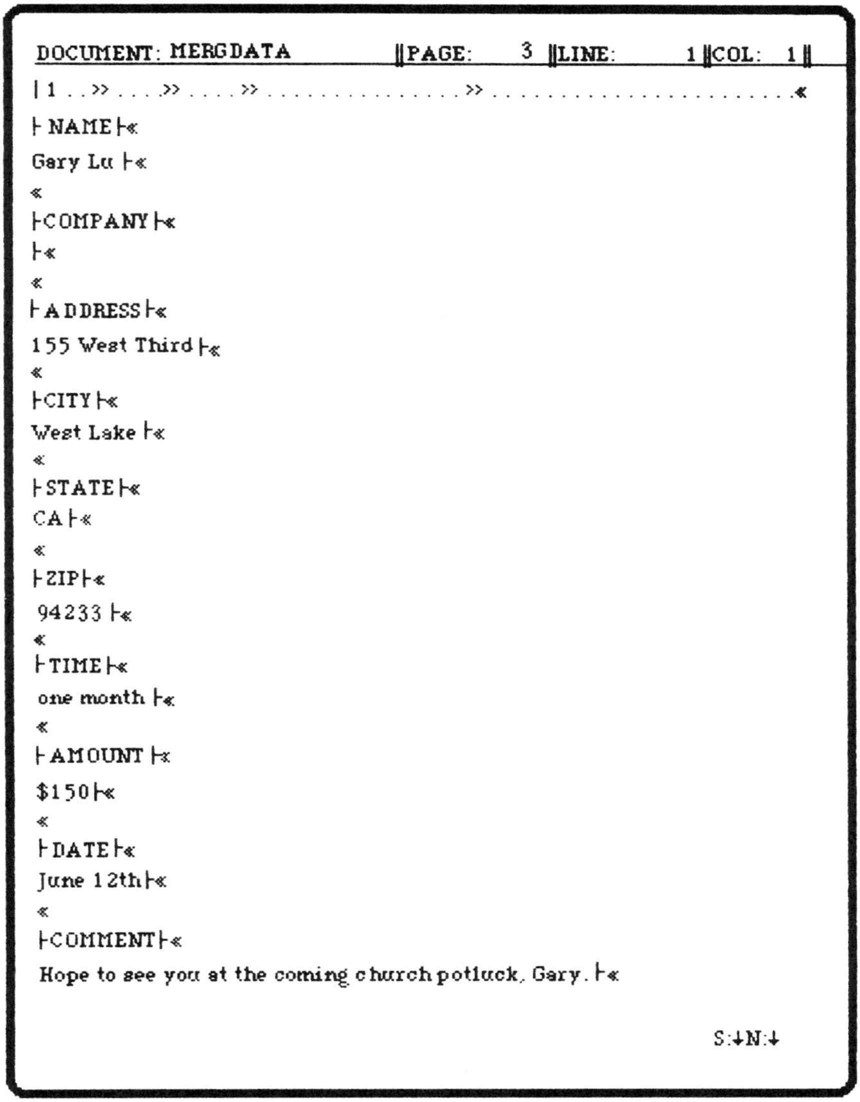

```
DOCUMENT: MERGDATA        ‖PAGE:    3 ‖LINE:     1‖COL:  1‖
| 1 . . >> . . . .>> . . . .>> . . . . . . . . . . . .>> . . . . . . . . . . . . . . . . . . .<
⊢ NAME ⊢<
Gary Lu ⊢<
<
⊢COMPANY ⊢<
⊢<
<
⊢ADDRESS⊢<
155 West Third ⊢<
<
⊢CITY⊢<
West Lake ⊢<
<
⊢STATE⊢<
CA⊢<
<
⊢ZIP⊢<
94233 ⊢<
<
⊢TIME⊢<
one month ⊢<
<
⊢AMOUNT⊢<
$150⊢<
<
⊢DATE⊢<
June 12th⊢<
<
⊢COMMENT⊢<
Hope to see you at the coming church potluck, Gary. ⊢<



                                              S:↓N:↓
```

Figure 12.3
Page 3 of MERGDATA
Document

has one hundred names and addresses, you'd have to insert the new code one hundred times. You can, of course, edit a merge data document this way. To save work, however, it's probably easier to create the list from the beginning with all the merge codes you expect to need.

Therefore, when you start a merge data document, type out the entire list of merge codes on the first page. Next, check that they are properly coded and copy them to the rest of the document. Because half the effort of creating a merge data document is typing the codes, save yourself work: either copy the set of codes whenever you need them or, better yet, *create a library document that automatically inserts merge codes for you.* (See chapter 11 for instructions on creating a library document.)

Each page of the merge data document corresponds to one printing of the primary document. A three-page mailing list (merge data document) results in MultiMate printing a form letter (primary document) three times. Every page of a merge data document should have a complete set of merge codes (and the information to be transferred).

MultiMate prints the entire primary document once with the information from one page of the merge data document. It then prints the primary document again with information from the merge data document's next page. The primary document is printed repeatedly until MultiMate runs out of pages in the merge data document.

What happens when the merge data document has more kinds of information than you need in a primary document? Suppose your mailing list has codes for all sorts of business information, but you're simply going to use it to address envelopes. No problem. You can pick and choose which codes to use in a primary document.

Although each page of a merge data document might contain dozens of codes, you can use as few or many in a primary document as you wish. To print envelopes, you might use two or three codes in a primary document, and only the information corresponding to those codes will be transferred from the merge data document. MultiMate doesn't care if extra merge codes and information appear in the merge data document.

A merge code must have a merge symbol at its beginning and end. You type this symbol by holding down the ALT key and typing "M" (for "merge"). In a merge data document, a typical merge code and the information it transfers might look like the following:

⊦COMPANY⊦≪
Westover Lumber Yard⊦≪

Notice that the COMPANY merge code has two merge symbols and ends with a carriage return. On the line beneath it appears the company name that will be printed in the primary document. The amount of information you transfer might be a single character or several paragraphs, but it must end with a merge symbol and carriage return. The final symbol tells MultiMate where to stop when transferring text.

Beware: if you forget a merge symbol somewhere in the merge data document, MultiMate will refuse to merge print. If you have such a problem, first check that your merge codes are spelled correctly and that all the required merge symbols appear. Because one missing merge symbol upsets the printing process and is difficult to detect in a merge document with many pages, be careful as you initially type the merge data codes.

Next, you'll type a primary document that uses the merge data document you just created.

The form letter you'll create here notifies people that they are behind in their rents. The letter and merge codes appear in figure 12.4. The merge codes are the same ones used in the MERGDATA document you created in the last exercise.

You type merge codes in a primary document wherever information from the merge data document is to appear. As in the merge data document, a merge code begins with a merge symbol (ALT M) followed by a code name; it ends with another merge symbol.

MultiMate also provides several merge commands. Because not

SETTING UP A FORM LETTER

Objective: Coding a Primary Document for Merge Printing

```
DOCUMENT: FORMLET          ‖PAGE:    1 ‖LINE:     1 ‖COL:   1‖
|1 . . . . . . . . . . . . . . . . . . . . . ≫ . . . . . . . . . . . . . . . . . . . . . ≪
⊦NAME⊦≪
⊦COMPANY⊦ ⊦OB⊦≪
⊦ADDRESS⊦≪
⊦CITY⊦,  ⊦STATE⊦ ⊦ZIP⊦≪
≪
Dear ⊦NAME⊦:≪
≪
Our accounts show that you are ⊦TIME⊦ behind in rental
payments.  Please  remit ⊦AMOUNT⊦ to us by  ⊦DATE⊦.≪
≪
⊦COMMENT⊦≪
≪
                         ≫Sincerely,≪
≪
≪
                         ≫Jack Jackson≪
                         ≫Metro Property, Inc.≪

                                    S:↓N:↓
```

Figure 12.4
Primary Document
FORMLET

all addresses have the same number of lines, you may sometimes need to use a merge command to make the primary document print correctly. In a mailing list, for example, some addresses may have company names and others may not, and you don't want an address printed with a blank line in the middle, if no company name exists. One merge command enables you to solve the problem by skipping a merge code if there is no information for it to transfer to the primary document. You'll learn more about these types of commands in the explanation to come.

Procedure

1. Type "2" and press ENTER to select "Create a New Document" from the main menu.

2. Type "FORMLET" and press ENTER at the Document Specification screen. (Check that the "Drive" prompt designates the drive holding the exercise disk.)

3. Press F10 at the Document Summary screen.

4. Press F10 at the Modify Document Defaults screen. A blank editing screen appears.

5. Press F9. You'll set up the following format line for single spacing: one tab stop at column 35 and a line length of 60 characters, as shown below:

```
                                        35             60
|1 ................................................ ≫...................≪
```

Set the line spacing to single spacing (if necessary) by typing over the number that appears at the beginning of the format line. Use the space bar to erase extra tab stops that may appear on the format line.

6. Move the cursor to column 35 and press TAB.

7. Move the cursor to column 60 and press ENTER to set the line length.

8. Press F9. You're ready to type the first merge code, NAME.

9. With the cursor on line 1, column 1, hold down ALT and type "M".

10. Type "NAME".

11. Hold down ALT and type "M"; press ENTER. Next, enter the merge code that transfers the company name. (From now on, explanations will assume you know how to type a merge symbol by holding down ALT and typing "M". The instructions will

simply show the merge symbol when you should type it.)

12. With the cursor on line 2, column 1, type "⊦COMPANY⊦". Next, you enter a merge command that tells MultiMate to skip the COMPANY merge code if no company name exists. The merge command looks like ⊦OB⊦, with "OB" standing for "omit if blank".

13. With the cursor on line 2, column 10, type "⊦OB⊦" and press ENTER. Next, type the rest of the merge codes that transfer address information.

14. With the cursor on line 3, column 1, type "⊦ADDRESS⊦" and press ENTER.

15. With the cursor on line 4, column 1, type "⊦CITY⊦, ⊦STATE⊦, ⊦ZIP⊦" and press ENTER twice. Be sure to type the comma and spaces between the merge codes as seen above. Next, type the merge code that produces a personal salutation.

16. Type "Dear ⊦NAME⊦:" and press ENTER twice. Don't forget the colon that punctuates the salutation.

17. With the cursor on line 8, column 1, type "Our accounts show that you are ⊦TIME⊦ behind in rental payments. Please remit ⊦AMOUNT⊦ to us by ⊦DATE⊦." Press ENTER twice. You can imbed as many merge codes in text as you want. Here you've imbedded three within just two short sentences. During merge printing, each letter will tell the recipient exactly how many months' rent is due, the amount due, and when it must be paid. As MultiMate inserts different amounts of text at each merge code, the text will automatically adjust to the correct line length.

18. With the cursor on line 11, column 1, type "⊦COMMENT⊦" and press ENTER twice. As you may remember from creating the merge data document, this merge code will transfer several sentence remarks into the letter to further "personalize" it.

19. Press TAB and type "Sincerely," and press ENTER three times.

20. Press TAB and type "Jack Jackson" and press ENTER.

21. Press TAB and type "Metro Property, Inc." and press ENTER. You've completed the form letter.

22. Press F10 to save it. With the work done, try printing the three-letter mailing.

23. Type "5" and press ENTER to select "Merge Print Utility" from the main menu. A Document Specification screen appears in which you can specify two documents for printing.

24. Type "FORMLET" and press ENTER at the "Name" prompt on the "MERGE DOCUMENT" side of the screen. The name you specify under "MERGE DOCUMENT" is always that of the document that is to receive information—the primary document. (Check that the drive specification indicates the drive holding the exercise disk.)

25. Press ENTER and type "MERGDATA" at the name prompt on the "MERGE DATA FILE" side of the screen. You have now told MultiMate where to find the information to be transferred into the letter. (Check that the drive specification indicates the drive holding the exercise disk.)

26. Press F10 to complete the document-name specification procedure. Next, MultiMate asks how many records to print and which ones. Much as you specify a specific range of pages to be printed, you can now specify which page of information in MERGDATA to start the merging process and which should end it.

27. Press ENTER, type "00003", and press F10 to print all three records in the list. A print menu appears on screen. You can now adjust the printing specifications as you do to print any other document.

28. Set up the print menu as is shown in figure 12.5. Move the cursor

```
           Print Parameters for Document    B: FORMLET

Start print at page number        001    Lines per inch : 6 / 8              6
Stop print after page number      001    Justification: N / Y / M(icro)     N
Left margin                       010    Proportional Spacing: N / Y        N
Top margin                        000    Char translate/width table     _____
Pause between pages : N / Y        N     Header/footer first page number   001
Draft print : N / Y               N      Number of original copies         001
Default pitch (4=10 cpi)           4     Document page length              066
Printer Action Table  Your Printer       Sheet Feeder Action Table  Your Feeder
Sheet Feeder Bin Numbers (0/1/2/3): First page: 0  Middle: 0  Last page:   0
P(arallel) / S(erial) / L(ist) / A(uxiliary) / F(ile)                      ?
                                         Device Number                    001

Print document summary screen: N/Y N Print printer parameters :        N/Y N
Background / Foreground:         B/F F  Remove queue entry when done:Y/N Y
Current Time is:     00:00:00     Delay Print until Time is: 00:00:00
Current Date is:     00/00/0000   Delay Print until Date is: 00/00/0000
Press F1 for Printers, F2 for Sheet Feeders - only the first 16 are displayed
        Press F10 to Continue,  Press ESC to Abort                     S:↓ N:↓
```

Figure 12.5
Print Menu for FORMLET

to an option and type the specification you see in the figure. Your print menu may have to be slightly different to suit the type of printer and paper that you're using.

Because three letters will print in a row, change the "Pause between pages" prompt to "Y" if you are using separate typing sheets or "N" if you are using continuous-form paper. The printer type, number, sheet-feeding device, and parallel or serial prompts must also be set for your specific equipment.

MultiMate can only merge-print documents in foreground mode. As you may remember, foreground printing means that you cannot edit other documents during a printing session. During merge-printing, MultiMate's attention is pretty much consumed with juggling information in and out of the form document. You can easily stop printing by pressing the ESC key.

29. Turn on your printer and load it with paper. MultiMate is set to print the three-letter mailing.

30. Press F10 to start printing. You can press ESC to cancel the printing at any time. Examine the letters as they're printed to see that different information appears in each.

Designing a form letter (or any other kind of primary document) is **Explanation** simply a matter of deciding where to put merge codes in the text. You might code and format a primary document to address envelopes by creating a document similar to figure 12.6.

In the rent letter, you used merge codes to print a name, address, and salutation at the letter's top. Other codes filled in pertinent facts within the letter's text. You also used a merge code to add a final message to the letter as a special note.

Most of this primary document was composed of merge codes and the three letters, when printed, bore quite different information. You can also use the same merge code as many times as you like in a primary document. A letter's text might directly mention the addressee's name several times, for example. As long as the merge codes in the primary document are identical to those used in the merge data document, MultiMate can churn out letter after letter without a hitch.

Notice the use of the ⊢OB⊢command that appeared in the primary document's second line. When the third letter (for Gary Lu) was printed, MultiMate found no company name to insert in the letter, so it skipped this item. The address came out printed correctly without a blank line appearing where the company name should have been. Without the ⊢OB⊢ command, the address would have printed like this:

Gary Lu

155 West Third
West Lake, CA 94233

Any time you have information that may or may not exist for a merge code in the merge data document, you can use the ⊢OB⊢ to prevent this kind of formatting problem.

MultiMate provides a set of three other merge commands that you might have occasion to use. You might, for example, want to print a list of 45 customer addresses per page, with each address in this format:

NAME   ADDRESS   CITY   STATE   ZIP

How can you tell MultiMate to merge-print 45 addresses in a row?

You use three merge commands: ⊢REPEAT⊢, ⊢NEXT⊢, and ⊢END REPEAT⊢. By placing a command such as ⊢REPEAT:45⊢ in the primary document, you tell MultiMate that it's going to do something

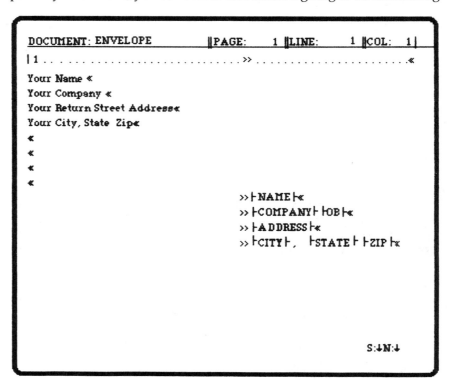

Figure 12.6
Primary Document
Formatted to Print
Envelopes

45 times. You tell MultiMate what to do by typing those merge codes that are to be repeated after the ⊢REPEAT⊢ command.

You must also tell MultiMate that with each repetition, it must use new information from the next page of the merge data document. To make MultiMate print the next address information in the merge data document, you use a ⊢NEXT⊢ merge command. You must also signal to MultiMate when it has reached the end of the information to be repeated. To put a boundary on the repeated information, insert an ⊢END REPEAT⊢ code in the primary document.

If that sounds like programming, that's what it is. The following example will help clarify the procedure. To print names and addresses of three different customers on a page, you'd code a primary document as follows:

```
1........≫ ............................. ≫...........≫.........≫......≪
⊢REPEAT:3⊢≪
⊢NAME⊢ ≫⊢ADDRESS⊢ ≫⊢CITY⊢ ≫⊢STATE⊢ ≫⊢ZIP⊢≪
⊢NEXT⊢≪
⊢END REPEAT⊢≪
```

The first repeat command tells MultiMate to print something three times. The second line specifies the merge code information that is to be printed repeatedly. After MultiMate prints the address information for the first customer in the merge data document, the ⊢NEXT⊢ command tells MultiMate to read the next set of customer information. Without the ⊢NEXT⊢ command, MultiMate would print the same name and address information three times. The last command, ⊢END REPEAT⊢, tells MultiMate not to repeat anything beyond this point.

Merge-printing a primary document coded as above with the three-address MERGDATA document would produce a page that looks like this:

Gail Strong	44 West Blake	Terre Linda	CA 91110
Blanche Ganner	333 Turnip Hill Rd.	San Rafael	CA 91222
Gary Lu	155 West Third	West Lake	CA 94233

If you foresee using merge printing to create such reports, you might experiment with these merge commands.

When merge-printing a mass mailing, you may not always want to print using the entire merge data document. You might want to send letters to a select number of addresses, for example. Unfortunately, you can't tell MultiMate to print information from some pages and skip others.

What you can do is create another merge data document. Create a document and then copy the coded information that you need from the original merge data document into the new one. In this way, you might select twenty addresses for printing out of a hundred. Simply use the external copy procedure (begun by pressing SHIFT F8) to copy coded address information from the merge data document to the new document.

SUMMARY

In merge-printing, the primary document and the merge data document transfer information as shown in figure 12.7. Merge-printing documents share a common set of codes. A merge code requires special merge symbols that are typed by holding down ALT and pressing "M".

In a merge data document, the information to be transferred to the primary document is typed directly under a merge code. The text must end with a merge symbol and carriage return:

Merge Code: ⊢NAME⊢≪
Transfer text: John Brown⊢≪

Merge-printing the merge data document and the primary document requires the steps shown in figure 12.8.

When coding a primary document you can also use the following merge commands:

⊢OB⊢   To skip merge codes if they are blank

and

⊢REPEAT:xx⊢   To print repeating sequences of
⊢NEXT⊢   merge code information
⊢END REPEAT⊢

Primary Document   **Merge Data Document**

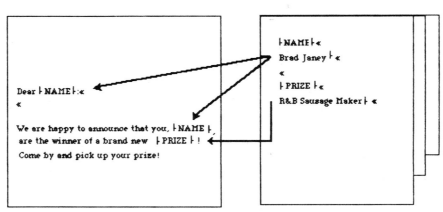

Figure 12.7
Information Transfers from Merge Data Document to Primary Document

1. After completing the primary
   and merge data documents,
   select "Merge Print Utility"
   from the main menu.

2. Type the name of the primary
   (merge) document, press ENTER
   twice, type the name of the
   merge data document, and press
   F10.

3. When the print menu displays,
   set the menu to print the primary
   document as you wish. Also set
   printing to occur in "Foreground".

4. Ready the printer and press F10.

Figure 12.8
Merge-printing Procedure

Chapter 13

SPECIAL-EFFECTS DEPARTMENT

Preparation

Your computer should be turned on and MultiMate's main menu should be on the screen. Your exercise disk should be in drive B and should contain the document called EFFECTS. Refer to appendix G for instructions for creating the document.

Your particular printer may not be able to perform the kinds of printing features described in this chapter. Some printers, for example, may not be able to underline words. However, if you have installed MultiMate using a print driver supplied with the program, you can perform all of the exercises.

Information about a printer's capabilities can most often be found in the printer's reference manual. If you've installed a custom print driver that you created with MultiMate's print driver program, you're probably already familiar with the types of printing your printer can do.

One exercise asks you to type special printer codes into text. The codes supplied here are for a Radio Shack Daisywheel II printer. If you have a different printer, you must look up and substitute codes for your specific printer in the exercise. If you don't have access to codes or are unsure about using them, feel free just to read over the explanation and skip ahead in the chapter.

MultiMate enables you to add some nice finishing touches to documents. You can make titles and subheadings print boldfaced, for example, or you can print math formulas and footnotes with super-

and subscripted characters (characters that print slightly above or below the line). In fact, depending on your printer's capabilities, you might use special characters, such as copyright symbols or Greek letters, in your text.

Activating these special printing features simply requires you to insert codes in a document. You might, for example, print a special quotation within a report in a different pitch (number of characters per inch), so that the text stands out. Pitch changes are easily invoked with MultiMate by inserting a code where the change is to begin and another where it is to end.

Boldfaced text appears darker on paper than surrounding text. MultiMate actually provides the ability to print in four shades, but it's unlikely that your printer will allow more than two or three different darknesses. MultiMate's four types of printing are:

Draft printing:	which prints text at the regular or standard darkness
Enhanced printing:	which prints text darker than Draft print
Bold printing:	which prints text darker than Enhanced print
Shadow printing:	which prints slightly enlarged letters darker than Bold print

You'll learn to invoke these different shades of printing by inserting codes in a document.

You can also underline text just as you can with a typewriter. Text appears underlined on screen and prints underlined on paper.

Most printers print at either 10 or 12 pitch. Some printers, however, may have several other pitches as well, ranging from 5 pitch to 17 pitch. (See "Print Pitch" in the MultiMate reference manual for examples of these different pitches.) You might print text at several different pitches within the same page. Again, this is a simple matter of inserting codes in the text.

In this chapter, you'll try out special printing features that you might use to enhance the looks of your documents.

DRESSING UP TEXT

Objective: Printing Text with Boldfacing, Superscripts, Underlining, and Shadow Printing

Text will normally be printed in draft printing mode. To specially invoke draft printing, hold down ALT and type "D". A screen symbol appears on screen. Text following the symbol will be draft-printed.

To use enhanced printing, hold down ALT and type "N" in front of the text to be affected. Type ALT D at the point in the text where enhanced printing is to end and draft printing is to begin again.

To use boldfacing, type ALT Z before and after the text to be boldfaced. To use shadow printing, type ALT X before and after the text to be shadow-printed. To print superscripted text (above the line), type ALT Q before the text and ALT W after it. Typing ALT W and then ALT Q after text causes it to print subscripted (below the line).

Underlining, the simplest of all these special effects, is carried out as it is on a typewriter. After typing text, you can underline it by positioning the cursor and typing underscores beneath characters. Text will appear underlined on the screen and on the paper.

Try dressing up the document called EFFECTS, shown in figure 13.1, so that you can see how these printing features are used.

Procedure

1. Type "1" and press ENTER to select "Edit an Old Document" from the main menu.

2. Type "EFFECTS" and press ENTER at the Document Specification screen. (Check that the drive specification indicates the drive holding the exercise disk.)

3. Press F10 at the Document Summary screen. The editing screen

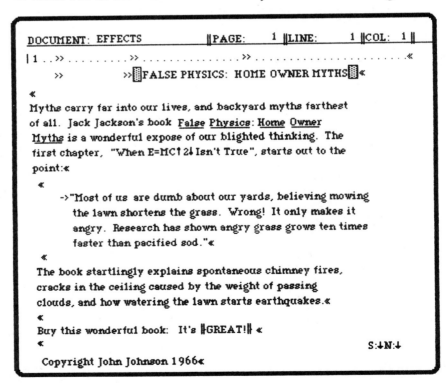

Figure 13.1
EFFECTS Document and
Printing Codes

and text appears. Because line 1 is a title, let's make it print boldfaced, or extra dark, on the paper.

4. Move the cursor to line 1, column 15 and press INS. You'll next insert the boldface print symbol.

5. Hold down ALT and type "Z". A block-like symbol appears on screen. This symbol tells the printer to start printing boldfaced text. You must tell the printer when to stop boldfacing as well. In this case, tell the printer to stop at the end of this line.

6. Press INS, move the cursor to line 1, column 47, and press INS. Here is where boldfacing is to stop, so you insert a second bold-face symbol.

7. Hold down ALT and type "Z"; press INS. The title on line 1 will now print boldfaced. Book titles are normally underlined, so try underlining the title on line 4.

8. Move the cursor to line 4, column 30, under the "F" of "False".

9. Holding down SHIFT, press the underline key (between the zero and the equal-sign key on the keyboard's top row) to underline these words:

    False Physics: Home Owner Myths

    Next, try superscripting the number appearing in the formula on line 6.

10. Move the cursor to line 6, column 26 and press INS. You'll now insert the superscript code. Text following the code prints above the normal line.

11. Hold down ALT, type "Q", and press INS. An up arrow symbol appears, telling you the text will print above the line. You must also tell MultiMate when to stop printing text above the line. You do that by inserting another symbol.

12. Move the cursor to line 6, column 28, and press INS.

13. Hold down ALT and type "W"; press INS. After you type ALT W, a downward-pointing arrow appears. This symbol tells the printer to print lower on the page, in this case returning to where text is normally printed. Next, try shadow-printing some text.

14. Move the cursor to line 18, column 32. To shadow-print the word "GREAT", you must insert the shadow-print code on both sides of it.

15. Press INS, hold down ALT, and type "X".

16. Press INS, move the cursor to line 18, column 39, and press INS again.

17. Hold down ALT and type "X"; press INS. You've now set up the document for boldfacing, underlining, a superscript, and shadow printing.

18. Press F10 to save the document. Let's print EFFECTS to see the results.

19. Type "3" and press ENTER to select "Print Document Utility".

20. Check that the EFFECTS document is specified in the Document Specification screen and press ENTER. (Type EFFECTS as the document name if it doesn't already appear there.)

21. Set up the print menu as shown in figure 13.2 with the exception of the "Printer Action Table" prompts. Use the cursor keys to move the cursor from prompt to prompt. Type over the characters of the print specifications to change them. At "Printer Action Table", supply the name of the MultiMate print driver for your printer.

22. Make sure the printer is turned on and paper is loaded.

23. With the print menu specification set, press F10 to begin printing.

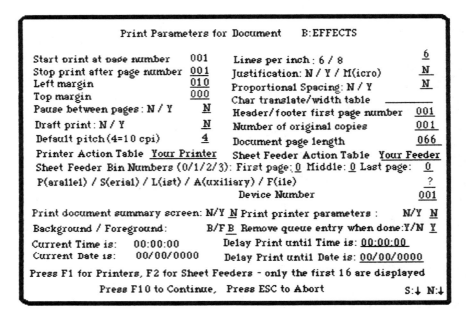

Figure 13.2
Print Menu for EFFECTS

Using MultiMate's printing features is a little like applying make-up. **Explanation**
A little cosmetic darkening here, an underline there, and model text
is produced ready to be admired.

To print extra-dark text on paper, you must insert codes before
and after the text during editing. To boldface text, for example, you
hold down the ALT key and type "Z". A boldface symbol appears
on screen. Any text typed after that will be printed boldfaced. To
turn boldfacing off again, you position the cursor where bold printing
is to stop, hold down ALT, and type "Z" again. The second use of
the boldface symbol turns off the printing feature. Each type of special
printing—draft, enhanced, bold, and shadow—must be turned on
and off this way with special symbols.

The secret to using special printing functions is remembering that
two codes are required: one to start the printing function and one to
stop it. Accidentally forgetting to insert a final boldfacing code, for
example, can result in all the remaining text being printed in boldface.

Normal printing is done in draft print. Enhanced printing produces slightly darker text, which you might use appropriately in a
formal business letter where a good impression counts. To print an
entire document in enhanced printing, you can simply set the "Draft
print" option of the print menu to "N" (for "no") before printing.

To use draft and enhanced printing in different parts of a document, you must use print codes. To start enhanced printing within
a page, press ALT N to insert an initial code. To return to draft
printing later in the text, you must press ALT D.

Bold and shadow printing produce even darker text. Not all printers are capable of these two print functions. Unlike draft and enhanced print, bold and shadow printing are started and stopped with
the same code. For bold printing, press ALT Z to insert a code that
initiates and stops boldfacing. You press ALT X to start and later
stop shadow printing.

Underlining is perhaps the easiest of the printing features to use.
You move the cursor under a character and press SHIFT and the
underline key to underline it. You can also automatically underline
words as you type. By holding down ALT and pressing the underline
key, you tell MultiMate to underline whatever you type. The SHIFT
and NUM LOCK key indicators in the screen's lower right appear
underlined when automatic underlining is turned on. All text that
you type, including spaces, numbers, and punctuation, will be
underlined. When you have finished typing underlined text, press
ALT and the underline key again to turn off the underlining feature.

You can also underline just letter characters (without automatically underlining spaces and punctuation). This type of automatic

underlining is called *alphanumeric* and is started and stopped by pressing ALT and the equal-sign key. You might use alphanumeric underlining to automatically underline a book title in which the spaces between words should not print underlined. With this type of underlining, you could simply type the title without worrying about improperly underlined spaces.

If you mistakenly underline something, you can erase underlining two ways. You can either retype the underlined text or underline it again. If you try to underline text that's already underlined on screen, the underlining is erased, leaving the original text as is.

With superscripts, you must remember the principle "What goes up, must come down". You direct the printer to print text a fraction of an inch above the current line by inserting the upward-pointing arrow code, which is done by pressing ALT Q. After printing several characters above the line, you usually want the printer to return to printing at the normal position. To tell the printer to come down again, press ALT W. A downward-pointing arrow appears on screen.

You reverse the code order to create subscripts. To print text just below the line, first press ALT W to insert the downward arrow code. To raise printing to the normal line level later, insert the upward arrow code by pressing ALT Q. Although super- and subscripts may not be routinely required, they do come in handy for printing footnote markers and formulas.

Once you've set up a page for special printing, you can erase any of the printing effects by simply deleting the corresponding codes. Although the codes appear in the text, they do not print and they do not take up space in the text. If codes appear in a line, and you're trying to be precise in placing your text, remember that the space the codes take up on screen will disappear during printing. To gauge how text will print, you must imagine text spaced on screen without the embedded codes.

In the next exercise, you'll look at changing pitch during printing and how you might print special characters and symbols.

SPECIAL EFFECTS

Objective: Changing Printing Pitch and Printing Special Characters

If your printer is capable of doing so, you might print text at any of nine different printing pitches. To change printing pitch, you insert a code in text where the pitch change is to occur. To insert a pitch code, hold down ALT and type "C"; a "Pt" character appears on screen. Next, type a code number for the pitch you desire. For example, to select between 10 or 12 pitch, you might insert one of the following symbols:

Pt4   for 10-pitch printing
Pt5   for 12-pitch printing

A table of different codes follows in the explanation section.

By default, MultiMate prints text at 10 pitch. Pitch codes must be put on a line by themselves (they may not work if they are located within a text line). You'll try out changing pitch with MultiMate by printing the quotation in the EFFECTS document at 12 pitch. You can see the codes you'll insert in figure 13.3.

Many printers can print special characters, such as accented letters or Greek symbols. To print a special symbol or give the printer a special command, hold down ALT and type "A". Then type the printer code for the desired character or command (always using three digits—for example, use 027 if the printer code is 27); printer codes are described in your printer's reference manual. When the printer reads this number, it prints the special character or executes the printer command that you specified. In the EFFECTS document, you'll imbed a code that tells a Radio Shack Daisy Wheel II printer to print a copyright symbol, as shown at the bottom of figure 13.3.

1. Type "1" and press ENTER to select "Edit an Old Document" from the main menu.   **Procedure**

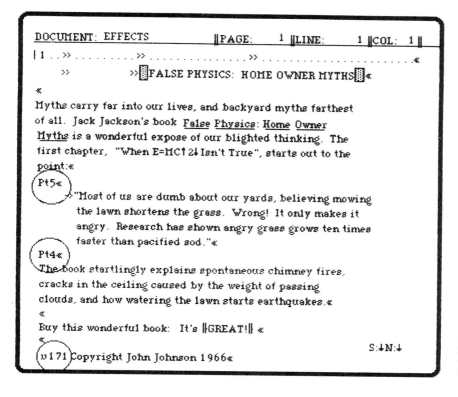

Figure 13.3
Pitch Changing and
Special Character Codes

2. Type "EFFECTS" and press ENTER at the Document Specification screen. (Check that the drive specification indicates the drive holding the exercise disk.)

3. Press F10 at the Document Summary screen. The editing screen and text appears. Try changing the printing pitch of the quotation (second paragraph) from the default 10 pitch to 12 pitch.

4. Move the cursor to line 8, column 1 and press INS. You'll next insert the print pitch symbol.

5. Holding down ALT, type "C". The pitch symbol appears on the screen. Next, you'll type a number for the pitch you wish (5 indicates 12 pitch).

6. Type "5" and press INS. From this point on all text will be printed at 12 pitch. You want the last paragraph to print at 10 pitch, however, so you must change pitch again.

7. Move the cursor to line 13, column 1. Insert the second pitch code here.

8. Press INS, hold down ALT, and type "C".

9. To change to 10 pitch, type "4" and press INS. Next, go to the bottom line and make the printer print a copyright symbol.

10. Move the cursor to line 20, column 1. Press INS, hold down ALT, and type "A". The printer-control code appears on screen. You must next supply a number for the special character or command you desire. To make a Radio Shack Daisy Wheel II printer print a copyright symbol, you type the number 171.

11. Type "171", press the space bar, and press INS. (If you have a different printer, you must substitute the number, in decimal form, that your printer requires. Refer to your printer's reference manual or skip this step and erase the printer code you just inserted.)

12. Press F10 to save the document. Let's print EFFECTS now to see the results of your work.

13. Type "3" and press ENTER to select "Print Document Utility".

14. Check that the EFFECTS document is specified in the Document Specification screen and press ENTER. (Type "EFFECTS" as the document name if it doesn't already appear there.)

15. Set up the print menu as shown in figure 13.2, with the exception of the "Printer Action Table" prompt. Use the cursor keys to

move the cursor from prompt to prompt. Type over the characters of the print specifications to change them.

At "Printer Action Table", type the name of the MultiMate print driver for your printer.

Accept the four time and date prompts, "Current Time", "Current Date", "Delay Print until Time is", and "Delay Print until Date is", as they are displayed on your screen.

16. Make sure the printer is turned on and paper is loaded.

17. With the print menu specification set, press F10 to begin printing.

Changing print pitch in a document is simple. You merely type ALT C and type a number for the pitch you want. The pitch code should be on a line by itself, not imbedded in text.   **Explanation**

The hardest part is remembering which number to type. Here's a list of the numbers corresponding to different pitches (you can also find this list in the MultiMate *Reference Manual* under "Print Pitch").

Code	*Corresponding Pitch*
Pt1	5 Pitch
Pt2	6 Pitch
Pt3	8.5 Pitch
Pt4	10 Pitch
Pt5	12 Pitch
Pt6	13.2 Pitch
Pt7	15 Pitch
Pt8	16.5 Pitch
Pt9	17.6 Pitch

MultiMate didn't do you any favors by making Pt4 correspond to 10 pitch and Pt5 to 12 pitch, did they? Pt10 might just as well have corresponded to 10 pitch, making it easy to remember. But that's programming (and programmers) for you.

You might use a variety of print pitches within a document. If you don't know (and can't find out) which pitches your printer can produce, you might simply experiment with the different pitch codes in a document. It's unlikely any harm will come to the printer.

Your printer might be able to print any number of special symbols. It might be able to perform special functions as well, such as printing in several colors or using extremely small increments of space. Most printers execute these types of functions when they receive a specific code from the computer. MultiMate enables you to send specific codes to the printer using printer-control codes.

A printer control code is created by typing ALT A and then typing a three-digit number. For example, with most printers, the code 010 (a decimal number) tells the printer to skip down a line. By imbedding these special printing codes within text, you can tell the printer to perform special commands or to print characters not found on the keyboard.

The number you supply must be a decimal number three digits long. If your printer's reference manual lists printer codes in hexadecimal or octal numbers only, you'll have to convert them to decimal to use these codes in your text. Explaining these complicated conversions would take too long to do here. Fortunately, most printers tell you the code numbers in several numbering systems, one of which will likely be decimal.

The code numbers range from 1 to 255. All numbers must be three digits, so the first code would be typed "001". Try to find out what special characters your printer can produce. You may be pleasantly surprised to find that you have access to printing functions you never suspected.

SUMMARY

You can produce special printing functions with the codes shown in figure 13.4.

Code	KEYS	Printing Feature
δ	Alt D	= to begin draft printing
∩	Alt N	= to begin enhanced printing (Use a draft print code to stop)
▓	Alt Z	= to begin and end bold printing
⊩	Alt X	= to begin and end shadow printing
↑	Alt Q	= to begin a super script (Use a subscript code to stop)
↓	Alt W	= to begin a subscript (Use a superscript code to stop)
∪	Alt A	= to use a special printer character

Figure 13.4
Special Printing Codes

Chapter 14

FASTER THAN THE SPEEDING HAND

Preparation

> Your computer should be turned on and MultiMate's main menu should be on the screen. Your exercise disk should be in drive B.

With MultiMate, you don't have to work hard; you can work smart. As you get accustomed to word processing, you'll find that you frequently repeat certain procedures. You might routinely complete fill-in-the-blank forms, set up a commonly used format line, or often specify documents to be printed in a particular way. Long documents especially require repetitive editing procedures at times. A small change, such as indenting headings instead of centering them, may require making the same sequence of keystrokes dozens of times.

What you need is a robot that can press the keys and repeat editing procedures endlessly without tedium, right? MultiMate provides some robotics in a function called a *key procedure*.

You can teach MultiMate to perform a sequence of tasks and repeat them whenever you wish. Simply perform the tasks to be repeated and record them as a key procedure. Begin by giving the key procedure a name (as you would name a robot); MultiMate memorizes the sequence of keys you press after that. You can create key procedures that make menu selections, print documents, move the cursor, insert or delete text—any function that you can carry out at the keyboard.

Once the key procedure is complete, you can have MultiMate repeat the procedure any time you wish (and it will usually be done faster than you could carry it out by hand). A procedure might combine many tasks in sequence and can be as long and complicated as you can think up. In this chapter, you'll create a procedure that leads you through the process of completing a simple invoice.

CREATING KEY PROCEDURES

Objective: Building Key Procedures for an Invoice

To build a key procedure, you essentially teach MultiMate which keys to press. Begin by holding down CTRL and pressing F5. Supply the key procedure's name (up to eight characters long) and press F10. Next, perform any key presses that you want MultiMate to learn. You can perform any function on the keyboard as you normally would.

At certain points in a key procedure, you may want the process to stop and allow you to type information. You can put a pause in a procedure by pressing CTRL F6.

To allow you to stop the key procedure at a specific point (or to go on with it), you can call a prompt to screen. The prompt enables you to type "S" to stop the procedure or "C" to continue it. To put such a prompt in a procedure, press CTRL F7.

When you've finished teaching MultiMate the key procedure, you end it by pressing CTRL F5 again.

Try creating two key procedures that produce an invoice like the one in figure 14.1.

Procedure

1. Type "2" and press ENTER to select "Create a New Document".

2. Type the document name "INVOICE" and press ENTER. (Be sure the drive specification is correct.)

3. Press F10 to bypass the Document Summary screen.

4. Press F10 to bypass the Modify Document Defaults screen. A blank editing screen appears. Next, you'll start creating a procedure called INV.

5. Hold down CTRL and press F5. A prompt appears on screen asking you to type a key procedure name.

6. Type "INV" and press F10. Space over any other letters that may appear on the line. At the screen's bottom right you'll see a "B" among the SHIFT and NUM LOCK indicators. The "B" tells you that MultiMate is building a key procedure. Any key presses you make now will be part of the procedure. Let's begin by setting up a format line for an invoice.

7. Press F9 and set up the format line you see below:

Column: 7   14   36   53   60
|1.........≫....≫ .... ≫..............≫......≪

8. Press F9 when the format line is finished. Next, you begin typing the invoice text.

9. Press F3, type "INVOICE", and press ENTER twice.

10. With the cursor on line 3, column 1, type "NAME:" and press the space bar. You want the procedure to pause here to allow you to type a name.

11. Hold down CTRL and press F6. The word "Pause" appears briefly at the screen's bottom. Once it disappears, you can continue creating the key procedure. Anywhere you want to enable someone to type in information, you'll create a pause in the procedure this way.

12. Press ENTER, type "STREET:", and press the space bar. You need another pause here to let you type in the street address.

13. Hold down CTRL and press F6.

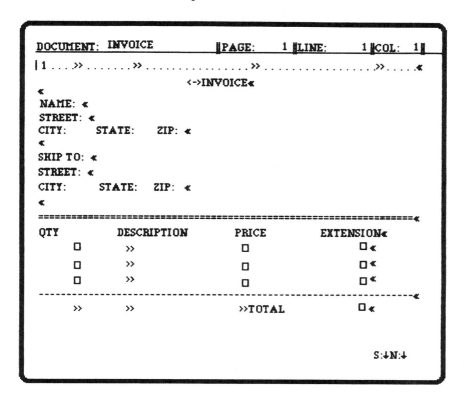

Figure 14.1
Key Procedure INVOICE

14. Press ENTER, type "CITY:", and press the space bar. You need another pause here to let you type in a city's name.

15. Hold down CTRL and press F6.

16. Space the cursor to line 5, column 11, type "STATE:", and press the space bar.

17. To make the procedure pause so you can fill in the state, hold down CTRL and press F6.

18. Space the cursor to line 5, column 22 and type "ZIP:"; press the space bar.

19. To create a pause, hold down CTRL and press F6.

20. Press ENTER three times.

21. With the cursor on line 8, column 1, type "SHIP TO:" and press the space bar. Each item to be completed in the shipping address must be followed by a pause.

22. Hold down CTRL and press F6.

23. Press ENTER, type "STREET:", and press the space bar.

24. Hold down CTRL and press F6.

25. Press ENTER, type "CITY:", and press the space bar.

26. Hold down CTRL and press F6.

27. Space the cursor to line 10, column 11 and type "STATE:"; press the space bar.

28. Hold down CTRL and press F6.

29. Space the cursor to line 10, column 22 and type "ZIP:"; press the space bar.

30. Hold down CTRL and press F6.

31. Press ENTER twice.

32. With the cursor on line 12, column 1, hold down the equal-sign key to create a line of equal signs stretching to column 58; press ENTER.

33. With the cursor on line 13, column 1, type "QTY".

34. Space the cursor to column 12 of line 13 and type "DESCRIPTION".

35. Space the cursor to column 34 of line 13 and type "PRICE".

36. Space the cursor to column 46 of line 13, type "EXTENSION", and press ENTER.

    You'll now type the section in which the product name and numbers for quantity, price, and extensions will be entered in the invoice. This information will line up in four columns. To align the columns, you'll insert tabs and Dectabs. After each tab or Dectab is inserted, you'll create a pause in the procedure so that a number or product name can be typed.

37. Holding down SHIFT, press F4 to produce a Dectab. This Dectab will line up the quantity figure for an invoice item. It's followed by a pause.

38. Hold down CTRL and press F6.

39. Press TAB and then hold down CTRL and press F6. This tab and pause will enable you to type a product name.

40. Holding down SHIFT, press F4 to produce a Dectab. This Dectab will line up the price figure.

41. Hold down CTRL and press F6 to create a pause.

42. Holding down SHIFT, press F4; then hold down CTRL and press F6. When you use this procedure to complete an invoice later, the key procedure will skip from column to column as you enter the quantity, description, price, and extension for the first item.

    If only one item were to appear on the invoice, you would want to stop the key procedure after the first item was completed. To give yourself (or another user) the option of stopping or going on, you use a prompt.

43. Press ENTER; then, holding down CTRL, press F7. The word "prompt" appears briefly on the screen. Now the procedure will let you stop adding items or continue with the second line of the invoice. From here on out, you'd repeat steps 37 through 43 to give the invoice as many lines as you wish. For this example, we'll simply add two more lines and call it quits.

44. Holding down SHIFT, press F4; then hold down CTRL and press F6.

45. Press TAB; then hold down CTRL and press F6.

46. Holding down SHIFT, press F4; then hold down CTRL and press F6.

47. Holding down SHIFT, press F4; then hold down CTRL and press F6.

48. Press ENTER; then hold down CTRL and press F7.

49. Holding down SHIFT, press F4; then hold down CTRL and press F6.

50. Press TAB; then hold down CTRL and press F6.

51. Holding down SHIFT, press F4; then hold down CTRL and press F6.

52. Holding down SHIFT, press F4; then hold down CTRL and press F6.

53. Finally, press ENTER; then hold down CTRL and press F7. The procedure is finished.

54. Hold down CTRL and press F5 to indicate that the INV key procedure is finished. Notice that the "B" at the screen's bottom right is gone. The INV key procedure will now enable you to easily complete a three-item invoice. (It could have been longer if you had continued adding lines.)

    Now you'll create a key procedure that finishes the invoice by drawing a line and totalling the extension column. Name this key procedure "TOT" (for "total").

55. Hold down CTRL and press F5 to start another key procedure. A prompt appears on screen asking you to type a key procedure name.

56. Type "TOT" and press F10. At the screen's bottom right a "B" will appear among the SHIFT and NUM LOCK indicators.

57. With the cursor on line 17, column 1, hold down the hyphen key to create a line of hyphens stretching to column 58; press ENTER.

58. Press TAB three times and type "TOTAL".

59. Holding down SHIFT, press F4 to create a Dectab.

60. Move the cursor to line 17, column 52 under the Dectab. Next, you'll tell MultiMate to do a column addition.

61. Hold down CTRL and press F4.

62. Hold down CTRL and press F5 to indicate that the TOT key procedure is finished. With the INV and TOT key procedures, you're now ready to automatically create and total invoices with MultiMate. In the next section (after the explanation), you'll try out both INV and TOT.

63. Press F10 to save the document.

Key procedures can be as simple or as complex as you wish. Creating a key procedure is a matter of teaching by example. To create a key procedure, you begin by pressing CTRL F5 and supplying a procedure name. You then perform the procedure that MultiMate is to learn. To end the procedure, press CTRL F5 again.

Explanation

Key procedures are special files that MultiMate records on disk. An extension of ".KEY" will be added to the end of the name you give to a key procedure. The invoice key procedure, for example, has the file name "INV.KEY". If you display a DOS disk directory, you can recognize key procedures by their ".KEY" extensions, whereas your word-processing documents have an extension of ".DOC". Key procedures aren't listed in MultiMate's document directories, so you can't see a listing of them as you edit or run the program. You can, however, copy, rename, and erase key procedures on disk using DOS commands.

Because key procedures are recorded on disk, they can be as long as disk space allows. A key procedure might insert a single word or provide functions as elaborate as those you created in this module.

One problem with key procedures is that you can't edit them as you type them. If you make a small typing error as you create the procedure, you might just correct it as you normally would during editing. Suppose that you're using a key procedure to insert a word (among other text) in a document, but you accidentally mistype the word. You can just fix the typing error and then finish the procedure as you intended. Because key procedures work fast, it's unlikely anyone will see the mistake as the procedure executes later.

Making a bad procedural blunder, however, may force you to stop building the key procedure and start all over or to edit it with a special program provided on MultiMate's utility disk. Unfortunately, editing a key procedure can seem like a course in programming. To learn to edit such files, read the "Key Procedure Files Edit Utility" section of the *Advanced User's Guide* provided with MultiMate's documentation.

You might think of key procedures as custom-made word-processing tools. Keep an eye out for situations in which a key procedure might help you—using such procedures you need never repeat any routine twice. An ideal application for key procedures is designing fill-in-the-blank forms, such as the invoice that you just completed. A key procedure can actually lead you step by step through completing a form (as you'll see in the next section). You might also use a key procedure to help create the coded address list used in merge printing. A key procedure can type the same set of codes repeatedly, pausing along the way to let you type address information.

As you create a key procedure, you must be aware of the times when its execution should stop to allow you to type information. To temporarily break off a procedure's execution, you press CTRL F6 to create a pause. After creating a pause, you continue building the procedure. When the finished key procedure executes later, it will halt at the point where you pressed CTRL F6. In the invoice procedure, you typed text such as "NAME:" followed by a pause so that you could type a person's name in the invoice.

Sometimes, you may want a procedure to stop before completion. On an invoice, for example, you may need to type a single product entry or dozens of entries. After the invoice key procedure helps you enter the quantity, description, price, and extended total for one invoice item, you need the option to add more items or stop. You can put such a point of decision into a key procedure by using a prompt.

A prompt is inserted in a key procedure by pressing CTRL F7. Like a pause, a prompt temporarily halts a key procedure's execution. The following prompt appears on screen:

DO YOU WISH TO CONTINUE OR STOP? (C/S)

You cannot edit or perform other word-processing functions when you see this prompt. You can only stop the key procedure by typing "S" or continue with it by pressing "C". Thus, a key procedure prompt simply allows you to end the key procedure when desired.

One important detail about the key procedure prompt should be explained. You can use it to make key procedures repeat. All you need to do is end a procedure with a prompt. If you type "C" for continue when the final prompt appears during execution, the key procedure will start over again from the beginning. That's a quite useful feature—here's why.

Suppose you decide to change the format lines throughout a 50-page document. Normally, you'd have to hunt through the document and change format lines one by one. With a repeating key procedure, however, you can change every format line automatically. You'd merely build a key procedure that starts by searching for the next format line. Once the next format line is located, you'd edit the format line as you continue building the key procedure. Last, you'd end the procedure with a prompt and turn off the key procedure function.

When you execute this key procedure, MultiMate finds the next format line, changes it, and then asks you if you wish to continue or stop. If you tell MultiMate to continue, the key procedure repeats and finds the next format line and changes it. With each repetition of the key procedure, another format line is changed. You need only repeat the key procedure until all format lines have been changed.

(You can also use MultiMate's search-and-replace function to change format lines, by the way.)

Any key procedure that ends with a prompt will repeat this way, no matter how complex the procedure is. With a little planning, you can design highly useful key procedures that loop through documents, changing them for you.

The next exercise allows you to try out the two key procedures that you just created and produce an invoice.

You can execute a key procedure any time while MultiMate is running. You might create a key procedure that starts at the main menu, print menu, editing screen, or some other screen.

EXECUTING KEY PROCEDURES

Objective: Completing an Invoice with Key Procedures

To start a key procedure, press CTRL F8, type the key procedure's name, then press F10. The key procedure starts immediately.

As a key procedure executes, it may pause to let you type, edit, or perform some other procedure. A message similar to the following one will appear on the screen:

PLEASE ENTER DATA, THEN CTRL-F6 TO RESUME

The message appears briefly then disappears. When you're ready to continue with the key procedure, hold down CTRL and press F6. The key procedure will continue from where it left off. (The first time you reach a pause, you'll have to type a "C" before performing the task for which the procedure paused.)

You also may see a prompt that asks you to type "C" to continue or "S" to stop. At that point you can decide whether to stop the key procedure. To continue with it, you type "C"; to stop, type an "S".

Try using your INV and TOT key procedures to produce the invoice you see in figure 14.2.

1. Type "1" and press ENTER to select "Edit an Old Document". **Procedure**

2. Type the document name "INVOICE" and press ENTER. (Be sure the drive specification is correct.)

3. Press F10 to bypass the Document Summary screen. When the editing screen appears, let's erase any text that might be there.

4. With the cursor on line 1, column 27, press DEL; hold down CTRL and press END; then press DEL a final time. All text should be erased from this page. With a blank page, you can now start the INV key procedure.

5. Hold down CTRL and press F8. A prompt appears asking you to type the key procedure's name.

6. Type "INV". Space over any extra characters that might appear on the line.

7. Press F10. Watch as the key procedure adjusts the format line

and types the invoice heading. It then pauses to let you type a client's name.

8. After "NAME:", type "C" and then type "Mary Blume". (At the first pause, you must type a "C" before you type the desired information. After that, no "C" is necessary.) You now want the procedure to continue.

9. Hold down CTRL and press F6. The key procedure types "STREET:" and pauses again.

10. Type "125 Jackson Ave." and then hold down CTRL and press F6 to continue.

11. After "CITY:", type "Spokane" and then hold down CTRL and press F6 to continue.

12. After "STATE:", type "Washington" and then hold down CTRL and press F6 to continue.

13. After "ZIP:", type "98270" and then hold down CTRL and press F6 to continue.

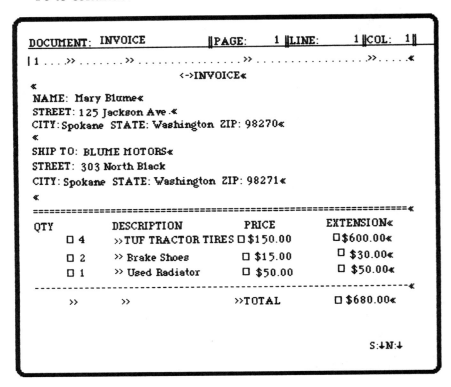

Figure 14.2
Completed INVOICE
Document

14. After "SHIP TO:", type "BLUME MOTORS" and then hold down CTRL and press F6 to continue.

15. After "STREET:", type "303 North Black" and then hold down CTRL and press F6 to continue.

16. After "CITY:", type "Spokane" and then hold down CTRL and press F6 to continue.

17. After "STATE:", type "Washington" and then hold down CTRL and press F6 to continue.

18. After "ZIP", type "98271" and then hold down CTRL and press F6 to continue. The key procedure now sets up the invoice to record invoice items. Mary Blume bought four tractor tires at $150 each. Let's record those now.

19. Type "4" and then hold down CTRL and press F6 to continue. The procedure tabs over to allow you to type a product description.

20. Type "TUF TRACTOR TIRES" and then hold down CTRL and press F6 to continue. The key procedure tabs over to let you type the unit price.

21. Type "$150.00" and then hold down CTRL and press F6 to continue. The key procedure tabs over to let you type the extended total.

22. Type "$600.00" and then hold down CTRL and press F6 to continue. Next, the key procedure asks if you wish to stop or continue the procedure. You want to add another invoice item, so you type "C" for "continue."

23. Type "C" to continue the procedure. The key procedure tabs over and waits for you to type the next quantity. Mary Blume also bought two brake shoes at $15.00 each.

24. Type "2" and then hold down CTRL and press F6 to continue.

25. Type "Brake Shoes" and then hold down CTRL and press F6 to continue.

26. Type "$15.00" and then hold down CTRL and press F6 to continue.

27. Type "$30.00" and then hold down CTRL and press F6 to continue. The key procedure again asks if you wish to stop or continue the procedure. You still want to add one more item, so you'll type "C" for "continue."

28. Type "C" to continue the procedure. The key procedure tabs over and waits for you to type the next quantity. Mary Blume also bought a radiator for $50.00.

29. Type "1" and then hold down CTRL and press F6 to continue.

30. Type "Used Radiator" and then hold down CTRL and press F6 to continue.

31. Type "$50.00" and then hold down CTRL and press F6 to continue.

32. Type "$50.00" and then hold down CTRL and press F6 to continue. The key procedure again asks if you wish to stop or continue the procedure. This time, you're finished, so you type "S" to stop the procedure.

33. Type "S". Because you've entered all the items for this invoice, you can now use the TOT key procedure to finish it.

34. Hold down CTRL and press F8.

35. Type "TOT" and press F10. The TOT key procedure draws a line and then adds up the extended total for you. The invoice is complete and should look like figure 14.2.

36. Press F10 to save the document.

Explanation

Before executing a key procedure, you must move the cursor on the screen where the key procedure is to begin. Your INV procedure, for instance, should always be started in a blank editing screen. A key procedure is actually just a sequence of keystrokes that runs MultiMate just as you do when typing at the keyboard. If you start a key procedure at the wrong place—the main menu, for example, when it's designed to begin at the editing screen—you may see some erratic results. It's just as if you sat down and typed random keystrokes and watched MultiMate go berserk.

To start key procedures, press CTRL F8 and specify the procedure's name. Sometimes other characters may appear on the line where the name is typed. You must space over them so that only the characters of the procedure's name appear. If an extra character appears on the name line, MultiMate won't find the desired key procedure. With the name specified, press F10; the key procedure takes control of the program.

While the key procedure is processing (that is, when it's not waiting for you to type information), you can cancel it by pressing ESC. If the key procedure reaches a pause, however, ESC will not cancel it. You will have to start the key procedure processing again (by pressing CTRL F6) and then try pressing ESC again.

During the execution of a key procedure, an "E" appears in the screen's bottom right corner. The "E" lets you know if the procedure has been completed. (Sometimes during a pause, you may think the procedure has stopped when it actually hasn't.) As long as the "E" is there, the current key procedure is not finished and you cannot execute a different one.

You can only use one key procedure at a time, and one key procedure can't execute another key procedure. For example, key procedure INV can't start key procedure TOT executing. (Sorry for those of you with complex hearts just dying to make interlocking key procedure masterpieces.)

Within these limits, key procedures can do anything you can do with MultiMate—and maybe better than you could do it.

A last word of advice about creating key procedures: start simple. Experiment with small editing procedures and try out making key procedures pause and using prompts. Make a procedure designed to repeat. Once you're familiar with how key procedures work, it's easy to create more complex ones.

If you're going to create a long procedure that involves complex tasks, first break down the key procedure into small units that perform one task. Once you have figured out how to create the individual tasks a key procedure is to perform, you can create a key procedure that does all of them in one sequence. Remember, you cannot edit a key procedure unless you use a special MultiMate program to do so. After ten minutes of creating a complex procedure, you don't want to discover that you've made a procedural mistake and have to start over.

To create a key procedure, you perform the steps shown in figure 14.3. To execute a key procedure, you perform the steps shown in figure 14.4.

SUMMARY

1. During editing, press Ctrl F5
   to initiate a key procedure.

2. Type the name of the procedure
   and press F10.

3. Perform the procedure as you
   normally would during editing.

   To create a pause in the procedure,
   press Ctrl F6.

   To create a prompt,
   press Ctrl F7.

4. When the procedure is completed,
   press Ctrl F5 to save it.

Figure 14.3
Creating a Key Procedure

1. With the cursor positioned in
   a document or on a menu or
   screen where the key procedure
   is to begin, press Ctrl F8.

2. Type the name of the key
   procedure and press F10.

3. If the procedure pauses for
   information, type the information
   and press Ctrl F6 to continue with
   the procedure. (For the first pause
   in a procedure you must type a
   "C" before you type the information.)

   If the procedure displays a prompt,
   type "C" to continue or "S" to stop
   the procedure.

Figure 14.4
Executing a Key
Procedure

Chapter 15

UNDER MULTIMATE'S SPELL

Preparation

> Your computer should be turned on and MultiMate's main menu should be on the screen. Your exercise disk should be in drive B and should contain the file called SPELL. (For hard disk users, the document should be on the default document drive, probably your C drive.) Refer to appendix H for instructions for creating the SPELL document.
>
> To perform the exercise, you must also have the dictionary disk ready for use. When you install MultiMate on your computer, you designate a drive (usually A) as the drive that will hold the dictionary disk. (Hard disk users may have transferred the dictionary to their hard disk, in which case the C drive would be the dictionary drive.) This exercise assumes that your A drive is the dictionary drive. To check which drive you must use, select "Other Utilities" from the main menu and then select "Edit Drive Defaults". The "Dictionary Drive" default can be changed to specify any drive you wish to use for the dictionary disk.

Human beings are divided into two basic categories: those who can spell and those who can't. Confess now, whose side are you on? Well, spelling may not be that important, but in a business letter it's everything.

MultiMate is an excellent speller. After you type a document, you can have MultiMate check the spelling of every word in it. MultiMate has a dictionary of over 80,000 words that it uses to check spelling. MultiMate will compare every word in a document against those in its dictionary and mark misspelled words in your text.

MultiMate can even correct misspelled words. Whether your document is a short letter or a long report, you can have MultiMate proofread it for basic misspellings and typographical errors. Although MultiMate can't catch all types of spelling errors, it can eliminate most simple spelling mistakes.

Checking a document's spelling falls into two phases. First, you spell-check the document. During spell-checking, MultiMate looks up words in its dictionary and marks words in your text that are possibly misspelled. You can spell-check a whole document at one time or spell-check small sections that probably hold questionable spellings. Once MultiMate has spell-checked the document, you can view the text on the editing screen. Any possible misspellings will blink on the screen.

After you've spell-checked text, you can spell-edit it. MultiMate provides a special function that will search out misspelled words that were marked and allow you to correct them. If a word is misspelled, MultiMate can provide a list of possible correct spellings. You can also have MultiMate replace the incorrectly spelled word with the correct spelling. Or, if your work uses a specialized vocabulary that isn't included in MultiMate's dictionary (law terminology, for example), you can add new words to MultiMate's dictionary. Thus, MultiMate can learn to check spelling for your specific types of documents.

As you spell-edit a document, MultiMate jumps through the text, finding misspellings and allowing you to change them easily. In this chapter, you'll spell-check and spell-edit a short text. Although not everyone may need this spelling feature, running MultiMate's spelling checker is one way of double checking your spelling.

CHECKING A DOCUMENT'S SPELLING

Objective: Spell-checking a Document from the Main Menu

Let's check the spelling of a short document named "SPELL" (see figure 15.1). You can spell-check an entire document, several pages of it, or smaller sections if you like. To start with, you'll try spell-checking an entire document.

You begin by putting the dictionary disk in the drive designated as the dictionary drive (usually the A drive). You then select the main menu's eighth option, "Spell Check a Document". You specify the name of the document to be checked. MultiMate then checks the document and marks possible misspellings in it. As it checks the document, it tells you how many words it has checked and how many are possible misspellings.

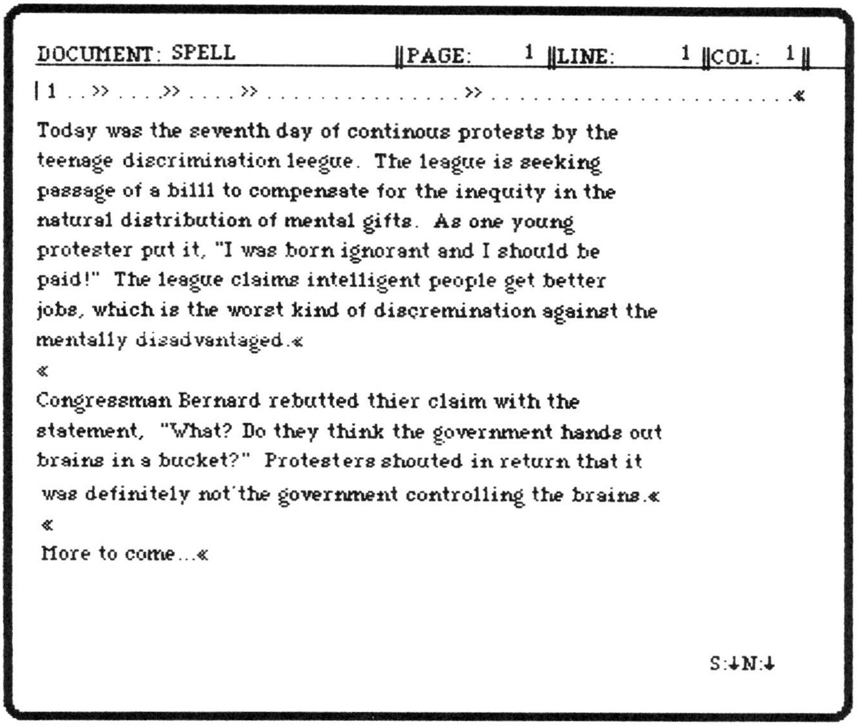

```
DOCUMENT: SPELL              ‖PAGE:    1 ‖LINE:      1 ‖COL:  1‖
│ 1 . .≫ . . . .≫ . . . .≫ . . . . . . . . . . . . . .≫ . . . . . . . . . . . . . . . . . . . . .≪
Today was the seventh day of continous protests by the
teenage discrimination leegue. The league is seeking
passage of a bill1 to compensate for the inequity in the
natural distribution of mental gifts. As one young
protester put it, "I was born ignorant and I should be
paid!" The league claims intelligent people get better
jobs, which is the worst kind of discremination against the
mentally disadvantaged.≪
≪
Congressman Bernard rebutted thier claim with the
statement, "What? Do they think the government hands out
brains in a bucket?" Protesters shouted in return that it
was definitely not'the government controlling the brains.≪
≪
More to come...≪


                                                    S:↓N:↓
```

Figure 15.1
Document to be
Spell-checked

To view possible misspellings after text has been spell-checked, you load the document as you normally do for editing.

Procedure

1. Type "1" and press ENTER to select "Edit an Old Document".

2. Type the document name "SPELL" and press ENTER. (Be sure the drive specification is correct.)

3. Press F10 to bypass the Document Summary screen.

4. Briefly examine the SPELL document. There are several spelling errors. Let's run the spelling-checker functions to find them all.

5. Press F10 to return to the main menu.

6. Place the dictionary disk in the A drive (or in the drive designated to hold this disk by your computer).

7. Type "8" and press ENTER to select "Spell Check a Document" from the main menu.

8. Type "SPELL" and press F10 at the Document Specification screen. (Make sure the "Drive" prompt designates the drive holding the

exercise disk.) After pressing F10, you see a prompt asking you to specify the pages to be checked. You can use the right or left arrow keys to move the cursor between the "Start" and "End" prompts to specify a sequence of pages to be checked. Because you want the entire document checked, you don't need to specify any pages.

9. Press F10. MultiMate starts checking the document. At the screen's bottom it displays the number of words it has checked and the number that are possible misspellings. Finally, the program will display a message saying that the operation is complete.

10. Press ESC to see the main menu. Don't remove the dictionary disk from the drive. Next, you want to see which words were misspelled, so you load the document for editing.

11. Type "1" and press ENTER to select "Edit an Old Document".

12. Type "SPELL" and press ENTER to specify the document name. (You can simply press ENTER, because the document's name is automatically displayed.)

13. Press F10 to bypass the Document Summary screen. The editing comes into view.

14. Read through the text and notice the words with blinking letters. Any word that is a possible misspelling has been marked this way. In the next exercise, you'll spell-edit this document to make spelling corrections.

Explanation

Spell-checking an entire document is simple. You insert the dictionary disk in the dictionary drive and then select "Spell Check a Document" from the main menu.

You can also spell-check the entire document from the editing screen as well. If you press ALT F8 during editing, a Document Specification screen immediately appears. Whether you start at the main menu or from the editing screen, the same Document Specification screen is displayed for you to complete. You specify a document name and press F10.

Next, MultiMate will ask which pages of a document should be checked. In a multi-paged document, you might want to check pages three through five, for example. You specify a beginning page number and the number of the last page to be checked. After specifying a range of pages, you press F10 to begin the spelling check.

MultiMate looks at every word in a document and checks its spelling. It may take MultiMate a minute to check several hundred words, which is fine for short documents. For long documents of thousands of words, however, you'll have to decide if spell-checking is worth the time MultiMate needs to check every word.

Any word that doesn't match an entry in MultiMate's dictionary is marked as a possible misspelling. A word is marked by making the initial letter blink. When you call a spell-checked document to the editing screen, possible misspellings stand out and are easy to find. You might simply review them and make corrections as you normally edit text. You can also correct misspellings systematically using MultiMate's spell-editing features, which you'll try out next.

Having a computer check your text doesn't insure that all the errors are correctly identified. Words that are not in MultiMate's dictionary (foreign words, Latin phrases, proper names, or specialized terminology, for example) may be marked as incorrect even if they're spelled correctly. MultiMate assumes that any word not in its dictionary is misspelled. (Fortunately, you can add words to the dictionary, as will be explained later.)

MultiMate may miss certain types of typographical errors as well. One example is a typographical error that produces a correctly spelled word. If you meant to type "at" and accidentally typed "fat", MultiMate will not catch this mistake. Its computerized mind simply sees "fat" as spelled correctly. Although grammatically the sentence might be obviously incorrect, MultiMate simply accepts "fat" as the word you meant to use.

Next you'll see how MultiMate can help you automatically make spelling corrections with its spell-edit feature.

Spell-checking the SPELL document marked six words as possible misspellings. Now you'll spell-edit the document to make the necessary corrections.

MAKING SPELLING CORRECTIONS

Objective: Using MultiMate's Spell-Edit Function

To spell-edit, you make sure the dictionary disk is in the dictionary drive. You also position the cursor where you want MultiMate to start the editing procedure. To begin spell-editing, hold down ALT and press F10. MultiMate will find the first marked word and display five options on the screen, as shown in figure 15.2.

If the marked word is spelled correctly but just isn't part of the MultiMate dictionary, you can add it to the dictionary by typing a zero.

If you're not sure about the located word and just want to skip it for now, you can type "1" to continue spell-editing with the next marked word.

If the word is correctly spelled and you don't want to add it to the dictionary (if, for instance, it's a person's name), you can type "2" to unmark the word and continue spell-editing.

If you wish to see a list of possible correct spellings for a word,

DOCUMENT: SPELL ‖PAGE: 1 ‖LINE: 1 ‖COL: 1‖

| 1 . . >> . . . >> . . . . >> . . . . >> . . . .«

Today was the seventh day of continous protests by the
teenage discrimination leegue. The league is seeking
passage of a billl to compensate for the inequity in the
natural distribution of mental gifts. As one young
protester put it, "I was born ignorant and I should be
paid!" The league claims intelligent people get better
jobs, which is the worst kind of discremination against the
mentally disadvantaged.«
«
Congressman Bernard rebutted thier claim with the
statement, "What? Do they think the government hands out
brains in a bucket?" Protesters shouted in return that it
was definitely not the government controlling the brains.«
«
More to come...«

Please enter desired function

0) Add this word to the Custom Dictionary
1) Ignore this place mark and find the next mark
2) Clear this place mark and find the next mark
3) Find a list of possible correct spellings
Esc) End Spell Edit and resume Document Edit S:↓N:↓

Figure 15.2
Spell-edit Options

type "3". MultiMate checks the dictionary and displays a list of correctly spelled words. You can select one of the spellings and MultiMate will automatically correct the word marked in the text.

To stop spell-editing, press ESC.

Try out a few of these options on the SPELL document.

Procedure

1. With the SPELL document on the screen, move the cursor to line 1, column 1 (if it isn't already there). Your dictionary disk should still be in the dictionary drive.

2. To initiate the spell-edit procedure, hold down ALT and press F10. MultiMate locates the first marked word ("continous") and displays the five options on screen.

3. Type "3" to ask MultiMate to display a list of possible spellings. There's a short pause as MultiMate tries to guess the word you meant to spell. It picks out a list of up to nine possibilities and then numbers and displays them for you. The first choice is usually the one you want.

4. Type the number corresponding to the correct spelling choice (continuous). MultiMate automatically replaces the marked word with the correct spelling. You can then press any key to continue the spell-edit process, or press ESC to stop it.

5. Press the space bar to continue spell-editing. MultiMate locates the next marked word, "leegue". Because you probably know the correct spelling, you might press ESC twice to simply retype the word. If you're feeling lazy, you can also ask MultiMate to compose a list of possible spellings again.

6. Type "3" to be lazy. Look at the new list. Notice that the first choice is the correct spelling. Notice also how different the other possible spellings are. MultiMate can't be sure how many letters are missing or misused, so it makes its best guess, sometimes with funny results. (How would the sentence read if you selected number 8?)

7. Type the number corresponding to the correct spelling choice (league), and press the space bar. MultiMate locates the word "billl". With this obvious typographical error, you want to simply delete a letter, so you need to stop the spell-edit procedure temporarily.

8. Press ESC. (You may have to press it twice. MultiMate asks you to replace disks. Don't replace disks, just press ESCAPE here.)

9. Delete one "l" from the word "bill" and retype the "b" so that it is no longer blinking. You retype the "b" to unmark the word.

10. Hold down ALT and press F10 to continue the spell-edit process. The next word located is "discremination". If this were a correctly spelled legal or foreign term, you might want to add it to the dictionary by typing a zero. The word is misspelled, however, so you should correct it.

11. Type "3". When the list of spellings appears, you select the correct spelling (if it appears).

12. Type the number corresponding to the correct spelling choice (discrimination). MultiMate next located the name "Bernard". This name is correctly spelled. You want to simply unmark the word and leave it as is.

13. Type "2" to unmark a word and continue spell-editing. MultiMate locates the next marked word "thier". Notice that the first letter of "Bernard" is no longer blinking. Because the word "thier" is a simple transposition of two letters, you'll probably want to just retype the word.

14. Press ESC and retype "thier" as "their". That takes care of the spelling errors.

15. Hold down ALT and press F10. MultiMate will search ahead through the rest of the document (not long, in this case), looking for marked words. When it reaches the document's end, you'll see a message saying that no more marked words can be found.

16. Press the space bar. You can now continue editing the document if you wish. Next you'll learn how to check specific sections of a document.

Explanation

Once your misspellings are blinking on the screen at you, Multi-Mate's spell-edit function can quickly get them out of sight.

You must keep the dictionary disk in the dictionary drive to activate the spell-edit function. When you start the spell-edit procedure, MultiMate first searches ahead from the cursor position for the next marked word. Make sure the cursor is positioned far enough toward the document's beginning that all marked words will be located. After positioning the cursor, you hold down ALT and press F10 to begin spell-editing.

Once a marked word is located, you decide what to do about it. Unusual words that are marked but that are correctly spelled can be added to MultiMate's dictionary. You select "Add this word to the Custom Dictionary" from the five options displayed. The next time you spell-check a document, the word added to the dictionary will not be marked as misspelled in the text. Adding words to the dictionary is helpful if you use specialized vocabulary. Customizing the dictionary makes spell-editing more efficient, because fewer correctly spelled words are needlessly marked.

If a marked word is located and you can't decide what to do about it, you can skip it for the time being by selecting the option "Ignore this place mark and find the next mark". MultiMate skips ahead, leaving the word marked so that you can find it later. When you want to find the word again, you can either restart the spell-edit procedure, or press CTRL and F1 to search for the marked word.

You'll find that MultiMate sometimes marks people's names, numbers, or letters that stand alone, as in outline headings. If these marked words or characters are spelled correctly, you can simply unmark them and continue spell-editing. To unmark a word, select the "Clear this place mark and find the next mark" option.

Looking up words in a dictionary can be an irksome chore. Fortunately, MultiMate can look them up for you. MultiMate will examine its disk dictionary and show you a list of spellings. Because the program can't be sure how badly you spelled the word, it makes an educated guess about the word you meant to use.

Based on the guess, it displays a list of correct spellings. MultiMate's list almost always has the correct spelling listed as number one among the possible choices. Each choice is numbered. You select your choice by typing a number; that choice then replaces the misspelled word in the text.

MultiMate does a good job of replacing misspelled words. If the marked word is underlined, the correction is underlined in the text as well. If the marked word uses capitals, the correction uses the same capitalization. Likewise, if the word ends in a period, the correction has a period as well. Marked words that have trailing punctuation such as commas or semicolons, however, may lose the punctuation when they are replaced.

Sometimes you'll spot misspellings right away and you won't want to create a list of possible spellings. You can simply edit the misspelled word by pressing ESC twice and then retyping the word. To stop the word from blinking, just type the initial letter over again.

As you stop and start the spell-edit procedure, MultiMate often suggests that you remove the dictionary disk and replace it with the system disk. If you're just editing a document, you can ignore the prompts telling you to switch disks and leave the dictionary disk in the drive. The MultiMate program can basically run without the system disk in the drive all the time. You must, however, insert the system disk in the drive when you want to edit another document or print any document. If you forget to replace the system disk in the drive, the program will remind you and no harm will be done, so don't be afraid to save yourself from having to switch the dictionary disk in and out of the drive as the program instructs.

Next, you'll learn how you can spell-check specific portions of a document.

CHECKING SPELLING AS YOU EDIT

Objective: Spell-checking Specific Portions of Text

When you spot a suspect word in your text, you can check its spelling right away. You might spell-check a single word, a sentence, a paragraph, or larger sections of text. With the dictionary disk in the dictionary drive, position the cursor before the text containing the word(s) about which you're uncertain. Hold down CTRL and press F10 to initiate a spelling check.

Next, you mark the amount of text you want checked. You use the same text-marking functions as you do to copy, delete, or move sections of text. Once the cursor is at the end of the text that you want checked, press CTRL F10 again and MultiMate checks the section's spelling. Words that don't match MultiMate's dictionary are marked and set blinking.

You can then take care of incorrect spellings by hand or by using

MultiMate's spell-editing feature.

Try misspelling a few words in the SPELL document (see figure 15.3) and then checking the spelling a paragraph at a time.

Procedure

1. Move the cursor to line 4, column 29, under the "a" in "mental".

2. Type an "o" to replace the "a" and create a misspelling.

3. Move the cursor to line 12, column 1.

4. Press the minus key to delete the "b" in "brains". Next you want to check the spelling of the first paragraph, so you begin by moving the cursor to the screen's top.

5. Press HOME.

6. To initiate the spelling check, hold down CTRL and press F10. The message "Check What?" appears at the screen's top right corner. MultiMate is waiting for you to mark the text to be checked.

7. Press ENTER to mark the entire paragraph. (Your dictionary disk

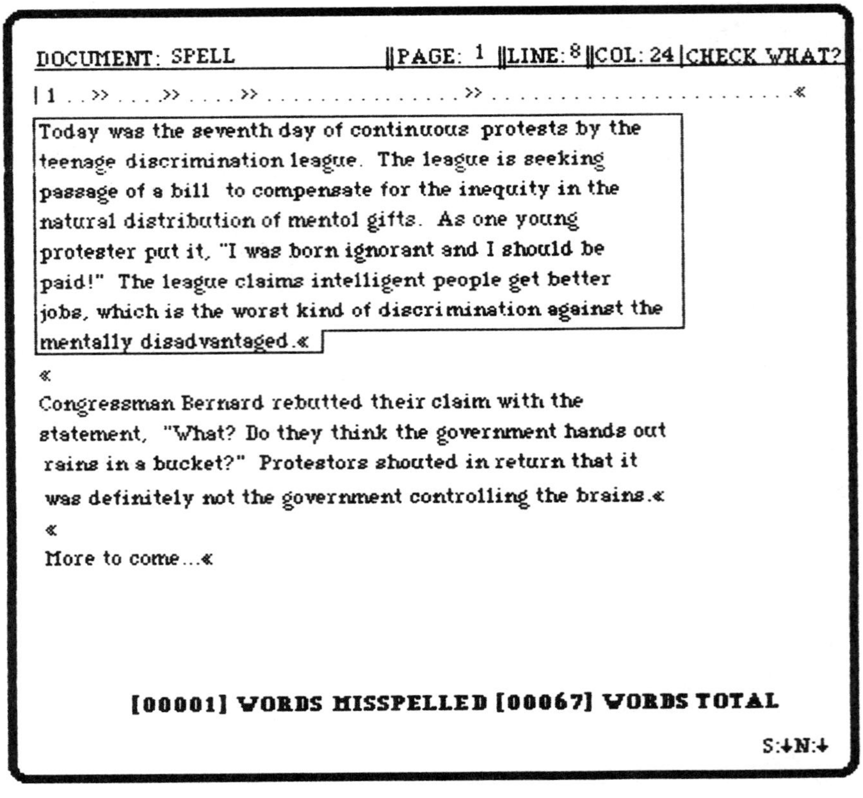

```
DOCUMENT: SPELL              ||PAGE: 1 ||LINE: 8 ||COL: 24 |CHECK WHAT?

| 1 . . >> . . . >> . . . . >> . . . . . . . . . . . . . >> . . . . . . . . . . . . . . . . . . . .«

Today was the seventh day of continuous protests by the
teenage discrimination league.  The league is seeking
passage of a bill  to compensate for the inequity in the
natural distribution of mentol gifts.  As one young
protester put it, "I was born ignorant and I should be
paid!"  The league claims intelligent people get better
jobs, which is the worst kind of discrimination against the
mentally disadvantaged.«

«
Congressman Bernard rebutted their claim with the
statement, "What? Do they think the government hands out
rains in a bucket?" Protestors shouted in return that it
was definitely not the government controlling the brains.«
«
More to come...«




          [00001] WORDS MISSPELLED [00067] WORDS TOTAL

                                                      S:↓N:↓
```

Figure 15.3
Spell-checking One
Paragraph

should still be in the dictionary drive.)

8. Hold down CTRL and press F10 to begin the check. MultiMate checks every word in the first paragraph. Sure enough, ''mentol'' is marked and blinking.

9. To check the second paragraph, move the cursor to line 10, column 1.

10. Hold down CTRL and press F10 to begin the spell-check procedure.

11. Press ENTER to move the cursor to the end of the paragraph. (You can mark as little or as much of the text as you like.)

12. Hold down CTRL and press F10. MultiMate checks the second paragraph. Unfortunately, MultiMate didn't find the misspelling this time. Why not? Because ''rains'' is a correctly spelled word by itself, and MultiMate didn't know you meant to use a different word. You've got to watch out for this type of misspelling.

13. Press F10 to save the document.

Explanation

Because spell-checking an entire document can take a long time, it's sometimes good to check just selected sections of text. You can home in on single words or text sections that you suspect harbor a few misspellings.

Checking a text section basically requires you to mark it just as you might if you wanted to copy or delete it. Begin by pressing CTRL F10; then mark the text. You can simply move the cursor ahead using the cursor-movement keys, or you can use MultiMate's search-ahead capability.

Once the text is marked, press CTRL F10 to initiate the actual checking process. When the check is finished, misspelled words appear blinking on the screen. You can then spell-edit them if you wish.

If you begrudge the time it takes to check an entire document, remember this spell-checking option. You may find it alleviates the need to suddenly cast around for a several-pound dictionary (often out of sight and out of reach). Although MultiMate can't catch all errors, as you saw in the last exercise, it can do the majority of your proofreading for you.

SUMMARY

To spell-check an entire document, you perform the steps shown in Figure 15.4. To make spelling corrections, you can use MultiMate's spell-editing function, as illlustrated in figure 15.5. You can also check specific sections of text. This procedure is illustrated in figure 15.6.

> 1. At the main menu, select "Spell Check a Document."
>
> 2. Type the name of the document to be checked and press F10.
>
> 3. Specify the page to start the spell-check on and press ENTER.
>
> 4. Specify the last page of the document to be spell-checked and press F10.
>
> 5. Wait until the spell-check process is completed and press Esc until the main menu appears.
>
> 6. Spell-edit the document.

Figure 15.4
Spell-checking an Entire
Document

> 1. Position the cursor in the document before the text to be spell-edited.
>
> 2. Press Alt F10 to initiate the spell-editing process.
>
> 3. When MultiMate locates a word marked during the spell-check process, select one of the five spell-editing options.
>
> 4. Continue spell-editing until all marked words have been processed.
>
> 5. Press Esc to end the spell-editing procedure.

Figure 15.5
Spell-editing Procedure

1. During editing, position the cursor in front of the text to be checked.

2. Press Ctrl F10 to initiate the spell-checking process.

3. Mark the amount of text to be checked by moving the cursor to the end of the text.

4. Press Ctrl F10.

5. When the spell-checking process is completed, press Esc until MultiMate is in editing mode again.

6. Spell-edit the text.

Figure 15.6
Spell-checking a Section of Text

Chapter 16

MULTIMATE
AND MORE!

Everyone likes short cuts. This chapter looks at some word-processing features that can help speed text editing. Now that you've been through the basics with MultiMate, you're ready to learn a few details that may come in handy.

ON YOUR MARK!

Marking text is one of the most common editing tasks you perform. Whether deleting, copying, moving, or spell-checking text, you must mark the text block to be affected. You've learned to mark text with cursor-movement keys and to use the search-ahead capability. MultiMate also provides some special keys that can quickly mark words, horizontal lines, sentences, and paragraphs.

Normally, when you mark a word, sentence, or paragraph, you must move the cursor to the beginning of the text to be marked. Moving the cursor is not always necessary, however. You can instantly mark text by pressing a function key combination, even if the cursor is in the middle or at the end of the text.

After initiating a procedure that requires you to mark text, you can press any of the following keys to mark a specific increment of text:

Function Key	Purpose
ALT F5	Marks the word in which the cursor is located.
ALT F6	Marks the line (across the screen) in which the cursor is located.

| ALT F7 | Marks the sentence in which the cursor is located. |
| ALT F8 | Marks the paragraph in which the cursor is located. |

Again, you can conveniently mark text this way without first moving the cursor to the text's beginning. For example, with the cursor in the middle of a paragraph, you can press ALT F8 to mark the entire surrounding paragraph all at once. In many instances, this method of marking text will be faster than the search-ahead method.

When you stop editing a document, you often return to the main menu and select another option. When you're ready to print a document, for example, you press F10 to save the document, which returns the main menu to screen. You select the main menu's "Print Document Utility" option (number 3) and specify the document's name; finally, the print menu appears. During editing, you can simultaneously save a document and make a main-menu selection. You can save yourself time by jumping directly from the editing screen to the print menu, for example.

JUMP!

With the editing screen in view, you can press ALT and 3, and the print menu will automatically come to view, ready to print the document on which you were working.

Here's a list of the keys used to make main-menu selections during editing:

Key Combination	Main-menu Selection
ALT 1	"Edit an Old Document"
ALT 2	"Create a New Document"
ALT 3	"Print Document Utility"
ALT 4	"Printer Control Utilities"
ALT 5	"Merge Print Utility"
ALT 6	"Document Handling Utilities"
ALT 7	"Other Utilities"
ALT 8	"Spell Check a Document"
ALT 9	"Return to DOS"

Notice that the keys correspond to the menu option—select ALT 1 to select the first option, ALT 2 to select the second, and so on. After word processing with MultiMate for a while, you'll know the main menu by heart and will find it convenient to jump directly from the editing screen into another menu option. Next time you finish editing a document and want to print it, try pressing ALT 3 at the editing screen. You'll appreciate the shortcut.

MARKING YOUR PLACE

As you edit, you sometimes need to jump the cursor to a distant corner of a document and then return to your original location. MultiMate allows you to use an electronic placemark to mark and return to where you were working. If you set a place mark at the desired point in a document, MultiMate will home the cursor back to it with just the press of a key or two.

The keys you use are ALT F1 (to set a place mark) and CTRL F1 (to home the cursor to the place mark).

Suppose you are on page 15 of a document and you need to check something on the first page and immediately return to page 15. First you press ALT F1 to mark your place on page 15. The cursor's current position will be marked (if the cursor is on a letter or number character, the character will begin to blink). You move the cursor to the first page. When you are done with page 1, press CTRL F1 and MultiMate will search for your place mark. After a few moments (depending on how far Multimate has to search), you'll find that the cursor has returned to the place mark's location.

You can set as many place marks in text as you wish. If you have a question or problem that you need to resolve later, you might mark the text position and use the place mark to find your place when you have an answer. MultiMate can only search forward through a document, however. It can't search for a place mark moving from the last to the first page.

COLUMN RIGHT!

Moving the cursor through columns of numbers can be jerky business. As you use the right or left arrow keys, the cursor jumps from column to column and you've often got to adjust the cursor position to line up on numbers for editing. MultiMate provides a handy Go To Tab function to help you move the cursor across tabbed columns.

Press ALT T to move the cursor to the first character after the next tab stop. After pressing ALT T, you'll see the cursor jump right and line up on the first character after the next tab stop. This tab function works with decimal tabs, indent markers, and normal tab stops. If you routinely work with columnar text, or intricately indented documents, try this Go To Tab function right away.

With word processing, you can run into some problems you probably never faced with a typewriter. In two cases, the culprit is the word processor's word-wrap feature. Word wrap can cause text to reposition on the screen inappropriately.

If you like to adjust the look of your text by hyphenating words, word wrap will occasionally cause problems. Suppose you hyphenate a word somewhere in a paragraph to make the text line up neatly between margins. Then it turns out that you have to erase or insert a word or two at the beginning of the paragraph. Word wrap will automatically readjust the paragraph, moving words between lines, and hyphenated words may move out of position. The hyphenated word now inappropriately appears at the beginning or middle of a line. You must find the hyphenated word and delete the hyphen. If you've done a lot of hyphenation, that can cause you considerable work.

MultiMate's answer is to use a "soft" hyphen. A "soft" hyphen is different from the normal hyphen in that if the word moves from the end of the line, the hyphen will disappear and not be printed. You don't have to worry about deleting hyphens if hyphenated words move out of position at the end of a line. To insert a "soft" hyphen, use SHIFT F7.

Suppose you have typed a sentence that looks like this:

The fifteen-ton truck loaded with garbage that
transportation authorities had proclaimed safe caught
fire.

Notice the gap after the word "that" in the first line. You want to hyphenate the word "transportation" on the line below to fill up part of this gap. You could simply type a normal hyphen and a space to hyphenate "transportation" as you would on a typewriter. Using a soft hyphen is a better idea, however, because you may edit this text later and "transportation" might move.

To divide "transportation" with a soft hyphen, you'd move the cursor under the "p" and press SHIFT F7. A soft hyphen screen marker would appear and the "trans" of "transportation" would jump up to the end of the first line. If later editing changed the position of the hyphenated word, the screen marker would disappear and "transportation" would print without a hyphen.

Another word-wrap problem can occur when MultiMate moves words between lines too soon. For example, look at the date in the following sentence:

The man jumped from the building at exactly noon July 25,
1984.

The date "July 25, 1984" is divided inappropriately between lines.

It's divided this way because MultiMate sees the date as three words (remember that a word to MultiMate is any group of characters followed by a space): "July", "25", and "1984". To avoid this type of inappropriate division, you can use a "hard" space. A hard space tells Multimate that a group of characters, such as this date, is not to be divided across lines. To keep the date from dividing improperly, you'd have to use a hard space after "July" and after "25,".

To insert a hard space, press ALT·S.

The same sentence with hard spaces would look as follows:

The man jumped from the building at exactly noon
July 25, 1984.

Whenever you need to keep a group of characters together on one line, use hard spaces.

A PAUSE IN PRINTING

Some printers enable you to use different size fonts and character styles simply by changing the print element. You might create professional-looking text, for instance, that prints quotations in a different font for contrast.

Changing print elements, however, usually requires you to stop the printer, pull one element off, replace it with another, and continue printing. If you foresee that you'll be switching print elements this way, you can set up documents to pause automatically during printing when a font change is required. You pause the printer by placing a special pause screen marker in the text.

To insert a printing pause in a document, press ALT P. After changing the print element, press ESC to continue printing. Pausing the printer this way also enables you to switch paper types or make printing adjustments as text is printed.

DISASTER STRIKES!

Someday something may happen to one of your documents. That "something", of course, is the unknown. Computers don't handle the unexpected very well, which can result in the ruin of a valuable document. A document might mysteriously lose pages or have unusual characters sprinkled through it, or the program might display error messages saying that MultiMate can't read the document from disk. It may sound a little fatalistic, but this happens to everyone who uses word processors a good deal.

MultiMate has provided you with a "last chance". If disaster strikes a needed document, you can run a special program to recover damaged documents. The Recover utility is supplied with the MultiMate utilities disk. After inserting the MultiMate utility disk in drive A, access the utilities by typing "util". A menu will appear that enables you to access the Recover utility.

After running the Recover utility, you may find that a good percentage of the document, perhaps even the entire document, can be used again. You should read about this valuable utility in the reference manual. It can get you out of tough scrapes when disaster looks total.

Because these days there are as many kinds of computers as cars in a used car lot, you may occasionally want to pass a MultiMate document to another computer different from your own. Or you might need to edit a document produced by a different word processor. Other word-processing programs are usually unable to understand MultiMate documents and vice versa. To exchange documents between MultiMate and different programs, you must convert them with a conversion utility also found on the utility disk.

PASSING THE GOOD WORD ALONG

The file-conversion program enables you to convert MultiMate documents to ASCII files. Most common computers and word-processing programs can use ASCII files. The conversion program also converts ASCII files into MultiMate documents, so you might use MultiMate to process text from other programs.

To incorporate figures from spreadsheet programs into your text documents, MultiMate can also convert spreadsheet files (DIF files) into ones MultiMate can process. This utility also enables you to convert files into a number of other formats that are used with large mainframe computers and networked computer systems.

Be sure to read about this utility if you expect ever to be exchanging documents between programs or noncompatible computers.

You may have noticed that your computer's disk drives turn on for several seconds each time you change pages with MultiMate. MultiMate is saving the old page and reading a new one from disk. If your computer has a hard disk, this disk accessing is fast and causes only a short delay. If your computer uses floppy disks, however, you may find MultiMate's constant turning on and off of the disk drives irritatingly slow.

SPEEDING UP MULTIMATE

You can speed up MultiMate's disk accessing as much as ten times. To do that, your computer must have a large memory capacity, probably more than 320K, and you must purchase a program called a disk emulator (also known as a RAM disk).

A lot of time is lost as MultiMate turns a mechanical floppy disk on and off. A disk-emulator program creates an electronic disk drive in your computer's memory that works many times faster than a mechanical disk. If your computer has 512K memory, for example, you can use a disk-emulator program to make a portion of the memory, say 160K of it, magically act as if it were an unseen disk drive.

Instead of having MultiMate store your documents on a mechanical disk drive, you can have MultiMate record documents on the electronic drive.

What's the result? Information is recorded on the electronic disk almost instantly. You can switch between two different pages as fast as you can press keys. Searches speed through an entire document without waiting for floppy disk drives to slowly read pages into memory. The speed of many editing procedures is increased considerably (perhaps five to ten times). The long delays associated with disk accessing are almost eliminated.

Many disk-emulator programs are available on the market. You might check with local computer user's groups, because they often have public-domain emulator programs available for free or for a negligible fee. If MultiMate seems too slow on your floppy disk system and if you have a good deal of memory in your computer, you should look into disk-emulator programs.

Disk-emulator programs have one drawback, however. When you use one, MultiMate keeps all your text in memory. If the power accidentally fails, you lose all the documents recorded on the electronic disk. *When you are using a disk-emulator program, you must copy the contents of the electronic disk onto a floppy disk regularly for safekeeping.* Until information is relayed from the electronic disk to a floppy disk, it's at risk and you could lose it.

Using an electronic disk is a blessing. You'll be surprised at how it increases your editing speed. You must simply remember to transfer the electronic disk's contents to a floppy disk from time to time. You can actually create key procedures that make the transfer automatically.

If you have a system with two floppy disks, inquire at a local computer store or computer user's group about a disk-emulation program. If you have a hard disk or use a network of computers linked to a central computer system, you needn't worry about using an emulator, because the disk-accessing speed will probably not improve greatly.

MOUSING AROUND

Moving the cursor about the screen is an almost ceaseless activity in word processing. Developers recently introduced a device, called a *mouse,* that is designed to facilitate cursor movement.

A mouse is a hand-held gadget that you attach to your computer with a cable. Electronic mice are about the size of a cigarette box and generally have a button or two on the side (see figure 16.1). By moving the mouse across a flat surface, you direct the cursor around the screen. Moving the cursor is a little like sketching with a pencil

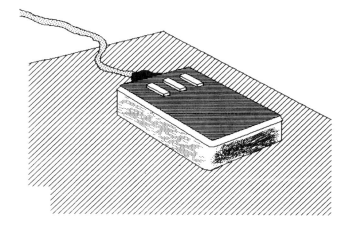

Figure 16.1
Mouse Pointing Device

on a pad of paper—the cursor moves in the same direction that you move the mouse.

Some people prefer using a mouse for word processing, others don't. One of the great advantages of a mouse is that you can move the cursor more directly to the place you wish to edit, without having to press complex sequences of keys. Moving the cursor with a mouse can be similar to pointing with your finger, whereas moving the cursor up, down, left, and right with cursor keys is a little like using an Etch-a-Sketch. With some mouse systems, you can also make menu selections quickly and easily. One mouse, developed by Mouse Systems, works with MultiMate and provides a system of pop-up menus for editing.

Pop-up menus are menus that suddenly appear on the editing screen and that are usually about the size of an open match book. The menus allow you to easily select editing functions that you might otherwise have to press function keys to perform. Because MultiMate provides you with a great many editing functions and function key combinations to remember, using a mouse and pop-up menus helps you avoid large amounts of memorizing.

Pop-up menus appear on screen, you make a selection, and then they disappear again. You never lose sight of the editing screen's text. Once they become proficient at directing the cursor with the mouse, many people prefer using mice over editing solely with a keyboard.

If you're interested in using a mouse with MultiMate, you might get a demonstration from your local computer dealer. The Mouse Systems mouse, which works with numerous spreadsheet and word-processing programs, has a special menu system designed for

MultiMate. Not all mouse devices work with MultiMate, so be sure to check.

Some people don't like to use mice for word processing. You're required to take your hand entirely off the keyboard during editing, which can be awkward and cause delay. Also, editing text often requires you to make fine adjustments in cursor movement (you often have to move the cursor letter by letter, for example), and that can be difficult with a mouse. Before investing in a mouse, be sure to try one out to get the feel of it.

MULTIMATE AND YOU

Learning to use a word processor is a complicated task and an initially irritating one. With so many functions to learn, so many key combinations to press, it takes some study and practice to get proficient at editing. Invariably, however, those who get to know MultiMate just growl when someone suggests that they use a typewriter.

One hint to reduce initial frustrations as you leave this book to "strike out" on your own: don't start using MultiMate for serious work, work that needs to be completed by a certain deadline, for example, before you feel confident about basic editing procedures. A good deal of learning MultiMate will be done as you work on real text that is valuable to you, but don't get yourself in a situation in which you must do two complex things at the same time: learn to word process and do your normal work.

Novices sometimes jump into difficult word-processing projects too soon. They end up frequently referring to manuals to remember which keys to press and which procedures to follow, and they make mistakes, all under the time pressure of their normal work. Give yourself a break; practice with MultiMate on documents that aren't important until you feel confident about applying MultiMate to your work. MultiMate is an excellent tool that will increase your productivity. Take the time you need to get used to it.

Appendix A
PRINTER DEFAULTS

Before you can use MultiMate to print a document, you must set printing parameters for such things as the top or left margin width that you desire. MultiMate enables you to store print parameters that you routinely use so that the program can automatically use them during printing (unless you specify otherwise). Such stored printing parameters are called *defaults*—they are the printing selections the program should use if you don't specify different ones.

To set up printing defaults, select the main menu's fourth option, "Print Control Utilities". A second menu will appear on screen, the print control utilities menu. From this menu, you select "Edit Printer Defaults" by typing "2" and pressing ENTER. A print menu like that shown in figure A.1 appears, displaying all the current printing defaults. Many defaults are listed, and their effect on printing is explained in chapter 3. To make a selection, you move the cursor to an option and type the desired number or letter. For now, you can simply set the parameters as you see them in figure A.1, with three exceptions.

The options marked "P(arallel)/S(erial)/L(ist)/A(uxiliary)/F(ile)", "Printer Action Table", and "Sheet Feeder Action Table" must contain information specific to your printing equipment. MultiMate must know if your printer is parallel or serial. (If you don't know, check your printer's reference manual to find out.) You should type a "P" (for "parallel") or "S" (for "serial") in this printing option.

MultiMate must also know which kind of printer you're using. Stored on the MultiMate system and utility disks are files that contain information for the most popular printers used today. These files are called "Printer Action Tables" in MultiMate's documentation, but are often known as *print drivers*. For MultiMate to properly communicate with a specific printer, you must use the driver supplied for it. For example, if you have an Epson printer, you must tell MultiMate to use the driver named "Epson." You specify the driver you want to use by typing the driver's name (for example, EPSON) at the "Printer Action Table" option.

A comprehensive list of driver names appears in the MultiMate *Reference Manual*. Look up the driver for your printer and type the driver's name (called a PAT file by the MultiMate documentation) in the option. You must also copy the driver to your system disk, if you haven't already. Then when you tell MultiMate to print a document, it will find the print-driver information stored on the system disk and be able to run your printer.

If you are using a sheet-feeder device, you must tell MultiMate the kind of sheet feeder you use. In the option "Sheet Feeder Action Table", you specify the driver that has been supplied for your feeder. Again, sheet-feeder drivers have been supplied on the utility disk and you should refer to the MultiMate *Reference Manual* to find out which driver is used for your device. The sheet feeder driver should also be copied to the system disk, if you haven't done so already. If you aren't using a sheet feeder, this option should remain blank.

Once your screen looks like figure A.1 (with the exceptions pointed out above), press F10 twice to store your printing defaults on disk and return to the main menu. From then on MultiMate will use your selections during printing. Before printing a document, MultiMate always gives you a chance to change any of these defaults, so you can still print documents using any parameters you wish. Your default selections will simply save you time by setting up your most commonly used printing options automatically.

```
                    MODIFY PRINTER DEFAULTS

Start print at page number    001    Lines per inch: 6 / 8            6
Stop print after page number  999    Justification: N / Y / M(icro)   N
Left margin                   010    Proportional Spacing: N / Y      N
Top margin                    000    Char translate/width table    _____
Pause between pages: N / Y      N    Header/footer first page number  001
Draft print: N / Y              N    Number of original copies        001
Default pitch (4=10 cpi)        4    Document page length             066
Printer Action Table Your Printer    Sheet Feeder Action Table Your Feeder
Sheet Feeder Bin Numbers (0/1/2/3): First page: 0 Middle: 0 Last page: 0
P(arallel) / S(erial) / L(ist) / A(uxiliary) / F(ile)                  ?
                                     Device Number                    001

Print document summary screen: N/Y N Print printer parameters:    N/Y N
Background / Foreground:     B/F B Remove queue entry when done:Y/N Y


Press F1 for Printers, F2 for Sheet Feeders - only the first 16 are displayed
      Press F10 to Continue,  Press ESC to Abort                  S:↓ N:↓
```

Figure A.1
MultiMate's Modify Printer Defaults Menu

Appendix B
CREATING BETTER

You are going to create a two-page document called BETTER that will be used in the exercises in chapter 5. The text for this document is shown in figures B.1 and 5.5.

To create the BETTER document, follow these steps:

1. Select "Create a New Document" from the main menu by typing "2" and pressing ENTER.

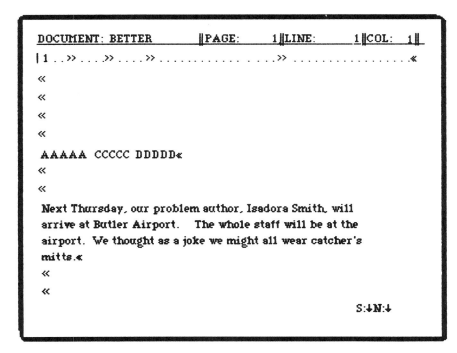

Figure B.1
Page 1 of BETTER Document

2. Type "BETTER" and press ENTER to name the document.

3. Press F10 twice to display the editing screen.

4. Press F9. The cursor jumps into the format line.

5. Backspace and type a "1" for single spacing at the far left of the format line.

6. Press the space bar three times and press TAB to set a tab marker at column 5.

7. Press the space bar four times and press TAB to set a tab marker at column 10.

8. Press the space bar four times and press TAB to set a tab marker at column 15.

9. Hold down the space bar until the cursor moves to column 42 and press TAB.

10. Hold down the space bar until the cursor moves to column 60 and press ENTER to set the right margin at 60.

11. Press F9 to finish editing the format line.

12. Press ENTER four times and type the row of letters as seen on line 5 of figure B.1.

13. Press ENTER until the cursor is on line 8 and type the paragraph you see in figure B.1. Remember to use word wrap and don't press ENTER to end each line of the paragraph.

14. Press ENTER three times to move the cursor down to line 16.

15. Press F2 once (don't hold it down) to create page 2.

16. Type the information shown in figure 5.5. (Remember, where you see a "≪", it means press ENTER, and where you see a "≫", it means press the TAB key.

17. Press F10 to save the document once you have finished typing page 2.

Appendix C
CREATING COPY

You are going to create a three-page document called COPY that will be used in the exercises in chapter 6. To create this document, follow the instructions below:

1. Select "Create a New Document" from the main menu by typing "2" and pressing ENTER.

2. Type "COPY" and press ENTER to name the document.

3. Press F10 twice to display the editing screen.

4. Press F9. The cursor jumps into the format line.

5. Backspace and type a "1" for single spacing at the far left of the format line.

6. Hold down the space bar until the cursor is on column 24 and then press TAB to set a tab marker.

7. Hold down the space bar until the cursor moves to column 60 and press ENTER to set the right margin at 60.

8. Press F9 to finish editing the format line.

9. Type the information shown in figure C.1.

10. After completing the information shown in figure C.1, move the cursor to the bottom of the page (as far as it will go) and press F2 to create the second page.

11. On the second page, type the information shown in figure C.2.

12. After completing the information in figure C.2, move the cursor to the bottom of the page (as far as it will go) and press F2 to create a third page.

13. On the third page, type the information shown in figure C.3. Remember to press the ENTER key four times to create four blank lines below the address.

14. Press F10 to save the document.

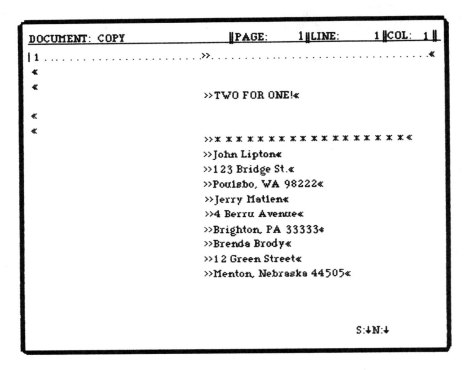

Figure C.1
Page 1 of COPY
Document

```
DOCUMENT: COPY            ‖PAGE:    2‖LINE:    1‖COL:  1‖
|1 . . . . . . . . . . . . . . . . .≫. . . . . . . . . . . . . . . . . . . . . .≪

 ≪
 ≪
                    ≫AAAA CCCCC BBBBB≪
 ≪
 ≪
 ≪
2. This is the second instruction of the day.≪
 ≪
3. This is the third instruction.≪
 ≪
1. This is the first instruction.≪
 ≪                                          S:↓N:↓
```

Figure C.2
Page 2 of COPY
Document

```
DOCUMENT: COPY            ‖PAGE:    3‖LINE:    1‖COL:  1‖
|1 . . . . . . . . . . . . . . . . .≫. . . . . . . . . . . . . . . . . . . . . .≪
Jane Towny≪
111 8th Ave.≪
Salem, OR  96000≪
 ≪
 ≪
 ≪
 ≪



                                            S:↓N:↓
```

Figure C.3
Page 3 of COPY
Document

Appendix D
CREATING SEARCH

You are going to create a two-page document called SEARCH that will be used in the exercises in chapter 7. To create this document, follow the instructions below:

1. Select "Create a New Document" from the main menu by typing "2" and pressing ENTER.

2. Type "SEARCH" and press ENTER to name the document.

3. Press F10 twice to display the editing screen.

4. Press F9. The cursor jumps into the format line.

5. Backspace and type a "1" for single spacing at the far left of the format line.

6. Press the space bar three times and press TAB to set a tab marker at column 5.

7. Press the space bar four times and press TAB to set a tab marker at column 10.

8. Press the space bar four times and press TAB to set a tab marker at column 15.

9. Hold down the space bar until the cursor moves to column 36 and press TAB.

10. Hold down the space bar until the cursor moves to column 60 and press ENTER to set the right margin at 60.

11. Press F9 to finish editing the format line.

12. Type ten "x"s and press the space bar. Rather than type many rows of "x"s, as you see in figure 7.1, just copy the "x"s that

you've just typed until they fill the screen. You'll perform the same copy procedure seven times to create all the "x"s you need.

13. Press HOME, press F8, press END, and press F8 twice.

14. Press HOME, press F8, press END, and press F8 twice.

15. Press HOME, press F8, press END, and press F8 twice.

16. Press HOME, press F8, press END, and press F8 twice.

17. Press HOME, press F8, press END, and press F8 twice.

18. Press HOME, press F8, press END, and press F8 twice.

19. Press HOME, press F8, press END, and press F8 twice. The screen should be full of "x"s now. Actually, you have four rows of "x"s too many, so delete them now.

20. Press HOME, press DEL, move the cursor to line 4, column 55, and press DEL.

21. Type the words "boy" and "Boyer" as you see them in figure 7.1. Sometimes you will have to press the space bar before or after the word to erase an "x" to make the screen look like figure 7.1.

22. Press END and then press F2 to create page 2.

23. Type the information you see in figure D.1. Notice that you'll have to press the TAB key three times before you type each line.

24. When your second page looks like figure D.1, press F10 to save the document.

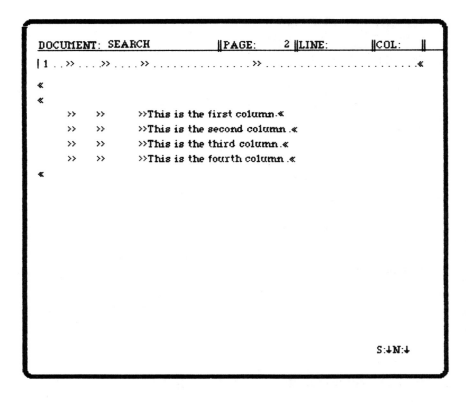

Figure D.1
Page 2 of SEARCH
Document

Appendix E
CREATING COLUMN

You are going to create a document called COLUMN that will be used in the exercises in chapter 9. To create this document, follow the instructions below:

1. Select "Create a New Document" from the main menu by typing "2" and pressing ENTER.

2. Type "COLUMN" and press ENTER to name the document.

3. Press F10 twice to display the editing screen.

4. Press F9. The cursor jumps into the format line.

5. Backspace and type a "1" for single spacing at the far left of the format line.

6. Press the space bar until the cursor arrives at column 24 and press TAB.

7. Press the space bar until the cursor arrives at column 36 and press TAB.

8. Press the space bar until the cursor arrives at column 48 and press TAB.

9. Press the space bar until the cursor arrives at column 60 and press TAB.

10. Hold down the space bar until the cursor moves to column 65 and press ENTER to set the right margin at 65.

11. Press F9 to finish editing the format line.

12. Type the text you see in figure E.1. Remember to press the ENTER key where you see the "≪" symbol.

13. When you have finished typing the text, press F10 to save the document.

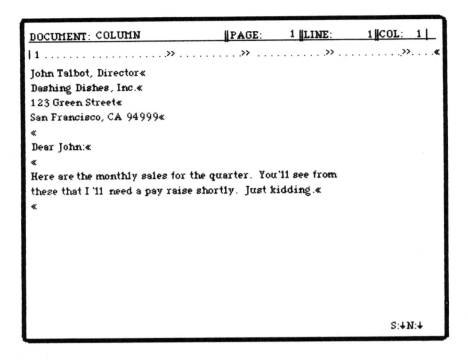

Figure E.1
COLUMN Document
Text

Appendix F
CREATING HEADER

You are going to create a two-page document called HEADER that will be used in the exercises in chapter 10. To create this document, follow the instructions below:

1. Select "Create a New Document" from the main menu by typing "2" and pressing ENTER.

2. Type "HEADER" and press ENTER to name the document.

3. Press F10 twice to display the editing screen.

4. Press F9. The cursor jumps into the format line.

5. Backspace and type a "1" for single spacing at the far left of the format line.

6. Press the space bar three times and press TAB to set a tab marker at column 5.

7. Press the space bar four times and press TAB to set a tab marker at column 10.

8. Press the space bar four times and press TAB to set a tab marker at column 15.

9. Hold down the space bar until the cursor moves to column 36 and press TAB.

10. Hold down the space bar until the cursor moves to column 60 and press ENTER to set the right margin at 60.

11. Press F9 to finish editing the format line.

12. Type the following line of "x"s and then press ENTER twice:

xxxxx xxxxx xxxxx xxxxx xxxxx xxxxx xxxxx xxxxx xxxxx xxxxx

251

You can type or just copy the "x"s as you wish. Next, you'll copy this line (and the return symbol under it) several times to create a two-page document.

13. Press HOME, press F8, press END, and press F8 twice.

14. Press HOME, press F8, press END, and press F8 twice.

15. Press HOME, press F8, press END, and press F8 twice.

16. Press HOME, press F8, press END, and press F8 twice.

17. Press HOME, press F8, *hold down* CTRL and press END, and press F8 twice.

18. Move the cursor to line 48, column 1, and press F2 to create page 2. You're all finished.

19. Press F10.

Appendix G
CREATING EFFECTS

You are going to create a document called EFFECTS that will be used in the exercises in chapter 13. To create this document, follow the instructions below:

1. Select "Create a New Document" from the main menu by typing "2" and pressing ENTER.

2. Type "EFFECTS" and press ENTER to name the document.

3. Press F10 twice to display the editing screen.

4. Press F9. The cursor jumps into the format line.

5. Backspace and type a "1" for single spacing at the far left of the format line.

6. Press the space bar until the cursor arrives at column 5 and press TAB.

7. Press the space bar until the cursor arrives at column 15 and press TAB.

8. Press the space bar until the cursor arrives at column 36 and press TAB.

9. Press the space bar until the cursor arrives at column 60 and press ENTER to set the right margin at 60.

10. Press F9 to finish editing the format line.

11. Type the text you see in figure G.1. Remember to press the ENTER key where you see the "≪" symbol.

12. When you have finished typing the text, press F10 to save the document.

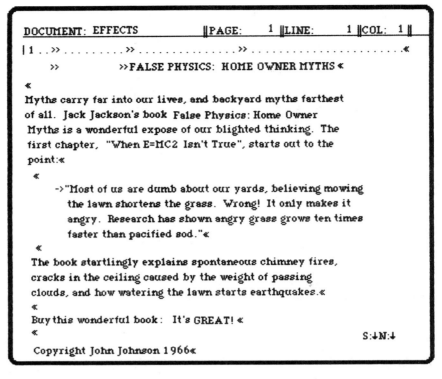

Figure G.1
Text for EFFECTS
Document

Appendix H
CREATING SPELL

You are going to create a document called SPELL that will be used in the exercises in chapter 15. To create this document, follow the instructions below:

1. Select "Create a New Document" from the main menu by typing "2" and pressing ENTER.

2. Type "SPELL" and press ENTER to name the document.

3. Press F10 twice to display the editing screen.

4. Press F9. The cursor jumps into the format line.

5. Backspace and type a "1" for single spacing at the far left of the format line.

6. Press the space bar until the cursor arrives at column 5 and press TAB.

7. Press the space bar until the cursor arrives at column 15 and press TAB.

8. Press the space bar until the cursor arrives at column 36 and press TAB.

9. Press the space bar until the cursor arrives at column 60 and press ENTER to set the right margin at 60.

10. Press F9 to finish editing the format line.

11. Type the text you see in figure 15.1. Remember to press the ENTER key where you see the "≪" symbol. Be sure to type the document just as you see in figure 15.1, including the words which are misspelled. You'll be correcting these misspellings during the exercise.

12. When finished typing the text, press F10 to save the document.

INDEX

Cursor arrow keys, 19, 33, 34, 36, 37, 39
Cursor movement, 71–76
   See also Cursor arrow keys
Cursor-movement keys, 71, 83

Date prompt, 9, 10, 42
Decimal tab. *See* Dectab
Dectab, 22, 125, 127–129, 132, 134, 139–141
Default(s), 14
   drive, 3
   printer, 239–240
Default directory, 17
DELETE (DEL) key, 16, 30, 35, 71, 78–81, 107, 113, 115, 129–131
Deletions, 84
   characters, 37
   columns, 125–126, 129–132, 142
   documents, 155–158
   sections of text, 35, 62, 78–82
   words, 62
Dictionary, 68, 217, 221, 224
   See also Spell-checking
Dictionary drive, 3, 4, 217
Directory, 17, 30
Discretionary search and replace, 105, 108
Disk(s):
   accessing, 235–236
   electronic, 235–236
   inserting, 9
Disk drive:
   delays with, 235–236
   floppy disks, 2–3, 235, 236
   hard disks, 2, 3–4, 7, 235
Disk drive defaults, 3
Disk emulator, 235–236
Disk operating system. *See* DOS
Disk-space-available notice, 16–17
DOC extension, 209
Document:
   accessing, 28–30
   back-up copies of, 13–14, 21, 22, 158

creating, 11, 12, 14–17, 26, 241–255
deleting, 155–158
duplicating, 85–89, 92–96, 99, 100, 155–158
editing, 11, 12, 26, 33–38, 70–84
library (*see* Library)
lost, 158–161, 234–235
naming, 14–17, 21
printing, 12–13, 40–54
renaming, 155–158
saving, 25, 35, 38
spell-checking, 14, 68, 217–221, 225–229
spell-editing, 217, 218–227, 255
transferring to other disks, 158
Document drive, 3, 4
"Document Handling Utilities," 13–14, 145, 155–161
Document specification screen, 8, 14–17
Document summary screen, 8, 17–20
   search of, 158–161
DOS (disk operating system), 7
   loading MultiMate from, 8–11
   return to, 14
DOS A > prompt, 9
Double-striking, 45
Draft print, 45, 193, 197, 202
Drive. *See* Disk drive
Duplicating, 85–89, 92–96, 99, 100, 155–158

Editing, 11, 12, 26, 33–38, 70–84, 125–143
   columns, 125–141
   cursor movement, 71–76
   deletions, 35, 37, 78–82, 84
   insertions, 35, 37, 76–78, 83
   making main-menu selections during, 231–232
   practice in, 96–99
   search and replace in, 109–110
   for spelling, 218, 221–225, 228
Editing keys, 39, 69